2184376

D1267656

THE COMPLETE GUIDE TO

LOW-BUDGET

FEATURE FILMMAKING

Films by the author:

Thou Shalt Not Kill... Except (1987)
Lunatics: A Love Story (1992)
Hercules in the Maze of the Minotaur (1994, TV)
Running Time (1997)
If I Had a Hammer (2001)
Alien Apocalypse (2005, TV)

JOSH BECKER has written and directed four independent feature films, *Thou Shalt Not Kill . . . Except, Lunatics: A Love Story, Running Time* and *If I Had a Hammer.* He has also directed nine episodes of "Xena: Warrior Princess," as well as the pilot TV movie for the series, "Hercules: The Legendary Journeys." His latest TV movie made for the Sci-Fi Network, *Alien Apocalypse* (2005), which he both wrote and directed, was Sci-Fi's highest-rated original movie ever. Mr. Becker resides in Bloomfield Hills, Michigan. For more info see www.beckerfilms.com.

THE COMPLETE GUIDE TO
LOW-BUDGET
FEATURE FILMMAKING

by
JOSH BECKER

INTRODUCTION BY

Bruce Campbell

POINTBLANK

Set in Bembo

POINT*BLANK* is an imprint of Wildside Press
www.pointblankpress.com
www.wildsidepress.com

Edited by J.T. Lindroos and Kathleen Martin

For more information contact Wildside Press

Contents

Part Four: Production

Part Five: Post-Production

To Ida and Bruce

JOSH BECKER:
Who Is This Guy and Why Do I Keep Running Into Him?

by Bruce Campbell

I'VE BEEN ASKING myself these very questions since I first met Josh Becker in suburban Detroit, Michigan, around 1971. For some reason, I was cast as King Creon in his student film version of *Oedipus Rex*. I'm guessing it was a combination of being in the same English class as Josh and supplying my own toga. While we were filming, I remembered thinking, *man, this guy takes filmmaking seriously.*

A year later, at a rather large assembly, Josh screened another amateur film of his called *Super-Student* and it brought down the house. I remember hating Josh for two reasons after that screening:

1. The bastard was able to show his movie in front of the entire school —and they liked it.

2. He didn't put me in it. *Had I failed as King Creon?*

Josh and I crossed paths again in study hall, and found ourselves in the 9th Grade school play, *The Lottery*. Josh had a leg up on the other actors when it came to portraying an adult—he already had a beard! He was, and still is, just slightly ahead of his time.

Once high school rolled around, Josh became an infrequent blip on my radar screen. In those days, he hung with a much faster, cooler crowd than my "theater" friends. He also had the audacity to graduate from high school early and head for Hollywood on his own.

The next time I saw Josh was about a year later at our local Howard Johnson's. He had returned to Michigan to get something done. That's kind of how it works—the further you get from Hollywood, the more likely you are to actually make a film. We met to talk about a slate of ideas he wanted to get into production. I had been making a lot of Super-8mm films with some other guys in our area (Sam Raimi and Scott Spiegel among them) so I was game to do anything.

That meeting spawned a slew of Super-8mm films we made together. Josh would, for the most part, write and direct. I would produce and do a role or two. We did a boxing flick, *The Final Round;* a goofy suspense thriller, *Holding It*, and a "What's the meaning of life?" film called *Acting and Reacting*. Teaming up with Sam Raimi and Scott Spiegel, we did more sappy comedies like *The Blind Waiter* and *Cleveland Smith Bounty Hunter*.

In the fall of 1979, Josh was one of the original crew members on the first *Evil Dead*. After suffering the tortures of the damned on that film, we shot a "pilot" for Josh's first feature called *Stryker's War*, which was eventually brought to life as his first feature film, *Thou Shalt Not Kill…Except*.

Josh and I stayed in touch, but the realities of the film business dragged us both out west at different times. For Josh, it was his fourth or fifth time in Los Angeles and he was the cagey veteran. He stayed busy writing scripts, selling some, optioning others while I cut my teeth in the genre world and started a family.

Next thing you know it was 1989. After a few bad experiences working on "Hollywood" projects, Josh and I longed for the chance to do another film where hassles were at a minimum. We officially reunited for the film *Lunatics: A Love Story*, which was shot back in Michigan. Josh wrote and directed, I produced, and Ted Raimi, long time pal and amateur film veteran, starred in the flick. Aside from horrible monetary restrictions, the experience was a glorious return to Super-8mm movie making—only with better equipment.

A few years later, Josh blazed a trail to the Southern Hemisphere, directing a *Hercules: The Legendary Journeys* TV movie and a boatload of *Xena: Warrior Princess* episodes for pals Rob Tapert and Sam Raimi. I joined the team a few years later, and although I never got to work with Josh directly during my stint (which was a mistake), we would run into each other passing through Auckland, New Zealand. It was great fun to meet up with an old pal half way around the world and get caught up.

The next time we collaborated was the film *Running Time*. This limited-release gem was extremely ambitious and unique from an actor's perspective, since most of it played out in real time. The film was shot in sequence (almost unheard of) so each day we could experience the unfolding drama. Every film student should watch this film closely to see what can be accomplished with very little money.

Josh and I bobbed up again in New Zealand, this time working together on the TV show, *Jack of all Trades*. Josh directed the pilot episode, while I starred and produced. It was very reassuring to work with a trusted filmmaker with similar sensibilities, especially when you're launching a new show.

Half a decade later, Josh and I found ourselves in the former Eastern Bloc (Sofia, Bulgaria), making a couple of films for the Sci Fi Channel. Josh will curse me until the end of time for making him go first, but his experience allowed him to adapt his story to the realities of where he was filming. I might add that when it aired, Josh's film, *Alien Apocalypse*, pulled the highest rating in the history of the Sci Fi Channel for its time slot.

What does any of the above have to do with what you're about to read? Well, a foreword is ultimately an endorsement of a given book, so I hereby endorse this product. There are plenty of folks putting out filmmaking "theory" books, but Josh got his know-how from over twenty-five years of being in the filmmaking trenches. I've worked with him during every phase of production—from generating the kernel of an idea, to putting on final touches in post-production—and he's as committed a filmmaker as you'll find.

As a writer, Josh enjoys making movies with stories, themes, irony, and conflict. As a filmmaker, he favors a well-planned, fiscally responsible approach to telling stories. As a person, he's encyclopedic, bright and brutally honest. What's not to love?

Filmmakers are eager to get right out of the box and make movies any way they please—structure and discipline be damned. I had the same approach when I started, so I can't blame you, but I could have saved a few years groping in the dark if a guide like this was available back then. Read this book and study it. You'll thank Josh after you read it, and Josh and I will both thank you when you go to Hollywood, because your movies won't be as crappy as they could have been.

Be original. Get busy.

Bruce Campbell
Jacksonville, Oregon

Shooting *Evil Dead,* L to R: Rob Tapert, Steve "The Dart" Frankel, Sam Raimi, Tim Philo, Josh Becker.

BRUCE CAMPBELL
in
Running Time
JEREMY ROBERTS
ANITA BARONE
A JOSH BECKER FILM
Thou Shalt Not Kill...
KEVIN SORBO
ANTHONY QUINN
LUNATICS
You have to be a little crazy to fall in love.
Hank's downright insane.
On Sunday, February 9, 1964, the world changed forever...
A Josh Becker Film
If I Had A Ha
A Panoramic Pictures Production of
BRUCE CAMPBELL
RENEE O'CONNOR
ALIEN APOCALYPSE
The Highest Rated

Introduction:

MOST BOOKS I'VE read about film production simply assume that you have an idea and a script to shoot. Most screenwriting books seem to be geared to how to write a script that you can sell to Hollywood (as though the authors of these books had the slightest clue) and do not take into consideration that you might be shooting the script yourself, possibly with your own money. This book will address both of these issues. It's about how to write a script properly that you can rationally shoot, and it's also about how to shoot it, how to finish it, how to sell it, and also how to get it shown.

Many things can be said about me, but not that I don't complete my films. I've started four independent feature films, and I've completed all four: *Thou Shalt Not Kill . . . Except* (1987), *Lunatics: A Love Story* (1992), *Running Time* (1997), and *If I Had a Hammer* (2001). Whatever the final adjudged quality of these films may be, the fact remains that I made them. I took four of my own ideas all the way to completed 35mm prints that were shown in movie theaters. All four films are presently available on videotape and DVD.

I've also written thirty-three feature screenplays, one of which I sold for $67,000. It's never been produced, but I'm not complaining because I used the money to make *Running Time*.

I've also directed nine episodes of "Xena: Warrior Princess," as well as one of the pilot TV movies for the "Hercules" series (with Anthony Quinn as Zeus), a recent Sci-Fi Network TV movie called *Alien Apocalypse*, and several other TV shows. I did lighting and sound for the classic low-budget horror film, *Evil Dead* (1983). (I have cameo parts in *Evil Dead 2* and *Army of Darkness*).

Admittedly, these are not spectacular credits by Hollywood standards. However, by authors-of-books-on-filmmaking standards, I think I'm do-ing pretty well, and I believe that I am particularly well-suited to the task of writing *this* book. If your goal is the same as mine, which is to make the highest quality feature films you can possibly make for the least amount of money, while still fulfilling all of the requirements of a distributor so that you can honestly make a deal, get your film released, and potentially get some money returned to you, then you need to read this book.

In the following pages I will take you through every single step along the way in the making of a low-budget independent feature film, from the intention behind the idea, through the story, the script, pre-production, production, post-production, distribution, and even film festivals. I will also define every term used in the making of a feature film. Many of these same ideas also apply to shorter films, but I'm concentrating on *feature length* films, which are usually 70 minutes or longer (although by the Academy of Motion Picture Arts and Sciences rules, 60 minutes qualifies as a feature).

Since this book is about the *reality* of making a low-budget feature film that can actually be sold when it's done—as of this day in June, 2005—it still must be shot on motion picture film, either 35mm or 16mm, not on digital video (DV), not on High-definition video (HD), and definitely not on super-8. Both HD and DV are now perfectly acceptable formats for documentaries, but they are still, for the most part, unacceptable formats for feature films. I've run into a lot of flak on this topic, and I know that this contention puts me in direct contradiction to almost every other filmmaking book presently out, which all now preach the gospel of digital filmmaking. But here's the thing—I'm right and they're wrong. But that's only if you actually want to have a chance of selling your movie once it's done.

If your film is purely a vanity project, and only to be shown to your friends at parties, then definitely shoot in DV and spend as little as humanly possible. But if you're really trying to make an honest-to-goodness, real, releasable feature film, one that will undoubtedly contain not only all of your own money, but all of your relatives' money, and all of your friends' money, too, you still have to shoot on film

The retort I generally next hear is, "But George Lucas shot the last three *Star Wars* movies on digital." Yeah? Well, guess what? You and I aren't George Lucas, or Danny Boyle (*28 Days*) or Robert Rodriguez (*Sin City*). You see, they have this thing called "a distribution deal" before they even started, which you and I haven't got, and can't get. We have to make a deal once our film is done, which means dealing with distributors, sales agents, and cable television movie channels, which presently are the biggest market for feature films in the world. I'm referring to: Cinemax, Flix, HBO, HBO2, HBO Family, HBO Signature, Independent Film Channel, The Movie Channel, Showtime, Showtime Extreme, Showtime Too, Starz, Starz Edge, Starz In Black, Starz Encore, Starz Encore Action, Starz Encore Drama, Starz Encore Love (where my film *Lunatics: A Love Story* found a home), Starz Encore Mystery, Starz Encore Wam!, Starz Encore Westerns, and the Sundance Channel. These are the people who actually pay money for movies, and all they presently show are 35mm feature-length films. Yes, there are a few exceptions on Sundance and IFC, but even they still mainly show feature films shot in 35mm or 16mm film (like my 16mm feature film *Running Time,* which has shown on IFC many times). I'm not making this up, tune in for yourself and take a look. Most of the movies at the movie theaters are still shot in 35mm, and most of the films on TV are still shot in 35mm. If you decide to shoot something other than 35mm (even 16mm), you are reducing your chances for selling your film by 90% at this point. This will all change, eventually, but it hasn't yet.

So, if you don't have a distribution deal in advance, which you don't (and you can't get), then you'd better have a viable, salable product at the end. If the biggest market for feature films still doesn't accept movies shot on HD or DV, then it's still not viable.

Yes, it's both easier and cheaper to shoot a movie on DV than on film. But the film business isn't about what's cheapest and easiest for you; it's about what will sell later. We could have shot *Evil Dead* or *Thou Shalt Not Kill . . . Except* on videotape, and it would have been a lot cheaper and easier, but neither film would have ever been released and you would never have seen or heard of either of them.

When you begin the process of producing a feature film you need to have a belief that somewhere down the road there will at least be a chance of recouping your costs—which still isn't all that good no matter what you do. But if you shoot on digital video, those chances just dropped to nearly nothing. I don't think it's rational to embark on as huge a process as a feature film having basically ruined your chances to recoup your costs from the outset.

To make a movie on DV that looks equally as good as film at this time will cost every bit as much money, and won't yield a decent *master,* which is the original, unless you transfer it back to 35mm film, which, at a present cost of $1.25 a frame (and there are 144,000 frames in a 100-minute movie), still makes it impractical. You might be able to cut a deal on this process, but at this time it will still cost at least $75,000 to $100,000, and that's a lot of money—too much for a really low-budget movie. You could shoot a feature film on DV and hope that a distributor will pay for your post-production, but that, in my experience, is an irrational assumption that in 99.9% of the cases will not occur, and therefore I can't deal with it as a legitimate possibility. This book isn't about the fantasy of becoming a star, it's about the reality of making a film.

Also, no professional digital video format to come out yet has stuck around long enough to be considered as a permanent, archiveable form of filmmaking. This too will undoubtedly change at some point, but it hasn't yet.

Nevertheless, I will still discuss features shot on digital video along the way, just because I know people are doing it, and it interests me. There are a few ideas I'd like to bring up. And whether you shoot on film or on a digital format, most of what I'm discussing in this book still applies.

Throughout this book I will be stressing the production of a $100,000 to a $200,000 movie shot on motion picture film, either 35mm or 16mm. I believe that with any film over $200,000 it will be very difficult to ever get your investment back, and anything under $100,000 (except where noted) is just impractical. When you hear a filmmaker say that they made a feature film for $7,000, they're just lying. You'll be spending at least $5,000 on film stock alone, and that doesn't include processing or taking it to a form where you can actually look at it. To end up with a finished film there is really no way on God's green earth to spend less than about $100,000, and still have the minimum required elements to make a distribution deal, which is what I keep coming back to.

Josh Becker

PART ONE:
WRITING THE SCRIPT

The Intentions Behind the Story:

WHY ARE YOU making this movie? Why do you want to tell *this* story? What's your intention behind telling this story?

If your intention is strictly to make money, you've chosen the wrong way to go about it. Go into real estate, the stock market, plastics, but not independent movies. You will assuredly end up with less money than you started with if you proceed with this crazy scheme. So, if money is not your motivation, what is?

If your intention is to tell a compelling, motivated story that could potentially be a quality movie, then keep reading.

Feature films are a narrative storytelling form, and a fairly long storytelling form at that. If you want to make experimental films, shoot shorts— features are the wrong place. Let's face it, most experimental shorts are too long and boring as it is. Feature films are about stories. If you actually want me to sit there and pay attention for 70 to 150 minutes, which is a long time, you'd better be telling me a story that's worth my time, which means it's a story that's worth telling in the first place.

Whether you're shooting a wide-screen epic, or sitting on a rock telling of the day's mastodon hunt, it's the same exact thing—you're telling a story. "The mastodon turned and looked straight at me. My blood ran cold. Just as it was about to charge, I lifted my spear and sighted in . . ."

If you intend to make feature-length films, you must have stories to tell. Just having the desire to make movies is woefully insufficient.

A huge misconception that I've heard many times over the years is—"it may not seem like a good story in script form, but you just wait until I shoot it." Well, just because you ever get to aim a camera at something doesn't mean it will ever be interesting and worth watching. An old expression that long predates movies is, "If it ain't on the page, it ain't on the stage," and no truer words were ever spoken. If your script stinks, you may well be the next Stanley Kubrick, and your film will still stink, too.

I'm sorry to be the bearer of ill-tidings, but movies *really* stink these days, and have been getting steadily worse for many years. I've watched a lot of recent movies, and there's nothing technically wrong with most of them other than the writing. It is so weak, and the stories are so poorly chosen, that I constantly feel like I'm looking into the empty vacuum of space.

Interesting stories have a tendency to begin the same way, and it's not

"Once upon a time . . ." The stories I like frequently begin with "Did you know . . . ?" For example: Did you know that the very first motorcycle gang was made up of World War II veterans? That's the basis of my script *Cycles*, which I sold. Did you know that Teddy Roosevelt's mother and wife both died on the same day in the same house? That's a key part of my script *Teddy Roosevelt in the Bad Lands*. I'm drawn to this type of story because I like history, and I also enjoy finding out new, interesting things, as I believe most other people do, too.

Then there's the "What if . . . ?" variety of story, which includes speculative fiction as well as science fiction. This is where my film, *Thou Shalt Not Kill . . . Except* began—what if the Marines took on the Manson family? You can also combine the "Did you know . . . ?" story with the "What if . . . ?" story and end up with something like my new film, *If I Had a Hammer*. Did you know that rock & roll was pretty much a dead issue in America between 1958 and 1964, which is why the folk movement was resurrected during that period? The *what if* aspect is that when The Beatles first appeared on "The Ed Sullivan Show" on February 9, 1964, I say it killed the folk movement dead as a doornail.

Did it really? I think so, but that's just my supposition.

Another perfectly viable form of a story is the fantasy. This is a variation on the "What if . . . ?" story and doesn't necessarily have to be the "Alice in Wonderland"-style fantasy; it can just as easily be a personal fantasy that takes place in the real world. My script *The Biological Clock* is my fantasy of what would happen if a single, nearly forty-year-old female friend of mine (who I'm secretly in love with in the script) decided to be artificially inseminated and wanted to use my sperm? Would this cause us to fall in love?

Other reasonable story beginnings are: "This is *really* cool . . . ," which usually doesn't live up to its introduction (just like, "This is the *funniest* story you've ever heard . . .") Or there is the perfectly standard and perfectly acceptable "There was/is this guy/gal . . . ," which is always a great beginning because it starts with the lead character.

If, however, you begin your story with "I don't care what story I tell, I just have to make a movie," you need to stop and rethink your position immediately. Your need to make a movie means *nothing* to the rest of us. The only thing that matters is the movie you make. You've got to want to tell a story or you have no reason to make a movie. I'm just a poor slob that's willing to shell out my hard-earned money on a good story, and it's your job to supply it.

Now, if you begin with "I don't care what story I tell, I just want to make money," you assuredly won't interest anyone and you probably won't make any money, either. If you begin with "I know you've heard this before, but now you're going to hear it again," you've killed most of the interest before you've even begun. If you begin with "I know you've heard this before—and didn't like it the first time—but now you're going to hear it again," well, that's about the worst beginning a story could have.

The only worse kinds of stories would be straight technical jargon about the inner workings of things you're not interested in, like a car mechanic explaining, in detail, what's wrong with your broken engine. More boring than that would be someone trying to sell you something you don't want, like life insurance.

Watching any remake, sequel, or highly-derivative or stolen story at this point for me is like listening to an insurance salesman drone on for two hours. This is when any chore that I've ever avoided in my life—cleaning the tub, weeding the garden, draining and flushing my radiator—seems preferable to listening to this story, and this is as far away as you can get from telling a good story.

Why am I being told this story? Is it because I might possibly enjoy it, or is it because I simply have the price of a ticket in my pocket? Many people will tell you that this doesn't matter, but I say it *completely* matters. You must *want* to tell a story. It's even better if you *need* to tell a story. But remember, the story's the thing.

Stories are crucial to societies, they represent our mindset, what we're thinking at a specific time, how we see things. As a storyteller, it's your primary job to tell an interesting story that's worth telling in the first place, that hopefully sheds some light on the human condition.

I honestly believe that we're all long overdue for some new, exciting stories that begin with, "What if . . . ?" "Did you know . . . ?" or "This is *really* cool!"

The Story:

So, choosing the basic story is the single most crucial choice you'll make during the entire filmmaking process, and to make matters more difficult, it comes right at the very beginning. This is where most people screw themselves before they've actually started. This is also where you will set the parameters of your budget—what sort of hurdles do you intend to make yourself leap over?

As the legendary MGM production head, Irving Thalberg, once said, "The success or failure of any picture is decided on the day you decide to make it. The choice of *subject matter* is everything. No matter how well your picture is written, directed, and acted, if the subject matter is inappropriate, you will have a failure." So, what's your story about? Is it a crime thriller, a western, a love story, about drug addiction, someone dying of a terminal illness, or the War of 1812? What story do you *need* to tell? What story do you know and think you can tell well?

The cheapest and most easily controlled thing to shoot is and always will be actors talking to each other, on *interiors*, meaning in someone's house or apartment or on a set you've built, where you control the lighting and it doesn't matter what the weather's like outside. My film *Lunatics: A Love Story* and Sam Raimi's film *Evil Dead* were both feasible low-budget productions because they mainly took place in one interior location and were subsequently very controllable.

When you are conceiving your story you must have your limited budget in mind from the very outset. Taking this seriously to heart, my story in *Lunatics: A Love Story* is about a guy who's an agoraphobic and afraid to go outside. I took the budget restrictions and built them into the story, just as you should do. However, not wanting to be stuck on the one set for the *entire* movie, I chose a girl who was set adrift in the city and had nowhere to go.

Bringing us to, what *is* a story?

A *story*, by *my* definition, is something causes something else, which frequently causes yet something else, etc. Just stating a genre like, a cop story or a film noir or a teen comedy, is *not* coming up with a story. You must think about how one thing causes another thing to occur within that genre.

Regarding the main character, I don't care what anyone else tells you or what you've read, you really *should* have a main character. Your *main character* is the audience's point of view, and without a lead character you have already failed to tell a good story on a very basic, fundamental level. More on this topic later.

So, if you begin, as I did, with "a crazy guy who doesn't like to leave his apartment" you know your lead character and your main location, but you still haven't provoked anything to happen, so it's not yet a story. But if the crazy guy should somehow lure the girl with nowhere to go back to his apartment, the two of them meeting will force something else to happen, which, in this case, is a love story. And then when she departs at the end of act two, he's finally got to leave his apartment and go get her back, which he does. That's the whole story.

Keep your budget in mind from the beginning when conceiving your story. What can you pull off? I felt that I could pull off either one or two actors on one set for over half of *Lunatics: A Love Story*. Whether I do pull it off or not, dramatically speaking, is beside the point, I pulled off the production, so it was a good, functional, low-budget idea. This basic idea made the film achievable on a very low budget with a very short shooting schedule, which is what you'll have, too.

Take my advice on this: unless you have a spare quarter of a million dollars in the bank that you're ready and able to blow, you do not want to make a movie that costs more than $200,000, no how, no way. It's possible to crawl from beneath the wreckage of a $100-200,000 movie WAY EASIER than you can from a $250,000 movie (or more), which could very well sink you *forever*. You should do everything within your means to keep your budget below $200,000, if at all possible. $150,000 is perfectly reasonable for an extremely-low-budget movie.

I know the average Hollywood movie now costs about $60 million dollars, with many exceeding $100 million, but that means nothing to the low-budget filmmaker. To us a thousand dollars is a lot of money, ten thousand dollars is a *huge* amount of money, and $100,000 to $200,000 is the maximum amount of money that you ever want to be gambling with, since you're probably not going to get it back, or, if you do, it will be so many years later it won't matter.

All the money you spend on the movie will be out for a long time, possibly forever. In fact, this is highly likely. I got ripped-off on my first film just as, Sam Raimi did on his. This happened to everyone else I know, and that's how you must view it. If you break even in fourteen years (which is two seven-year deals), you'll have done very well.

Therefore, you can't *really* be making this first film for the possible monetary pay-off. It's got to be for other reasons. It could be for the love of movies and the need or desire to try and make a good one, or the challenge of just getting a feature film done, or the hope that this film will get you noticed. It just can't be for money.

A feature film is such an enormous process—even small ones—that many people who start to make them never end up finishing their films, and it's always sad because there's already a lot of money tied up in the project. I know a guy who has started and shot large parts of four different feature films, none of which has he yet completed.

Before everything else must come the resolve that you will absolutely complete your movie. If you don't have that resolve, don't begin. I've started and completed four low-budget features and it's been a struggle each and every time. All I can tell you for a fact is that my film *Running Time*, which was the cheapest of the four films, was also the least painful and the least struggle. My last film, *If I Had a Hammer*, which came in at $350,000, tried to kill me, and I'm still licking my financial wounds six years later.

Don't let this happen to you. Make the cheapest movie you can think of making—two people in a room, five kids in a cabin, a heist in one office, etc. If you don't take this into consideration right at the start you will more than likely get severely burned somewhere down the road. Limit the cast and limit the locations, and build the limitations right into the script, like Sam did with *Evil Dead* and I did with *Lunatics: A Love Story*.

However, *Lunatics: A Love Story* was my second film. In my first film, *Thou Shalt Not Kill . . . Except*, I have the marines battling the Manson family in 1969. In retrospect this was a very ridiculous script to shoot first—a big cast, period costumes, military uniforms, period cars, a lot of weapons, a foreign location (Michigan standing in for Vietnam). It's absurd. That I shot anything resembling the script is a miracle, and I don't recommend this route to anyone else. My production did a disservice to my script. In fifty out of a hundred scenes I found myself totally over my head on a production level. So I *implore* you, limit your cast and limit your locations. It's imperative, and you'll thank me for it. You must set up a situation that you can afford to pull off.

What most people don't realize, I think, is that there are literally tens of thousands of independent feature films sitting around that nobody will touch with a ten-foot pole. All you need to do is go to a film market, like the American Film Market (AFM) in Los Angeles, or MIFED in Milan, and look around—most of the films you'll see advertised and shown will never see the light of day, not in theaters, not on TV, and not even on video. And those are the films that found representation; there are thousands and thousands of others that didn't even get that far.

So leave the big sprawling stories to Hollywood. Low-budget features shouldn't be cheap attempts at making Hollywood films; they're their own animal, and compression and limitations should be treated as good things that you ought to embrace. Many of the finest stories ever told, regardless of the budget, are very limited in scope: *Rosemary's Baby*, which is primarily in one apartment; *The Apartment* which is also mainly in one apartment;

The Magnificent Ambersons, which is primarily set in one house. One of my very favorite films is *The Member of the Wedding*, which takes place almost entirely in a kitchen with three people, and it's brilliant. Any of these films could have been made on tiny budgets.

Orson Welles' **The Magnificent Ambersons**, with Agnes Moorehead and Tim Holt, photographed by Stanley Cortez.

Don't let the limitations limit you, let them inspire you. That may sound like nonsense, but it's possible and you need to do it.

If you write a script where you end up having to change locations two, three, or four times a day, you will regret it. You want to get all of the myriad of crap it takes to make even a small movie, plop it down somewhere, then be able to shoot all day. Every time you have to pick all that gear up and move it, you've wasted an enormous amount of precious time you could have used for rehearsing, blocking, or shooting, which are the important parts of filmmaking, not schlepping the equipment around. On "Hercules" and "Xena" we almost never changed locations more than once a day, and frequently not even then if everyone could help it.

All of this comes into play immediately by what story you decide to tell. Accept the fact that you will be telling a story about just a few characters in just a few places. What locations can you get cheap or for free? Remember you will be clogging this place up all day long for two, three, or maybe four weeks. If it's a functioning business then it probably won't work. How about your own house? Or your summer cabin. Or your friend's barn. Or the woods nearby. The easier the better.

I shot half of *Running Time* in my own apartment. I shot quite a few scenes for *Thou Shalt Not Kill . . . Except* in my friend Bruce Campbell's garage, as well as my parents' house, and their backyard. We shot quite a bit of *Evil Dead* in Sam's parents' house and backyard, as well as Bruce Campbell and the producer, Rob Tapert's, family's summer cottages.

Ask yourself: What's available? What's cheap? Or preferably: What's Free?

Let this be the starting point for your story. What location is most accessible? That's where the main action of your story should take place.

Having written thirty-two feature screenplays, as well as having spent my entire life watching and studying movies, I'll give you piece of information that seems to have gotten lost somewhere down the road: the best stories are the deep ones, not the sprawling, action- and special effects filled ones. The more action and special-effects you have, the more the film will cost. Writing doesn't cost anything but time.

A serious mistake I've watched many young filmmakers commit is being so eager to start shooting that they blow off the entire writing process. They either begin shooting with their hastily written first draft, or *before* they have finished the first draft. If you do this you *will* be sorry later. The writing process is the cheapest and most important part of the filmmaking process, I kid you not. And since you will inevitably end up rushing through the shooting, why rush through the writing if you don't have to?

A common misconception among filmmakers of all ages is that something more than what is embedded in their script will somehow magically occur when they shoot it. *Wrong*. Magic does not occur on movie sets very often or at all. A movie set is a hectic, confusing, pressure-filled, and often aggravating place to work. Just getting to the position where you can actually shoot the shots you have in mind is hard enough. That you are now depending on magic to spontaneously combust is, quite frankly, ridiculous. That's why your script has to be as good as you can possibly make it before you shoot.

There's an old expression that goes, "Writing is rewriting." Just because you got a script written doesn't make it good. In fact, no first draft is *ever* worth shooting. If you can't improve your script by writing a second draft, you're not trying. *Think* about your story. *Consider* your character's motivations. This cannot be stressed enough

Where Do Stories Come From?

There's another old expression that goes, "If you're not directly inspired by something, then you're just stealing." Some ideas have come to me completely out of nowhere, but generally they are inspired by some story I've heard or seen. And just because you're inspired by another story doesn't mean yours has to resemble the original at all. There is a world of difference between being inspired by something and stealing it.

I've always admired the concept behind *The Magnificent Ambersons*, which is about the end of one time period and the beginning of another. The author, Booth Tarkington, chose the end of the 19th century and the beginning of the 20th century. I was inspired by this to come up with my own end-of-an-era story, *If I Had a Hammer*, which is about the end of the folk era and the beginning of the rock era, which I say occurred on February 9, 1964, when The Beatles first appeared on "The Ed Sullivan Show." That there is a connection between *The Magnificent Ambersons* and *If I Had a Hammer* would never even be suspected by anyone anywhere if I didn't mention it here. No one could ever say that *If I Had a Hammer* is a *Magnificent Ambersons* rip-off. Not that I'd mind. But, nevertheless, I was directly inspired by it.

My film *Running Time* was directly inspired by Alfred Hitchcock's film *Rope*, although there isn't one plot similarity between the two films other than their time frames, meaning they both play out in real time where a minute on the screen is actually sixty seconds long. *Rope* is about two young men who commit a murder, *Running Time* is about a heist at a laundry company. But once again I was directly inspired by another film. I had no interest in telling the same story, but I was moved by it to write my own.

In all honesty, stealing stories and dressing them up differently is perfectly legitimate, and it's done all the time. I'm against it, but that doesn't mean it isn't a viable method. *Gladiator* is a slightly redressed version of *Spartacus,* and *Dances With Wolves* is a somewhat altered (and elongated) version of *Broken Arrow* (1950). Both of those films won Best Picture Oscars. There was a while there when samurai movies regularly became westerns, like *Seven Samurai* into *The Magnificent Seven*, and *Yojimbo* into *A Fistful of Dollars*, and that cross-fertilization was interesting. The short story "The Most Dangerous Game" by Richard Connell, about a man being hunted by a mad hunter, has been redone in *every* genre. Although I don't recommend stealing, I say it's better to steal a story than to have no story at all. But I do think that originality counts for something in filmmaking, even if it now shunned as heretical in Hollywood.

Several of my non-writer friends read the above paragraph and one said, "I would like to see you come down a little harder against stealing stories," and another said "I think stealing stories is despicable." Well, stealing stories is part of writing. Perhaps it's the word stealing that's upsetting them. In the end it all comes down to just what it is you're appropriating. You can just take the whole story, with its setting and characters; or you can take the concept behind the story, like I did with *The Magnificent Ambersons* and *If I Had a Hammer*, which I believe is perfectly acceptable. Either way, you're still taking something, which is just a milder way of saying you're stealing something.

The place I've found most of my story ideas is from reading. I enjoy reading history, and I also enjoy historically based stories, particularly action stories, and there are a million of those that haven't been filmed yet. It has been said that you should write what you know, which is obviously good advice. However, every bit as good, I think, is to write about something that you'd *like* to know, then read up on it. Let the writing process inspire you to learn. When I decided to attempt to write a script about the Battle of Belleau Wood in World War I, I'd only come across references to it in several other books. It sounded like a completely fascinating battle—the first big battle the Americans were involved in during World War I—and there didn't seem to be any other movies about it (ostensibly, King Vidor's silent classic *The Big Parade* is set at Belleau Wood, but it never says so in the film). So I read every book, article, and reference I could find about that battle, which really wasn't all that much, and then the rest I made up.

However, period stories are not advisable for low-budget movies since they automatically cost more to costume and art direct. I've done it twice already with *Thou Shalt Not Kill . . . Except*, set in 1969, and *If I Had a Hammer*, set in 1964, and take my word for it, it's exceptionally difficult with a very low budget. You can no longer just steal an exterior shot that has cars in it because they all have to be in the correct period. I rented seven old cars on *If I Had a Hammer* and it's a big expense. It's an even bigger hassle clearing away the modern cars that are already parked there—you need permits and postings, and you have to have a rented cop to back you up. To keep costs down, I say stay in the present day if you can.

An obvious place to look for stories, that I have personally always found rather difficult to deal with dramatically, is your own life. Two very important points to keep in mind about true stories are: 1. Just because it's true doesn't mean it's interesting, and 2. Just because it's true doesn't mean it's believable. Fact can well be stranger, and far more difficult to believe, than fiction. Real life rarely offers well-worked-out dramatic situations, which means you'll often need to change things. Once you start changing events from the real situation, is it still true? No, and it won't be true anymore the second you write it down. As soon as one person takes a true event, puts it through ones own memory, and applies ones own sensibilities, it's no longer true. In fact, there are no true stories in movies, not even documentaries, because the filmmaking process is a lie. By compressing time, and choosing to show one thing over another, it all becomes slanted. Truth is a much more difficult goal to achieve in drama than by just depicting actual events. As Pablo Picasso said, "Art is a lie that shows us the truth."

I just had an interesting discussion with my former webmaster, Gerry. He was complaining about *The Bridge on the River Kwai* (one of my very favorite films) because it isn't true. Well, it never said it was a true story, and it is based on a novel, so what's his problem? Gerry thought it would be better if it were true. I said that I didn't think so. The novelist, Pierre Boulle, as well as the screenwriters, Michael Wilson and Carl Foreman, were going for what I believe were greater truths than they would have found in a true story. *The Bridge on the River Kwai* is about duty and what it means to a number of different people, particularly a British Colonel and a Japanese Colonel. The dramatic situation that Boulle conceived—a Japanese prisoner of war camp during WWII where a bridge must be built by a certain day—is a perfect setting for the exploration of this concept. It's true enough to be completely believable, but it's fictitious enough to allow the writers to seriously explore their theme, much more so, I believe, than a true situation would have offered.

The truth of a story does not come from the fact that it actually happened, it comes from the believability of the dramatic situation and the characters' responses to it. If the audience believes it, it's true. As a friend of mine once said, "If I can believe it, I can have fun. If I can't believe it, I can't have fun." I'll take this one step further, because I think you not only need to believe the story, you need to *care*. There are many stories that I believe that I don't care about at all. And if I don't care, I can't have any fun. So a good story not only needs to be believable, but it must also make you care. This is called *empathy*, and without it a story doesn't matter.

Another place to look for story ideas is in your own beliefs and interests. Is there anything that really matters to you? Nuclear disarmament, child literacy, gay rights, save the whales? Think about this seriously because there is rarely anything better than a passionate belief in what you're saying. Stories that express your point of view are often the best stories to tell.

Genre:

Genre is a French word that means kind, type, or sort, which is exactly what it means in English, too. The genre of a film is its type, like a western, or a teen comedy, or a crime thriller, or science fiction, or a family drama. A genre is not a story; it's a category in which stories are written.

How to Come Up With a Story:

Here's a perfectly rational, workable method for coming up with a story. First, choose the genre in which you'd like work. Let's take the genre of the teen comedy as an example. Second, go immediately to . . .

The Three Acts and the Act Ends:

Each act always ends at a dramatic conflict that will cause a point of no return for your lead character, either physically, emotionally, or both. Given that, now envision how act one of your story ends, and then what act two will be, keeping in mind that act two is the main action of the story. Now you can quickly see if you even have a story. If your potential story idea can't pass this first simple test, you can be reasonably sure it's not much of a story.

Okay, what if a group of teenagers take a road trip from Maine to California. We'll call this film *Which Way Is West?* However, that in and of itself is not a story. Nothing has caused anything else to happen. Nor do you have three acts. And you really don't want to have teens in a car driving for all three acts, because all three acts should be different. If the three acts are the same—teens driving in a car—that's bad storytelling, and will assuredly become boring.

If something crucial doesn't occur to your lead character in about thirty-five minutes, which is the end of act one, you still haven't come up with a story. A group of teens driving in a car is not a story, no matter what they may talk about. However, if a group of teens are driving in a car, stop to eat, then come out and find their car gone—that's a story, or the beginning of one anyway, because now something else *must* occur. Something happened that will now cause something else to happen. Will the teens walk home? Call the cops? Call their parents? Hitch? Try to find out who stole their car? Something's got to happen.

As we all now know, we need something to cause something else to legitimately have a story. Therefore, if you begin with teenagers on a road trip, your next thought should be, how does act one end? And what's the main action of the story that this has just led me into? If, however, you want the road trip itself to be the main action of the story, which it seems like it ought to be to me, then you don't want to begin with the road trip. Instead, you'd begin with the teens at home, and their reasons for wanting to go on a road trip. Now, what crucial event causes the main character to decide to leave? Did he break up with his girlfriend? Have a fight with his parents? Get his girlfriend pregnant? Realize he was gay? Steal the money from his college fund? Whatever dramatic conflict you choose, something must cause the main character to do something, which in this case is hitting the road.

So, by immediately thinking about how the acts end, and what that causes, a story will naturally develop. This is a perfectly rational method for taking an idea and molding it into a story. It's also a perfectly rational way to take what you think is a story and find out if it's functioning properly, and what it still needs to do so.

Now, since the three acts of a story are three entirely separate ordeals, and should be viewed as such, we've now made act one and act two completely different items that neither look nor sound alike, and there's a dramatic conflict at the end of act one that caused our character to hit the road. This should then lead us to what ought to be our next nagging question—what dramatic conflict occurs at the end of act two? If, for instance, the character is driving his older brother's beloved, cherry, 1959 Studebaker Hawk, and it gets totaled at the end of act two, this will lead us into an act three that's entirely different from the first two acts, which is good, since the three acts need to be entirely different.

It's almost like you're telling three different stories. In *Running Time*, for example, you have: Act One—leading up to the heist, which is in a prison and in a truck; Act Two—the heist, which is in an office; and Act Three—after the heist, which is in various alleys, and a girl's apartment. These are three entirely different dramatic situations—that hopefully all fit together—but don't look the same, nor do they function the same way. The three acts of a story are like the three parts of a house: the foundation, the walls, and the roof. They don't have the same appearance, nor do they have the same purpose. But they do all fit together, and they go in a specific order. The foundation can never go on top of the roof, nor can the roof go under the foundation. You can put the walls on top of the roof if you must, but you'll just end up with a pile of lumber, not a house.

Act One is the setup: Why did the chicken cross the road, or, in this case, why did the teenager hit the road? It's a question that needs to be answered. In *Running Time* they plan a heist and get a bunch of guys with guns. But that doesn't necessarily mean these guys can pull off that heist. Can they? That's the question. You now feel compelled to watch the rest of the film to find out. You might think it's a better idea to go directly to the heist and begin your story with action, but you'd be wrong. The audience is not only happy to sit through the setup, *they absolutely need it,* and subconsciously they demand it. If you don't give them a good setup, you've blown it before you've even gotten going. If Act One isn't a proper setup of about thirty to thirty-five minutes, and doesn't end properly with a dramatic conflict, that's the exact moment the audience will get bored. Deep in their guts every human being understands how an Act One works, and how it's supposed to end, on a moment of no return for the lead character. So, like *Running Time*, if you walk into a place with a gun and say "Give me the money!" you can't take it back. If you steal your brother's priceless Studebaker Hawk and hit the road with your buds, then your brother realizes his car is gone, you can't take it back. The end of the act must be decisive, and if it isn't, you haven't discovered an exciting new way to tell a story, you've simply got an act with a weak ending, of which we've all seen more than our shares.

Act Two is confronting the situation, which in *Running Time* is the heist.

This is the main action of the story. In our teen comedy it's the road trip. Frequently, this is the longest chunk of the movie, and could well be an hour or more of a two-hour movie.

Act Three is the resolution, or the punchline, if you will. At the beginning of Act One of *Citizen Kane*, Charles Foster Kane mumbles, "Rosebud" on his deathbed; in Act Two reporters try to figure out what Rosebud means; in Act Three we see that Rosebud was Kane's childhood sled. A story without a proper resolution is like a joke without a punchline—it ain't much of a joke. Lengthwise, Act Three is the loosest of the acts—it can be a third of your story or it can be shorter. In my film *If I Had a Hammer*, which is 117 minutes long, Act Three is only 17 minutes, but it does seem sufficient to me. However, too short of an Act Three isn't good. The audience wants to be let down slowly and gently from a story, and to pull the plug too fast is unsettling. So, in *Which Way is West?* Act Three would be back in Maine, or out in California, but either way, not on the road trip anymore.

If you look at your story in three acts, I also believe it's much easier to grasp because, very simply, it's in smaller chunks. It's now in three sections that are approximately thirty-five pages each. If one act is twenty-five pages and one is forty, it doesn't matter, it's the concept behind it that's important. And any joke can become a shaggy dog story by inordinately dragging out the setup, but it generally won't make the joke any funnier. As Shakespeare said, "Brevity is the soul of wit."

Telling a story is completely analogous to telling a joke, because a joke is just a little story. First, you set the joke up, then you pay it off. If you don't tell a joke right, it's not funny. If you don't tell a story right, it's not compelling. It would be like telling the joke this way: "To get to the other side. Chickens. On the road." If you don't give the information in the proper order it loses all of its impact.

And I believe that *compelling* is the key word to keep in mind at all times when writing a motion picture story. If things keep causing other things to occur, it will be compelling. If things stop causing other things to occur, it will be boring. You never want your story to be boring. The worst filmmaker in the world can be boring, so that's not a worthy goal.

The real goal is to tell a compelling story, no matter where it's going, no matter what it's about. And this can be achieved with very limited resources because it's a concept and doesn't cost anything. And, as we low-budget filmmakers always keep in mind, anything that's free is good and should be taken advantage of.

However, if you ignore this information because you believe that you are really an "artist" and you need your "freedom," that rules and structure will restrict your creativity, we need to have a little talk.

A Note About "Freedom" and Creativity:

Art is not about freedom, it's about the restriction of freedom. And the more restrictions, the better the art. As the great Pulitzer Prize-winning author, Willa Cather, once said: "Every artist knows that there is no such thing as 'freedom' in art. The first thing an artist does when he begins a new work is lay down the barriers and limitations; he decides upon a certain composition, a certain key, a certain relation of creatures and objects to each other. He is never free, and the more splendid his imagination, the more intense his feeling, the farther he goes from general truth and general emotion."

I will not read scripts submitted to me on my website, and I have a bold, well-displayed notice saying so. Nevertheless, one fellow pestered me and pestered me to read his script. As I began to relent I told him that he'd better read all of my posted essays on screenwriting and see if his script followed the rules. He scoffed that my essays were nothing more than "Screenwriting 101" and he knew all of that silly stuff. He sent me the script and in the first thirty-five pages he had not established a lead character, nor had he set up any kind of story that was going anywhere. I summarily tossed his script in the wastebasket. I wrote back to him saying that even though he might very well know all the rules of screenwriting, he wasn't following any of them. He replied, "I'm a rebel." Well, sadly, he's confused—he's not a rebel, he's just a bad writer, or more likely not a writer at all.

This is exactly why there are so many bad movies these days, because so many people think that they're rebels and artists, whereas in reality they're just amateur bad writers. Don't let this happen to you. If you don't put the time in on the script it absolutely will show in the final film. As Bruce Campbell once said, "If you've got script problems and you haven't fixed them by the time you shoot, your script problems then become forty feet tall."

This may very well be the most difficult concept of all for writers who are just starting out (I've been confronted on this issue on my website over a hundred times over the past eight years)—that following these structural rules will somehow hinder your creativity, and that freedom and creativity have something to do with one another.

The structural rules of drama were first analyzed and written down by Aristotle in his treatise "Poetics" in the third century B.C. These are the same concepts that every writer since then has had to wrestle with, from Euripides to Shakespeare to Tennessee Williams to David Mamet. That's the game, wrestling with the rules, and the more rules you master the greater the writer you are. Just like in martial arts, boxing, basketball, or any sport, the more moves you master, the greater the athlete you are. You can absolutely be certain that ignoring the rules won't make you a better athlete or a better writer.

Quite simply, the professional writers are constantly trying to restrict themselves to their point and their theme. Just how specific and structured you can make your script is indeed the challenge. The idea isn't to fly crazily out at the edges, it's to go specifically to the center.

The One-Gimme Rule:

The One-Gimme Rule goes like this: the audience will go anywhere with you once—to a galaxy far, far away; to the center of the Earth; believing that a caveman who was frozen a hundred thousand years ago can be woken up and is still alive, etc.—*but they'll only do it once.* This is the definition of the completely overused term "the suspension of disbelief." An audience will happily suspend their disbelief once, and only once. The second time the audience is asked to do so—like if you say the thawed caveman has telekinesis—they will begin to mentally bail-out on the story. If they are asked a third time, they are lost for good—the story is no longer believable and therefore no longer any fun, and has now become a burden to watch.

The Outline and the Ending:

The process of making movies is essentially about coming up with a complete story, then breaking it down into its smallest individual parts, then putting them all back together again. First, you have a whole story; then you break it down into three acts; then you have fifty to one hundred scenes at a minute to two minutes each. Obviously, some scenes will be longer, and a few may be shorter, but that's a rule of thumb. And each of those scenes will subsequently be covered in at least one shot, but probably several to many shots. A *shot*, by the way, is the same thing as a *camera setup*, meaning it's from the time you turn the camera on until you turn it off, from action to cut. Those shots will all get edited together and hopefully combine back into one whole thing (with the aid of blessed music to fill the holes).

Now you're going to take your story and break it down into its various scenes. This is done by creating an outline.

The form has been simplified to this:

Act One:
1.
2.
3.
4.
5.
etc.

Act Two:
1.
2.
3.
4.
5.
etc.

Now fill in the slots with brief scene descriptions—one sentence, possibly two. Write down absolutely any scene you can think of, letting one scene lead you into the next one. Since you already should have figured out how act one ends and how act two ends, plug those in, and keep noodling with this outline until you reach the ending.

The end of act three, which is the end of the movie, should be another crucial moment for the main character, as well. And it's imperative that you know your ending before you begin writing the script. In a well-told story everything should be leading inevitably toward the conclusion, which is the joke's punchline, so if you don't know your ending, on some basic level you won't know what you're writing about in any scene. Use the outline to construct your story, scene by scene.

The Author Is God:

Here is my theory as to why people enjoy watching and hearing narrative stories: in a well-told story everything is leading inevitably to the conclusion. That means that the characters' actions actually affect their outcome. I suspect that we would all love to believe that about real life, too—that our actions actually effect our life's outcomes. Sadly, on some visceral level, I think we all doubt that it's true. We all suspect that life may just be meaningless chaos, with no real rhyme or reason, and there is no God looking out for us, leading us to our logical, inevitable destinies. During the course of a story, however, there absolutely is a God—the author, who in fact does know the fate of these characters, and is leading them to their logical conclusions. Therefore, on some deep level, a good story reassures us that life is meaningful. That's my theory, and I'm sticking with it.

The Treatment, Step-Outline, or Beat Sheet:

Another step used by many writers before writing the script, which I personally find more useful than an outline and always do, is to write a treatment before writing the script. A *treatment* is just like a short story version of the film, in regular prose, and is usually somewhere between three and twenty pages long. If you call this item a Step-Outline or a Beat Sheet, it simply has more headings. Frequently, writers will go from the outline to the script. However, if you write a treatment in between you'll know a lot better what you're going to write in the script. You can just as easily write the treatment and skip writing the outline. But here's the real reason for writing a treatment: it's the easiest place to just let yourself go. Easier, I believe, than the outline. Since it's in plain old prose, not in script form or outline form, you can just write and write without feeling constrained. I think it's a good idea to put in the act demarcations, and if it's a Step-Outline or a Beat Sheet, then it must have them. Some people will tell you not to put in any dialog, but I say put in anything and everything. When it's done, if you've gone to the trouble of fully describing certain scenes, you can now appropriate those sections to use in the script and just cut and paste them in.

The Pitch:

Yet another technique in the storytelling process is to tell your story out loud to other people, which in Hollywood is called a *pitch*. Here's the big question: can you tell the story all the way through, or are you getting stuck? What's fascinating, I've found, is if you've got people listening, and you hit an illogical section of your story, you'll get embarrassed and quickly attempt to fix the problem on the spot, frequently finding a workable answer you hadn't thought of before. Try it, it really works. On some level, stories were meant to be told, and I personally love telling people the stories of movies. A friend once told me that after the nuclear war, should I be among the survivors, my job would be to sit on a rock and tell a different movie every night. I felt this was a great compliment and I've cherished it for years. So I highly recommend telling your story out loud. You'll probably get embarrassed at some point, but it will be good for your story, and you'll probably come up with some new ideas.

The Screenplay:

Since it's important that your screenplay be understood by many different people, like the actors, all the department heads, and possibly even investors, and location owners, it's essential that it be clear and comprehensible by one and all. A screenplay is not the place for technical information. You may be both the writer and the director, but the screenplay is not the place to describe the shots you intend to use to cover the scenes. Nor is it a place to ever mention film equipment. Just because as the director you intend to shoot the scene from up in a tree with a wide-angle lens doesn't mean anything to the reader.

Here are two examples:

Wrong: The camera starts up high in the air in a wide shot on top of a crane, then it swoops down on a group of U.S. marines who walk stealthily along a jungle trail.

Right: A group of U.S. marines walk stealthily along a jungle trail.

Telling me about cameras and cranes doesn't put me into the story, it puts me into a movie production and removes me from the story. In this instance you want the reader to feel that they are a part of a group of U.S. marines in a tense situation, not that they are part of a movie crew shooting a film about marines. So be clear and just tell the story.

As a basic rule of thumb, one page of the script equals one minute of screen time. If the page is mainly dialog, this is basically true; if it's mainly action, however, it's not true at all. It's very easy to write "the Japanese attack Pearl Harbor," but it's a lot more difficult to show it, and will probably take more screen time than the one sentence indicates. That's why you need to explain what you mean in as much detail as you can, keeping in mind that no one will grade you on your prose, and a screenplay isn't a novel.

Feature-length screenplays are for the most part 90-pages to about 130-pages, with most clocking in between 110- and 120-pages. But remember, 85-minutes is a perfectly acceptable length for a feature film, and it's definitely cheaper to make a shorter film. I recommend making between an 80- and a 100-minute movie, so your script really shouldn't exceed 100 pages, and it's just foolish to shoot scenes you won't use. Figure that out in advance, that's why you're writing a script. It costs nothing to cut pages out of a script, it costs thousands of dollars to cut scenes you've shot out of the movie.

Screenplays are written in the *present tense*, as though it were happening at this moment. Patton *slaps* the private, not Patton *slapped* the private.

Some writers seem to think that because it's a screenplay they are no longer required to work in whole sentences. They write, "Open door. Go in. Look around. Darkness." Writing like that drives me crazy, and makes me not want to read it. You shouldn't be flowery, either, but you still have to follow the basic rules of grammar.

I've seen scripts where the writers somehow feel the need to capitalize all of the props, like this: "The marine holds an M–16 AUTOMATIC RIFLE in his hands, has a HELMET on his head, and BOOTS on his feet." The art department will go through the script on their own, as will all the other departments, and highlight what they consider to be important themselves, you don't need to do it for them. Anything that's in caps seems like it's being yelled to me, and looks foolish.

Some screenwriters will also put "(Continued)" at the bottom and the top of every page if a scene continues from one page to the next. I also find this annoying and don't do it myself. Every TV script I've ever read has had this, so maybe it's required. The authors of books don't write "(Continued)" at the bottom and top of every page when a chapter continues over several pages. We readers all realize that things continue until we're informed otherwise, and when we get to the last page, they're not continued anymore.

Slug-lines:

Slug-lines are the capitalized sentences that begin every scene, such as:

```
EXT. NAVAL BASE (PEARL HARBOR) - DAWN
```

The *slug-line* is the physical description of the scene. Slug-lines do not describe shots. I've read a number of scripts over the years that have mistakenly done this and it's a big mistake. If the script should ever get filmed, it will cause a lot of trouble later on.

There is a school of thought that says there are only two possible time periods in a script, DAY and NIGHT. I disagree because DAWN and DUSK, particularly on real exteriors, means a specific lighting effect, and potentially early or late scheduling, and should be considered along with everything else. Yes, you can always add an orange hue in post production, or you can put on an orange filter while you're shooting at anytime during the day, but the actual dawn and dusk are frequently spectacular and are often used as a lighting effect. However, on an interior you would probably achieve the orange light of dawn or dusk with gels on the lights, so it's not as crucial, but it is still worth mentioning so you can plan for it. Therefore, I say you have four choices: DAWN, DAY, DUSK, and NIGHT.

EXT. means exterior or outside.

INT. means interior or inside.

Why bother with this stuff? you might ask. Because in the real world of production, the very first people to start work on a production will be the 1st Assistant Director and the Production Manager or Producer, who will begin the script breakdown and budget (which I'll get to). Just seeing how many interiors there are compared with how many exteriors means a lot, as well as how much day shooting and how much night shooting there is.

Next comes a more detailed description of what the slug-line says.

```
EXT. NAVAL BASE (PEARL HARBOR) - DAWN
```

```
The sun is just rising over the naval base at Pearl
Harbor, Hawaii. Misty tropical orange light il-
luminates eight enormous battleships, and eighty-
four other naval vessels, that all sit quietly in
port. The ship's crews are all waking up, just like
it was any other day . . .
```

```
A title appears onscreen that reads, "7:00 AM, De-
cember 7th, 1941."
```

In screenplays you never use any film terms like close-up, long shot, tracking shot, or anything else. First of all, it's not the writer's place to choose those things; secondly, it doesn't help the reader visualize the story. If you simply state what things are, the reader will do the visualizing (just as I do with everything else I read), but don't do it for me because it's annoying. If you're also the director you'll do the visualizing later on as a shot list or storyboards, but in the script itself it's inappropriate.

Script Formatting:

The *formatting,* or spacing, of a screenplay consists of four tab stops and a margin. It's really very simple and shouldn't be difficult for anybody of any age.

The far left margin is where the slug-line begins, as well as the scene descriptions.

Tab stop #1 is twenty spaces in, and is where the dialog begins. It should end at eighty spaces, before the right margin.

Tab stop #2 is twenty-five spaces in, and is where the emotional description of the line goes, in parentheses. These are adjectives, like (annoyed) or (amused), and go below the character's name, but above the dialog. I've heard actors gripe about them as though they were an infringement on their domain, but I like them and I use them a lot.

Tab stop #3 is thirty spaces in, and where the character's name goes, in capital letters.

Tab stop #4 is eighty spaces in, and where the transitions are stated, in capital letters.

All together it looks like this:

```
INT. MESS HALL - DAWN
Tired, sleeping-looking soldiers wander into the
mess hall and line up to get breakfast. A COOK
slops a ladle full of green slop on PRIVATE JONES's
tin plate. Jones looks down at the mush and winces.

                    JONES
               (disgusted)
          You gotta be kidding.


                    COOK
               (offhandedly)
          I wouldn't shit you, you're my
          favorite turd. Next.

Private Jones keeps moving.


                              DISSOLVE:
```

The first time you introduce a character with dialog, his/her name is both capitalized and underlined.

Another thought to keep in mind when writing a screenplay is that none of your paragraphs should be too long. A paragraph that's over a quarter of a page long looks too dense and isn't inviting to read. Work in short paragraphs that are made up of entire sentences.

Script Software:

To achieve four tab stops it seems kind of foolish to need any computer software's assistance, but if you find it helpful go ahead and use it. Some of these software programs also offer up a whole variety of plots. Soon they'll write the script for you, too, while you just kick back and take a nap. Then *all* movies will seem like they were created by machines, instead of just most.

The Lead or Main Character:

Your *main or lead character* is your story, plain and simple. If your lead character is flat and dull, your story is flat and dull, no matter how many plot twists you may dream up. Who this person is trumps what they go through. If your lead character is pointless, your story is pointless. If your lead is obnoxious, so is your story, etc.

As it was explained to me many years ago by a man who had written thirty-five pictures back in the 1940s and 50s, Big Bad Bart is in a saloon in the old west, pulls out his pistol, slams it down on the bar and says, "The next son of bitch that walks through that door is a dead man!" Now, whoever walks through that door is the story: if it's Clint Eastwood, we have a serious western and a shoot-out; if it's Woody Allen, we have a comedy. Your lead character *is* your story. Without a lead character, you don't have a story. You have nothing more than a series of events.

More and more often I see films with either no lead character, or the wrong character chosen as the lead. The film *15 Minutes* stars (in this order), Robert DeNiro and Edward Burns, and for the first two acts Robert DeNiro is in fact the lead character. Sadly, DeNiro dies at the end of act two. I have no doubt that the filmmakers thought Edward Burns would then *become* their lead character for act three, except that it doesn't work that way. You can't change lead characters in mid-stream and you can't kill your lead before the very end—it's not different and it's not daring, it's just plain old bad storytelling, and dramatically weak. Therefore, *15 Minutes* has no lead character for the final third, and subsequently falls to pieces and becomes a bad movie. You can switch leads in Act One if you care to, as Alfred Hitchcock daringly did in *Psycho*, but I don't recommend it unless you really, really mean it, as Hitchcock and writer Robert Bloch clearly did.

Your lead character must desperately need or want something, which is what will compel the entire story forward. If the lead character doesn't need or want something, the audience will not need or want to know what happens next in your story. Without a strong lead character you will never have a strong story, because, once again, the lead character *is* the story.

You can certainly have several lead characters, but you really must choose one of them as the main character. You have to take sides. You may not think you do, but you do. If you choose several characters as equal leads without specifically choosing one as the main character, that's weak storytelling, and a mushy dramatic point of view. Strong drama comes from a strong, specific point of view, which can be anything, including weakness, for instance, as long as it's specific to the lead and they feel the emotion strongly.

The main character is the story, and the audience is the main character. There's always a good solid reason why your main character is your main character, too, it's not a mistake and it's certainly not arbitrary. In *Thou Shalt Not Kill . . . Except,* for instance, I have four marines as the lead characters, so why did I specifically choose Sgt. Stryker as the main character? Because he's the character most suited to command the battle at the end of the story. Once I decided that, I then also made that his personal issue, as well—he's suited for command, but in Vietnam he never got to, and then he was wounded and sent home. However, as fate would have it, the battle now comes to him.

This method is known as working backward. It's a very logical way to work a story out dramatically. That's why you need to know your ending, then go back through all the events of the story getting them to lead to that ending.

In my script *Devil Dogs: The Battle of Belleau Wood,* there were 28,000 American soldiers fighting 40,000 Germans, so who the heck was the main character? There were 68,000 choices! So, I began eliminating. I could immediately cut it down by 40,000 Germans because I didn't want to be on their side. All right, how about the American commanding officer, Gen. James G. Harbord? Well, he didn't actually do any fighting himself and I wanted to be in the action. I considered creating an anonymous everyman soldier, but I quickly decided against that because it's a true story and it seemed like it should have a real character for the lead. As I kept researching the battle, one soldier's name kept coming back up in every account— Gunnery Sgt. Dan Daly—who was not only the most decorated soldier at the Battle of Belleau Wood, but was the most decorated enlisted marine of all time. So I chose Sgt. Daly as my main character, because on some level the most heroic soldier at the battle was the most crucial character to be there. Suddenly, the whole story fell into place for me because I now knew whose story I was telling. You can't tell the story of 28,000 against 40,000, but you can tell the story of one sergeant and his platoon of men.

Characterization and Motivation:

Characterization is that which identifies and differentiates your characters, that which makes them specific and unique. *Motivation* is their reasons for doing what they do.

Human beings don't necessarily do things for good or rational reasons, but, nevertheless, *there are always reasons for their actions.* There is a chain of logic, even if the events themselves are entirely illogical, that has caused us to do all the things that we've ever done. People don't just act for no reason, unless they happen to be characters in a bad movie.

The motivations for many of the things we human beings do is often not based on altruism or good intentions, but is instead based on the concept that we are our own worst enemies. Given a choice between doing what's best or what's worst for ourselves, we will frequently choose the worst. Why? Good question, it's one of the enduring human mysteries, and probably why, whether we realize it or not, we are all deeply intrigued by the idea of irony (more on this later).

Let's keep going with my several year process to figure out who Gunnery Sgt. Dan Daly was. This was not achieved by research because basically there's almost nothing written about the man. The most information I could find anywhere after an extensive search was in a 30-year old copy of Leatherneck Magazine, formerly the official magazine of the U.S marine corps. This was the only complete version of Daly's life I could locate, and it contained no motivations for why he had done what he'd done, just the facts, which I already knew—he stood up in the middle of machine-gun fire and got his trapped men moving.

Gunnery Sgt. Dan Daly, the most-decorated enlisted Marine of all-time, with two Medals of Honor

Well, fine, this was just a screenplay anyway, not a history book. All I needed was a motivated character to make my script work, right? Sadly though, just saying he did what he did because it's true, or something silly like, it needed to be done, flatly don't cut it as good motivations. I mean, why *did* he do it? That's what everyone in the audience are asking themselves all the time.

This is why a writer is like a detective. They are both trying to deduce why people did what they did, or do what they do. What are their motivations, the reasons behind their actions?

To say that Sgt. Daly stood up in machine-gun fire for the love of his country or because it was the right thing to do is ultimately lame and insufficient. I don't believe it, and I'm sure it's not true. If you're in the middle of a battle, with bullets whizzing past your head and soldiers being blown to bits all around you, with your face pressed into the dirt, sweat running into your eyes, and hoping upon hope that the next bullet or shell doesn't hit you, I'm convinced that no one is thinking about abstractions like patriotism, God or country. Under those circumstances everyone is functioning on a much more basic survival level: crouch lower; don't crap in shorts; is the rifle's safety off?

Several years later I ran across a quote from the 1600s that said, "Anger is the whetstone of valor," and an epiphany occurred to me. Circumstances can certainly make some people so angry that they'll do insane things, like maybe even standing up in machine-gun fire. And anyone that can get *that* angry, must have some sort of an anger problem. So I went back several years later and rewrote the script, and suddenly Sgt. Daly's character made all kinds of sense to me. So then I finally knew what the script was about: the theme was anger, and the drama was now Daly's inability to control his anger and his efforts to try. The irony of the story was that his inability to control his anger was also what caused him to be a hero. Whether or not this was actually the case I can't say, but it sure made a whole lot of sense as a motivation for his actions in a screenplay.

Also, a good character is a developing character—he/she is learning something over the course of the story. Sgt. Daly is learning how to cope with his anger, and failing. Sticking with military characters, General George Patton learns that as high-ranked as he may be, he still can't slap his men around. These may not be huge, important lessons, but they're enough for one character in a single movie.

George C. Scott as George S. Patton in *Patton* (1970)

Rocky, for instance in the film *Rocky*, is a dopey character, but he's still developing and learning a few things during the course of the film. First and foremost is his realization at the end of act two that he cannot beat the champ under any circumstances, and the best he can possibly hope for is to go the distance in the fight. And, as important as this fight is to him, his girlfriend is even more important to him.

A terrific example of a developing character is Michael Corleone (Al Pacino) in *The Godfather*, and his development is in fact what the whole film is ultimately about. At the beginning Michael doesn't want anything to do with the family business ("That's my family, Kay, not me"). By the end he's running the family business. Watching Michael transform into the Godfather is the *dramatic arc* of the story, which is based on the developing needs and desires of the lead character.

At the beginning of *Running Time*, Carl (Bruce Campbell) thinks he still needs his old high-school buddy, Patrick (Jeremy Roberts), even though he's kind of an idiot. By the end, Carl realizes that he no longer needs Patrick, and that part of his life is now over.

When you are creating your characters it's important to look around yourself at all the people you know and observe what makes each of them so specific? And clearly something does. People are all different, and nobody does things for the same reasons. So go ahead and steal your friends and relatives' character traits, that's what they're there for.

Most of the characters I create are based on me to some extent. I am forever looking to my own motivations, then using them for my characters. So writing is also a form of self-analysis. What would I do in this circumstance?

As the writer Harlan Ellison has said, "We're all the same person under different skins." Finding truthful motivations for your characters is what connects them to the rest of humanity and makes your story universal.

Dialog:

There's an old concept that in a well-written script you ought to be able to remove the character's names and still clearly know who's speaking because their voices are so unique. It's an important thought to keep in mind. Do all of your characters speak differently? Or do they all sound like you?

Life is basically a series of questions and answers. If one of your characters isn't curious and asking questions, you've chosen dull characters. When the crazy girl first comes into the apartment of the crazy boy in *Lunatics: A Love Story*, not only is he entirely wrapped in tin foil, but all of the walls of the apartment are covered in tin foil, too—this is to stop the X-rays that he believes doctors shoot at him through the walls. Well, you can bet that she has quite a few questions, many of which he has great difficulty answering sanely, and this translated into pretty good dialog, if I do say so myself. But in any given dramatic situation, someone ought to have at least one decent question about what's occurring, and that's where the dialog frequently begins.

If you are Paddy Chayefsky, who wrote *Network* and *Altered States*, then your characters will climb up on soap boxes and make speeches. This is difficult to do unless you're a really good writer with many salient points to make. To just have people talking for the sake of talking without any points to make is called *blather*. Chayefsky rarely reverted to blather because he really did have a lot of points to get across, and created interesting characters to make them. Sadly, however, many movies do revert to blather and it's painful and dull and to be avoided.

Almost every time I have written a line of dialog over three sentences long, I've ended up cutting it down, either during rehearsal or during editing. People in real life may well go into diatribes that are longer than three sentences all the time, but in movies it's hard to watch. To have a character speak for an entire minute in a movie is a very long time, and usually interminable. Snappy dialog is generally made up of quick exchanges that keep us moving toward the next scene and the conclusion. Lousy dialog is when a character has to state or recap the plot, or come out and tell you his autobiography. If you can't figure out a way to have this information come out naturally in short exchanges, it's probably not important enough for you to stop your narrative. The second I feel like I'm not moving forward anymore—which a long speech generally causes—I begin to get bored. Remember, the key word is *compelling*. Also, keep in mind that you don't have to reveal all or even part of your characters' histories right away. Let information come out gradually over the course of the script.

If you have one hundred scenes in a 100-minute movie you won't have a chance to revert to blather. But if you start writing longer scenes of two or more pages, and you will, stay alert: just what the heck are these people talking about anyway? Are they talking about the plot, their own motivations, or are they just talking for the sake of talking?

The Plot:

When I say that a story is something causes something else, that's the *plot* I'm referring to—the plot is the story in its most basic form. You can do away with the plot, but then you must have an absolutely great lead character so everything is coming directly out of them, and characters like that are *really* hard to come up with. Most movies do have plots and I think you need one, too (I know I always have). However, I contend that for the most part, the simpler the plot the better. Convoluted plots are really for the birds. Just stick with something causes something else, that generally causes yet something else. The end. That's a plot.

Many people mistakenly believe that the plot is the most important thing in a story, but I heartily disagree. I say the characters are the most important thing in a story. You can make a great movie without a great plot—or any plot, for that matter—but you can't make a great film with flat, dull characters no matter how good your plot is. A plot can ultimately only be so good. Almost any character, given enough scrutiny, can be fascinating.

A pretty good plot-oriented movie is *The Guns of Navarone*. The plot is about a group of Allied partisans who must blow up some big German guns on the island of Navarone so that Allied ships will be able to get through the straits. Luckily, it also has reasonably well-developed, though shallow, characters, so it's a pretty good movie. On the other hand, *Patton* hasn't got much of a plot at all—it's WWII and the allies would like to win the war—but it's got an intriguing, developing, lead character, and is therefore a much better movie. The problem with a plot-oriented story is that once you know the plot, you know it (like in *The Sixth Sense*, for instance). Yep, in *The Guns of Navarone* they blow up the guns all right. And yep, Bruce Willis is really dead. Once you know how it ends, you've got it. Whereas, watching George Patton's character develop I think is endlessly fascinating no matter how many times I see it. That one of our most powerful generals in the midst of a huge war was nearly busted for slapping a private is far more ironic and interesting to me than blowing up some artillery.

However, I'm not for one second intimating that you don't need a plot because I think you do. The trick is the balance. If you have a strong, interesting, developing lead character, you don't want to hamper them with too dense of a plot. Plots don't have to be tricky.

I've seen a whole spate of recent films with tricky plots, which seems like a trend, and they were all boring. It's as though they were saying, I'm allowed to be dull throughout most of the film because I have a good explanation at the end. Sorry, but being dull is failing, no matter how clever of an explanation you may come up with.

If you want to see a large array of one-sentence plots laid out in front of you, just look at the last 75 pages of any TV Guide where there are literally hundreds of plots in alphabetical order. It's kind of amazing what you can construe from a single sentence, like, do I want to watch this movie or not? And you can almost smell the plots that aren't going anywhere, which is because they seemingly have no cause and effect aspect to them.

The Scene:

The dictionary definition of a *scene* is: 5. a division of a play, or an act of a play, now commonly representing what passes between certain of the actors in one place. 6. a unit of dramatic action within a play, in which a single point or effect is made.

So, recapping for a moment, a shot is from when the camera goes on to when the camera goes off—from action to cut, which is also known as a *setup*. A *master shot* is when the shot covers the entire scene, and usually everyone in it. So a master shot is a whole scene.

A scene can be as simple as someone getting out of a car and going into a house with no dialog. This is known as a *transitional scene*. Or a scene can be the entire twenty-five minute heist in *Running Time*.

It is said among the Hindus, "As it goes with the smallest, so it goes with the largest." An atom is a miniature version of a solar system, and a scene is a miniature version of an entire story, with a beginning, a middle, and an end.

In *Rocky*, Rocky asks Mickey (Burgess Meredith) why his locker was taken away. Mickey offhandedly tells him he doesn't want to know why. Rocky loudly demands to know why. Everyone in the gym goes silent and listens. Mickey says, "You could've had something. You could've been a contender. But now you're nothin' but a cheap leg-breaker for the mob." Rocky shrugs, "It's a living." Mick growls, "It's a waste of life!" and turns away. Everyone returns to his/her workout, and Rocky slinks out of the gym.

It's short, it's dramatic, it's confrontational—based on a question and an answer—and I learn new information about both Rocky and Mickey; Rocky wasn't always a loser, in fact he had potential, and Mickey respected that even if he never told him and doesn't respect Rocky now, and it also sets Mickey up for when he comes to ask Rocky for the job of manager later on. It's a good scene, it's dramatic, it's fun to watch, it illuminates the characters, it moves the plot along, it sets up something in the future, and it has a beginning, a middle, and end.

A good scene also frequently leads you right into the next scene, and inevitably toward the conclusion.

When the great stage director, Elia Kazan, came to Hollywood to direct his first film, *A Tree Grows in Brooklyn*, the head of 20th-Century Fox Studios, Darryl F. Zanuck, gave him this advice: "Make every scene in the movie the best scene in the movie." This is great advice and should be taken to heart.

You've got fifty to a hundred scenes in your film, and that means you've got that many tries to get your drama to come to life, and how often you succeed determines the ultimate quality of your film.

Meanwhile, I did three uncredited rewrites of a film called *Hit List* (1989) with Jan-Michael Vincent, Rip Torn, and Lance Henriksen. The director, Bill Lustig, read one of the drafts and got mad because there was a half-page scene on a high-rise rooftop. He said that he would not drag a whole crew and all the equipment up to a rooftop to achieve only a half-page scene. This was really good advice and I've always kept it in mind ever since. If you can't get an entire page out of a scene—unless it's a transitional scene—then it's probably not a very good scene to start with, and may well not be worth doing. The bottom line is that if you are going to go to all the trouble it takes to shoot a scene—any scene—you'd better minimally get a minute of screen time out of it, otherwise you're ripping yourself off. Also, actors generally need at least a minute and a few lines to just warm up and get going.

So try to make each and every scene the best scene in the script, and even if you're only right occasionally, at least you're thinking the right way, and it should make for a decent script.

Flashbacks:

A *flashback* is a memory. Unless what you're flashing back to is crucial for the upcoming story, it's not wise to flashback too often. A compelling story should always be moving forward, and in a flashback you're basically moving backward. Most flashbacks stop your narrative dead in its tracks. Often, a quick flashback or two is needed in act one to set up the story, and that's fine. But to keep flashing back in acts two and three is generally a mistake. Flashbacks at the very end to explain some part of your mystery is done all the time, though, and it always seems to me like a cheap way out of not having set up your story properly.

Flashbacks have been used well and creatively over the history of cinema, but not all that often. Flashbacks are put to brilliant use in *Citizen Kane*, but that's because the entire plot is based on who is Kane and what did his last words mean. Each flashback is filling in a piece of the puzzle of Kane's character and driving us forward as we learn who he is. But most flashbacks don't work that way. Usually when it dissolves into a flashback, I feel like the writers have run out of story and are now padding things out. So, if you don't need to flashback, don't. Stay in the present time and keep moving forward. Remember, the key word is *compelling*.

Flashbacks can be used as a structure, too, like someone remembering something at the beginning, then the whole story is a flashback. This has been done a million times and each time I see it I find it ever more wearisome, and think to myself, "Is that the best they could come up with?" An interesting spin on this structure (and I'm sure there are more) is what screenwriter Abraham Polonsky did with *Body and Soul* (1947). At the beginning, the boxer is in a fitful sleep and remembers acts one and two, then wakes up at the start of act three and has to go fight for the world championship in the present time, which made it feel very immediate.

Script Transitions:

There are four legitimate *script transitions* (as opposed to the many transitions that can be dreamt up in directing), which are the film techniques you're suggesting should be employed to literally get us from one scene to the next scene. The possible script transitions are: *dissolve*, when one scene starts to go away and the next scene comes in over the top of it; *fade out*, when the screen goes to black; *fade in*, when the screen goes from black into the picture; and *cut*, which is to go directly from one scene to the next. Personally, I think "cut" or "cut to" are a waste of time and never need to be used. If there's a new slug-line, obviously we got there somehow, and if it doesn't say dissolve, fade in, or fade out, then we're clearly cutting, it's understood. I have seen the term *smash cut* used, but I don't know what it means. A cut is a cut is a cut. One image is stuck to the next image. You could put a loud smash sound effect right on the cut, but otherwise I don't know what's smashing.

I have a problem with fades during the course of a movie, and this may just be me. I accept fades at the very beginning and the very end of the movie, and I don't mind them at the end of an act, but otherwise I think fades are an intrusion and an annoyance that remove me from my involvement in the story. Anything that pulls you out of the story I say is bad and a mistake. Once you've gone to the extreme difficulty of drawing me into the story, don't do anything foolish to lose me, like using fades. Long fades are particularly aggravating. When the screen goes black for any length of time, I always take the opportunity to look around the theater at the other patrons.

I much prefer dissolves because they never let go of your attention. Before the scene you're watching is gone, the new scene appears on top of it and keeps you interested. Dissolves are frequently used to indicate a loss of time, meaning later that day or night, or at some point in the future. Dissolves are also often used to go in or out of a flashbacks. Dissolves can be used creatively as well. If employed imaginatively, the dissolve itself can be a thing of beauty. In the opening sequence of *Apocalypse Now*, with Martin Sheen going stir-crazy in the Saigon hotel room, there are numerous long gorgeous dissolves, which not only indicate how much time he's spent in that room, but just look spectacular.

Irony:

What is *irony* exactly? *Webster's New Twentieth Century Unabridged Dictionary* defines it as "a combination of circumstances or a result that is opposite of what might be expected or considered appropriate." The really surprising twists and revelations in stories do not come from the plot, they come from the irony in the characters.

Irony is my favorite thing in stories, and it's what I'm always searching for on some level in the stories I write. I think it's ironic that Sgt. Daly is constantly trying to control his anger, but his anger is what keeps making him a hero. His biggest shortcoming is his greatest attribute, which is ironic.

On occasion people will do the right thing for the wrong reason, or the wrong thing for the right reason, and that's good irony. In *Taxi Driver* (1976), Travis Bickle (Robert DeNiro) has gone insane, buys an arsenal of handguns and tries to assassinate a senator, but is foiled by the secret service and he gets away. Instead, Travis then goes out and kills a mobster and a pimp, and is hailed a hero. He mistakenly did the right thing for all the wrong reasons, and it's both highly ironic and scary.

In *The Bridge on the River Kwai,* Col. Nicholson decides to build a proper bridge for the Japanese to keep up the morale of his men. He is doing the wrong thing for the right reason. When he hears there is wood in the forest there that could last for five hundred years, he sighs wistfully, "Five hundred years, think of it?" Of course, the bridge is blown to smithereens in the first sixty seconds after its official opening.

Theme:

Writer-director Frank Tashlin said that he always boiled the *theme* of his scripts—the subject or topic—down to one word, which I think is a good way to go. In his film *Will Success Spoil Rock Hunter?* the word was *success*, and every single scene is about success in one way or another. Sadly, the theme of most films is generally not found in the title (if they were, writers would probably have to think a lot more about it). A really good theme not only covers the actions of the lead character, but those of as many other characters as possible, and that's *really* hard to do.

Just like with irony, a writer ought to be considering the story's theme constantly. Used properly, the theme ought to be touched on in every single scene if possible, but certainly every scene the lead character appears in. In fact, every line of dialog the lead character speaks ought to refer to the theme in some way.

The Point:

The *point* of a story comes out of theme. *Will Success Spoil Rock Hunter?* No, it won't. In *Running Time* the theme is trust, and the point is who you trust is who you are. It's not important to make a big point or say anything earth-shaking, but I think it's crucial that you actually believe the point you're making. To make a point you don't believe is called *lying*. To have no point at all makes your story pointless, and that which is pointless is dull, and being dull is unacceptable in a good story.

I have run into the same problem with many screenwriter wannabes that I've encountered over the past twenty-five years—they won't be hemmed in by any of the rules—they're all rebels. Subsequently, all of their scripts have been pointless, with poor characterization, no theme, no irony, and worse still, these wannabes are under the preposterous delusion that they are forging new ground in drama and boldly going where no man has gone before. It's utterly ridiculous.

You do not have to be a rocket scientist to figure out how to write a decent script, thousands have figured it out before you. But you do have to be willing to put in some plain old hard work. A script isn't going to come out the ends of your fingers properly structured, with a functioning theme, and fully formed characters—it just ain't gonna happen. If you don't put in the time confronting each of these issues and working them out, your script won't be any good, just like the eight million other crummy scripts floating around Hollywood. If your script's no good and you actually shoot it, your film won't be any good, either. You're no exception, we're all dealing with the same set of variables. If you think what you're experiencing is entirely new and unique to you, that it's so unlike what the other six billion human beings are experiencing, as well as all those who went before them, you're missing the big picture. The point of drama is finding the points of connection between all of us pathetic humans.

Perhaps it's the word *rules* that makes people so uneasy. Look, I was as rebellious and anti-authoritarian as any young person ever was—I graduated after one year of high school, as an example, and started college a month after I turned sixteen. However, when I seriously decided that I wanted to be a screenwriter, I had to finally come to accept the disciplines of the craft. I wrote four entire feature-length scripts thinking it was just a free-for-all, that anything went, and you could just sit there and type and a script would come out. Well, I got four scripts out before I began to get a grasp on any of these ideas, and those scripts are completely worthless.

I'm not saying you have to write four bad scripts before the first decent one emerges. What I am saying is that these are concepts that you simply *must* confront to write a script well. Ignoring these concepts does not make you a unique, one-of-a-kind artist, it puts you into the much larger category of Thoughtless Bad Writers.

The concepts of dramatic writing, as I've mentioned, are thousands of years old, and nothing has significantly changed during that time. You are not going to reinvent drama, nor will you reinvent the wheel, and if you think you will, you're immature. Get with the program. Drama is about motivation, characterization, plot, irony, theme, and the point. Those are the materials a dramatist has to work with, it's their clay. Don't try to come up with the formula for clay, make a better statue.

Writing is a discipline, like weightlifting. The structural and thematic rules are the weights. You certainly have the right to proclaim, "I'm a rebel, and I won't lift those weights," but then you're not a weightlifter; you're a blob standing around the gym getting in other people's way.

Copyrighting the Script:

When your script is completed you need to copyright it with the Library of Congress in Washington DC (you can get the forms from: Register of Copyrights, Library of Congress, Washington DC, 20559. Request form PA, or you can download them from www.loc.gov/copyright). You can also register your script with the Writer's Guild of America, but if you're going to choose just one, copyright it, that's the official, legal version. Should you end up in court with a copyright suit, you're much better off with an official copyright than a registration with a trade union. Presently, a copyright for a script costs thirty dollars, and they ask that your script be unbound, meaning remove the fasteners (this is so they can more easily microfilm it, then discard it). You should state your copyright on the cover page of the script, and include the copyright symbol ©. Since most typewriters cannot make this symbol, a small c with parentheses around them works, too. On some word processing software now, like this one (MS Word), if I put a small c in parentheses, it will automatically make it into a copyright symbol. Stating your copyright up front is as important as registering your script. Stating a copyright is in essence saying, "Don't steal this or you're breaking the law."

The Bridge on the River Kwai: **A Study Guide**

In my opinion no one has yet written a better script than *The Bridge on the River Kwai*. Yes, it's based on a good book, but the script is actually better than the book, and that's certainly a rare occurrence. Since screenwriters Michael Wilson and Carl Foreman were both blacklisted due to the communist witch-hunts of the 1950s, neither writer got screen credit until the film was restored in 1997, sadly after both of them had died. What makes this script so special? That it's a World War II POW camp story? I don't think so, there are plenty of those. That the prisoners build a bridge? Or perhaps that commandos blow it up? I'd say it's none of those things. That's all plot stuff, and it's important, but it's not what makes the script so good.

Irony and theme are what make it so captivating—plus, it's beautifully directed, shot, and cast (oh yeah, those things). The story's basic great irony appears on page 1 of Pierre Boulle's book—he purports that a Colonel in the military is the same person in any country in the world: an uptight, unbending, humorless prig, with such an extremely overdeveloped sense of duty, that's it's to the exclusion of everything else including common sense.

Alec Guinness as Col. Nicholson and Sessue Hayakawa as Col. Saito in *The Bridge on the River Kwai* (1957)

You may have watched this film a hundred times and never noticed that, and it doesn't matter in the slightest because it's there. The main irony as well as the theme (which is the meaning of duty) and the main dramatic conflict all occur in the first ten minutes of the film. You just can't do any better than that. Most films these days do not have these issues figured out over the course of two or more hours.

So, let's say that Pierre Boulle began conceiving this story with his ironic observation that colonels are the same the world over (it is on page one). Okay, maybe that's true, but it's not a story. For it to be a story you must have a *dramatic conflict*, which is minimally two people confronting each other. To make Pierre Boulle's point you would need two colonels from different countries confronting each other. Well, how about a battle? Realistically, two colonels will never end up face to face in a battle; if they did, they'd just kill each other. How and where do you get them to face off and have a chance to speak? How about in a prison camp in the middle of the jungle, where one of the colonels is God and the other colonel is a prisoner? And, since World War II had ended just a few years earlier (the book was written in 1952) and was still on people's minds, why not situate the story during WWII? Thus, we have a setting, a subject, and a theme, and we haven't mentioned bridges, escape attempts, espionage teams, or anything else about the plot.

What *The Bridge on the River Kwai* is about—and you absolutely can't believe you've gotten there in the first ten minutes—is Colonel Saito (Sessue Hayakawa) smacking Colonel Nicholson (Alec Guiness) across the face with the Geneva Convention rule book. The two lead characters have reached a major dramatic conflict on the meaning of duty and the front titles just ended! Where can this possibly be going? Well, that's *exactly* what you want the audience to be wondering at the beginning of your story and it's what makes this narrative so breathtaking.

Because it's so sweetly ironic that these two colonels should ever possibly end up face to face in a dispute over the meaning of duty (which is not a true story, but artfully better than the truth), that which the original author felt he had to point out on page one of his book, the screenwriters spend thirty-five minutes illustrating and milking, and don't actually state until near the end of act one when each colonel independently proclaims the other colonel to be "mad." The screenwriters don't tell us the colonels are the same, *we observe it ourselves.*

But that's not the only irony inherent in this situation; there is yet another, bigger irony looming. The prisoner, Colonel Nicholson, wins the dispute with his captor, Colonel Saito, because Saito is actually in a worse situation than Colonel Nicholson—if Saito doesn't get that bridge built on time so that a troop train can come across it on a specified day, he will have to kill himself. He informs Colonel Nicholson of this and asks, "What would you do?" Nicholson shrugs, "I suppose I'd have to kill myself." Now the prisoner is in command over his captor. Then you have an even bigger irony: Once Col. Nicholson has won his dispute with Col. Saito and Nicholson takes charge of building the bridge, he decides to build a "proper" bridge to keep up the morale of his men. This is quickly bordering on aiding and abetting the enemy, which is the wrong thing for the right reason.

The Bridge on the River Kwai is not great because it has soldiers and machine guns and explosions or even because it's beautifully directed and photographed; it's a masterpiece because it's got such a terrific sense of irony and an incredibly strong and true theme, and the situation is the perfect one to exploit these things.

That screenwriters Wilson and Foreman are then able to take the theme of duty and weave it back through every other major character—James Donald, the idealistic doctor; William Holden, the apathetic prisoner; Jack Hawkins, the ruthless lead commando; and Geoffrey Horn, the young inexperienced saboteur—then tie up every one of these stories in the same sequence at the end is so brilliant that it's utterly astonishing. That a bridge blows up (in real time, without slow motion) is almost more than you can bear.

The Bridge on the River Kwai has been more important to me as a struggling screenwriter than any book I've ever read on the subject, and it's not that several books haven't been quite important to me. But everything you need to know about screenwriting is right there, gorgeously photographed on location in what was once called Ceylon, which is now called Sri Lanka.

Motivation, theme, irony, and the story's point ought to be the main subjects you think about when you're writing, then comes the plot. With these concepts in mind it is possible, given you've chosen an interesting story and an intriguing main character to begin with, to write a great script.

PART TWO:
RAISING MONEY

A Limited Partnership or a
Limited Liability Corporation:

Before you can legally begin raising money, you must start a company.
You could start a corporation, but that's a rather permanent arrangement,
and it costs a lot of money to have a lawyer set it up. That's why nearly all
movies are produced using either a limited partnership or a limited liability
corporation.

A *limited partnership (LP)* or a *limited liability corporation (LLC)* is a legal
entity, registered with the state, that clearly outlines the deal for the production of your proposed movie, the percentages of ownership, and an
assurance of limited liability for the investors. That means that no investor
is liable for any more money than they have already invested. There are
two kinds of partners in this kind of deal: *limited partners*, who are the investors, and *general partners*, who are the ones who have put the deal together
and will co-own it for their effort and expertise in making the movie.
Frequently it is a fifty-fifty split between general and limited partners, but
not always. The split is decided by the general partners, and it's all based
on what you think you can sell. Some folks feel that giving the limited
partners a larger percentage will make the deal more enticing to them, but
I don't think so. I believe that a fifty–fifty split is both fair and reasonable.

The difference between a limited partnership and a limited liability corporation is that an LLC also offers the limited liability of a corporation to
the general partners as well, and it costs more money. That way neither side
is liable, and God forbid anyone in the modern world should actually take
responsibility for his own actions. Personally, I've always used LPs because
I'm not a corporation.

So, why do you need a limited partnership or a limited liability corporation? Because, given the very remote possibility that your film actually
does make money, you have to know who gets what. Why would people
with money possibly invest in a deal that didn't outline how they'll recoup
their cash? Very simply, they won't. Also, this is the only way you have to
show potential investors that you're not a complete idiot and that you are
performing to the minimum standard requirement for legally doing business. If you're meeting with lawyers, doctors, and dentists, who are hit on
for money all the time, you must have some credibility; and if you haven't
made a movie before, having done your paperwork properly is just about

all you've got. Potential investors don't want to see your script, they want to see your *partnership agreement*, which is the contract between you and them. If you don't have one, you're boned before you've started.

Also, you can't open a business bank account without the paperwork showing you're actually a business. Without a business bank account you can't cash checks written to your company name. You don't want people writing checks to you personally, because it will put you in a future tax nightmare.

Therefore, you will certainly be using a limited partnership or a limited liability corporation to form the company to make your movie. With those forms of partnership there is often a limit of twenty-five to thirty-five investors, depending on the rules of the state where you live. To go beyond the limit, you must register with the Security Exchange Commission (SEC) just like any other stock on the stock market, and that's an enormously expensive ordeal that you absolutely don't want to deal with.

With a thirty-five share (called *units*) limit at $1,000 each, you would have $35,000. However, if your proposed budget is $150,000, the shares would then have to be $4,285 each. The limit on the number of investors divided by the amount of your proposed budget equals the cost of your units.

Well, $4,285 isn't the end of the world, but it's not peanuts, either. Right now I wouldn't want to part with four grand under almost any circumstances. How about you? So, the smaller you can make the shares the better, which means the smaller you can make the budget the better.

As a note, if you spend more than about $500 to $1,000 for having a lawyer draw up your limited partnership or LLC, you're getting ripped off. It's a totally generic, boilerplate document that any lawyer should easily be able to plug your name and numbers into. You can even do it yourself if you really want to save money, but then you have to know the state regulations. It's better to get a lawyer to do it, but don't get taken for a ride. It's nothing more than some word processing for a legal secretary, and it's not worth more than $500 to $1,000. If the lawyer suggests turning the legal work into anything more than that, they're taking advantage of you. Just having the legal work done properly is sufficient; it doesn't need to be fancy.

How to Raise Money:

Getting the financing to make a movie is by far the trickiest and most difficult part of the filmmaking process, whether it's an independent or a studio film. In my considered opinion it's more difficult to get a deal in Hollywood, which I've never gotten, than raising the money yourself, which I've done four times. In over twenty years in Hollywood I never discovered the logic of making film deals, as I observed most people in Hollywood never do (even though I have made TV movies and TV shows, but that's different).

Even the people I know that have been very successful in Hollywood are not allowed to make the movies they want to make. If the studio is putting up the money, they have the power to say what gets filmed and what doesn't. All scripts in Hollywood have to be passed before large committees of executives that all have their own agendas, generally that have little or nothing to do with the making of quality films. So, if quality or personal filmmaking is your objective, Hollywood is not a logical route to follow.

Since I desperately need to make movies, and I specifically want to keep making movies my own way, I concluded many years ago that I had to raise the money myself.

There are two basic routes to raising money independently: 1. earn it yourself, 2. get it from other people. There is a large school of thought among independent filmmaker wannabes that says you should never use your own money. I say, nonsense! If you won't invest in yourself, why would you expect anyone else to do it? And since you can be 99.9% certain that all of the money that's put into this first film will be lost, it's exceedingly hard to convince anyone with any sense that it's a good investment, particularly business people who understand investments. I spent nearly five years of my life trying to raise money for two different movies, and finally ended up with a paltry $18,000 for all my efforts. This is the money I used to shoot my first film, which was painfully insufficient.

If you own anything, like a house, you'd better be willing to mortgage it. If you own anything worth any amount, you'd better be willing to hock it. Movies are the biggest money-suckers that I've ever encountered in my life. I've poured every extra cent I've ever had into my own movies, four times now. And I'll do it again, too, should I even slightly recover from the last one.

In all honesty, and in retrospect, had I just worked at a decent, mid-level job for those five years, lived frugally, and intentionally saved my money to make a movie, I would probably have put away more than $18,000, and would have also spared myself thousands of headaches and tons of heartache. It was a grueling, depressing, learning experience to have about five hundred meetings over the course of five years with all sorts of various folks trying to hustle them out of a few thousand bucks each to make a movie. However, when everything was said and done, it wasn't worth it. Working hard at a potentially unrelated job where you can make a halfway decent living, combined with enough sense to start a secure, interest-bearing account, like a CD for a college fund, will much more logically get you to the goal of having money than trying to raise it. At least, that's what I think. And if you can get a high-paying job, even better.

However, should you decide to go out and solicit funds, here are some lessons I learned along the way:

People are not eager to part with their money, and if it seems like they are, they're pulling your leg. Anyone that acts like $5,000, $10,000, or $100,000 isn't a lot of money, probably doesn't have any money at all. They may dress well and even live in a nice house, but they probably don't have two cents to rub together. People with money respect the difficulty it took to get that money, even if they didn't earn it themselves, and they will not part with it easily.

Anyone that says, "A hundred thousand dollars? You got it, babe," or anything like that is totally full of it.

Anyone that starts to tell you how to change your story and hasn't yet put up any money is to be avoided in the future at all costs.

If you've met with someone three times and they haven't cut you a check, and now they want to meet again, they just like taking meetings. You may get some free lunches out of it, but you will never get any money.

Who do you go to for money? Anyone that will meet with you, that's who. It's only going to be the oddball, nutty people that will end up investing anyway, because remember, *it's not a good investment*. Therefore the smart people probably won't do it unless they're into movies or the arts or some artsy-fartsy kind of thing, and this must be exploited. Make them think they're a patron of the arts and that investing in your film is like a large PBS donation. Make them think you're a struggling genius who desperately needs their help. Do anything you have to do.

When everything else is said and done, the very best scheme for raising money is spreading guilt among your relatives and friends. Convince them this is your big shot at stardom and if they don't invest they're sabotaging you and holding you back. Be inventive. It's your best bet next to earning the money yourself, which will take years. Obviously, wealthy relatives and friends are the first ones to hit, and hit hard. And repeatedly. And just because they said no once doesn't mean you can't ask them again.

If you feel like you have too much pride to do things like that, then you're probably right, and you do, and you probably won't raise any money, and then you won't make a film. The most important part about raising money, I'm sorry to say, is eating shit. If you're not willing to crawl for this money, you'd better go get that job and start earning it right away, because that will be your only chance.

When soliciting money, if you let a potential investor get a sense that you are unsure of what you're doing, you'll never get the money. You must make potential investors feel secure, that they are investing in experts that intimately know of what they speak. You cannot just toss your partnership agreement on the table and say "read this." You have to know every point in it thoroughly and be able to explain it. If you can't then you'll come off as a putz, and no one will invest in a putz. Also, if you let the potential investor feel that you may or may not actually make the film, they won't invest. You have to make them feel like this is a train leaving the station, and they can either climb aboard or not, but the film will be made regardless of their participation. This isn't an easy stance to pull off. People with money, who are approached to invest in all sort of schemes constantly, can smell a faker. Just because you *want* to make a film means nothing, you have convince everybody that you *are* making a film, and the first one you have convince of this is yourself.

If you don't get any money out of someone, at least do your best to get the name of one other possible investor, that way you won't leave empty-handed.

A Pilot Version or a Trailer:

I made a super-8 pilot, or short, version of my first film, *Thou Shalt Not Kill . . . Except*, called *Stryker's War*, that was 45-minutes long. Sam Raimi made a super-8 pilot version of *Evil Dead*, called *Within the Woods*, which was 30-minutes long. Joel and Ethan Coen made a 35mm *trailer*, or coming attraction, for their first film, *Blood Simple* (I mention this because Joel was the assistant editor on *Evil Dead*), and it was four or five minutes long. Showing potential investors that you can actually produce something similar to your proposed film is not only a wise idea, it gives you some badly needed credibility. Digital video is much better format for this now than super-8. Even if you don't do a pilot version of your film, at least stage some scenes. Put something together. Give everybody a hint as to what you've got in mind. And if you can't pull off the production of a short pilot version, you'll *never* pull off a feature, so this idea has value in several ways.

Credit Cards: A Cautionary Tale

Financing an independent movie with credit cards is now part of the mythology of the form, and so I got suckered into it myself. However, unless you have a well-paying job so you can stay ahead of the minimum payments and eventually pay the cards off, or unless you have no qualms about declaring bankruptcy, I'd say be very careful in your use of credit cards. Also, with the recent changes in the bankruptcy laws, which now favor the credit card companies, just declaring bankruptcy isn't so easy.

If you put $100,000 on credit cards to finance a film, as I did with *If I Had a Hammer*, you will be paying about $1,000 a month in minimum payments that are making no dent in the *principal*, the actual amount you owe, you'll just be paying on the *interest*, the accruing finance charges. The second you're late with any payment, the minimums suddenly double (or more), and the whole situation goes from bad to worse.

I didn't even have a single credit card until I was thirty-five years old—they made me get one when I was directing "Real Stories of the Highway Patrol" so I could rent vehicles. However, once I had a credit card, every other credit card company began sending me applications, all of which I promptly filled out and sent back. Soon I had ten credit cards, which I made sure to pay off entirely every month to prove I was a great credit risk. After I had done that for about a year, I began having my credit limits raised until I had at least a $10,000 limit on every card. At that time I was gainfully employed on "Xena," and making a good living, and it all seemed like an amusing game.

Then I went and made *If I Had a Hammer*. I put up $100,000 of my own money, raised another $100,000, then put yet another $100,000 on credit cards. And, as fate would have it, "Xena" was then canceled and there went my well-paying gig.

My initial plan was to always pay more than the minimum payments so that I would be constantly diminishing the principal. I kept this up for a year, while simultaneously personally paying for all of the post-production costs on *Hammer*.

Before I knew it I was out of money, I had no income, I still wasn't done paying for the post-production costs, and I still owed the credit card companies $1,000 a month in minimum payments. And so my life began to fall apart. I met with a credit consolidator (like you see on TV all the time), and they said that I was so far in debt that they couldn't help me. Nor would any of the credit card companies lighten up on the interest charges—I was (and still am) paying between 16% and 22% interest.

I somehow miraculously completed the film, while I simultaneously began discussing bankruptcy with an attorney, which seemed like my only recourse at that point. The year 2000 wins for me as the worst year of my life in the last fifteen years.

Very luckily for me, kindly relatives of mine leant me enough money to continue making the minimum payments, as well as paying into the principal somewhat. And so I continue to pay, and continue to pay, and so far, over four years after the film's completion, I'm still paying (I'm now down to four credit cards, and I've paid off a bit over half the principal).

Since you cannot depend on, nor even expect, getting any money back, how on earth can you keep making all those payments? You can't. Therefore, using credit cards to finance a film is a foolish idea. And if you do declare bankruptcy, there's a chance the bank will try and seize your movie, which is yet another good reason for having created a limited partnership or LLC, so then the partnership is the film's owner, not you, so the bank will have a more difficult time taking your film (not that they want it, because they don't).

PART THREE:
PRE-PRODUCTION

Starting a Business Bank Account:

ON SOME WEIRD level starting a business account at the bank is what makes a movie into a reality. Now you can do what movies do almost better than anything else on earth (except possibly military defense systems) which is, *spend money*. If you're spending money then you really are making your movie.

Generally, the business name is based on the film's title. For instance, the company for *If I Had a Hammer* was Hammer Partners, L.P. *Running Time* was originally called *Blood Money* and the company was Blood Money Partners, L.P. A bank teller at Bank of America in LA looked at the check and asked, "Is this a real estate offering?" I said, "Yes, it's for a subdivision called Blood Money Estates."

Locking the Script:

Some people never lock their scripts until they shoot them. To lock the script is to say it's done, this is the finished script we're shooting. For some folks the script is in a constant state of being rewritten until it's frozen on film. TV is notorious for this, but so are many, many movies. I say it's a bad idea that almost always makes for a worse film or TV show in the long run.

As a director, the most important thing you've got going for you is preparedness. If the script is rewritten right up to the night before you shoot, you're flying by the seat of your pants. Nothing made me more nervous working in TV than getting rewritten pages either the day before shooting, or in a number of nerve-wracking instances, the day of the shoot. It makes everyone feel insecure, particularly the director, as well as the actors, who now don't know their lines. Forget any kind of subtlety or depth of performance, the big goal now is can the actors get the words out of their mouths without blowing it.

There's absolutely no reason to do this to yourself on a low-budget independent film. If you don't have a release date, you don't have a deadline. There's no reason to start pre-production until your script is in good enough shape so that you feel secure enough to lock it. That doesn't mean you can't change things in rehearsal or even on the set, but stop rewriting.

The Breakdown:

The *breakdown* is the vital analytical stage between the script and the budget. Without a breakdown you cannot create a realistic budget, and it's imperative to have a realistic, believable budget. Without it you won't know how much you think you'll be spending, and to not know that in any business venture is insanity.

You can buy legitimate breakdown (and budget) forms from Samuel French Bookstore in LA, or perhaps you can find them for free somewhere on the internet. But you don't need a form to do a breakdown, just the script and the time to give each scene some analysis.

To do a breakdown you simply go through the script, scene by scene, in order, and write down which actors are needed, how many extras, and, beyond your regular crew and standard film equipment, what special personnel and extra equipment you think you might need. It's not really a big deal, it isn't very hard, but it must be done.

Here's a section of my breakdown for *If I Had a Hammer*, which I did on my own form:

Sc. 13   EXT. STUDENTS FOR POLITICAL ACTION OFFICE – DAY

Characters:	Extras:	Special Equipment/ Personnel:
Lorraine, Lorraine's Mom, Lorraine's Dad	5	Cadillac, 2 old cars

---

Sc. 14   INT. CADILLAC – DAY

Characters:	Extras:	Special Equipment/ Personnel:
Lorraine, Mom, Dad	0	Car lights, possibly a towbar & truck

Sc. 15   INT. PHIL'S BEDROOM – DAY

Characters:	Extras:	Special Equipment/ Personnel:
Phil, Mr. Buckley	0	Special Newspaper

Sc. 16   INT. PHIL'S HOUSE/ LIVING ROOM - DAY FOR NIGHT

Characters:	Extras:	Special Equipment/ Personnel:
Phil, Dan, Mr. Buckley, Mrs. Buckley	0	Day for Night lighting

Sc. 17   EXT. PHIL'S HOUSE - DAY FOR NIGHT

Characters:	Extras:	Special Equipment/ Personnel:
Phil	01	Old Car (Falcon)

Sc. 18   EXT. PHIL'S HOUSE AND BLOCK - DAY FOR NIGHT(also a special effects plate)

Characters:	Extras:	Special Equipment/ Personnel:
Phil	23 Old	Cars(including Falcon), Day for Night lighting

Sc. 19   EXT. PURPLE ONION - NIGHT

Characters:	Extras:	Special Equipment/ Personnel:
Lorraine, Phil, Terry, Alvin, Debbie	408	old cars, Night lighting, Additional Hair, Wardrobe & Makeup

Sc. 20   INT. PURPLE ONION/ WIDE SHOTS -- NIGHT (Various) (includes Sc. 41, Part)

Characters:	Extras:	Special Equipment/ Personnel:
M.C., Lorraine, Phil, Moustapha, Alvin, Debbie, Terry, Bobby Lee, Ronnie, Lee, Pete, Fred, Mindy, Brian, Tim, Cheryl, MaryLou, Dean, Bill	40	Playback, Stage lighting Additional Hair, Wardrobe & Makeup

I've chosen seven different scenes of varying sizes that sort of cover the gamut of possibilities, day, night, interior, exterior. Let's go over them.

Scene 13 was an exterior of the Students For Political Action office. This was shot at a storefront we rented in Tujunga, California. I also used the actual office interior for the SPA interior. Then I also used this same location, both exterior and interior, as a café by repainting it and completely redressing it. In scene 13 we are on a day exterior of the office, and Lorraine, the lead female character, is handing out fliers to passing pedestrians when her mother and father drive up in a big Cadillac and take her out to lunch. I indicated in the breakdown that I needed: Lorraine, Lorraine's Mom, and Lorraine's Dad—the three speaking characters—as well as five extras, whom she offers fliers to as they walk past, the Cadillac her parents will drive up in, and also two other old cars to park on the street. Now, as long as the regular crew with the regular equipment show up, combined with what I also said I needed in the breakdown, I then theoretically have everything I need to shoot that scene.

Scene 14 is Int. Cadillac – Day, and was in a moving automobile. Since this was a period story that took place in 1964, it was imperative that I not see any new cars go by or parked on the street. Since I shot this film in LA, it wasn't all that easy finding this location, nor could we possibly afford enough old cars with which to line the streets. So I chose a side street that runs parallel to the LA river and has foliage blocking the street from the river, and anything else we might see. I then had to apply for a permit from the city to post notices on this street that there was no parking on the street that day, then I had to hire two LA city cops with motorcycles to enforce this posting, as well as to keep any new cars away from us while we shot. I also tried as hard as I could to angle all the shots toward the wall of foliage and away from the inhabited side of the street. In the Special Equipment category I requested: car lights, a towbar, and a truck. To light inside a moving car you need special lights that run off a battery. Using a towbar and a truck to haul the car is a standard way of shooting a moving car so that you don't have to actually have the car's engine on so you get better sound, particularly in an old car which usually has a loud old engine and a bad muffler. As fate and the budget demanded, I didn't get the truck or the towbar, so all of my shots were either in the car, mounted to the side of the car (with special camera *car-mounts* that need to rented), or on the street with the car going past the camera. We also ended up renting a convertible so we could just lower the top and not have to light inside. But with the noisy old engine running and the top down, the sound came out pretty lousy, as we all expected it would. It's the worst sound recording in the entire film, but it's understandable so I used it anyway. Hell, it is a low-budget movie after all.

Scene 15 was in Phil, the lead male character's, bedroom, with he and his dad. When we first see Phil in this scene he's reading a newspaper which I wanted to be able to actually see and read with a specific reference to the events transpiring in my story. Therefore, I needed to have the art department make a fake newspaper with the information I wanted to see on it. Using computers and laser printers, this wasn't a huge issue, but it still had to be thought about in advance so it was ready on the day I wanted to shoot.

Scene 16 was in the living room of Phil's house and was meant to be shot *day for night*, meaning it would be shot in the daytime, but would pass as nighttime. Why do this? you might ask. Because I had a number of other scenes in this same location, mostly to be shot in the day, and I wanted to get them all on the same day. Why not actually shoot them at night?

If I Had a Hammer, INT. LIVING ROOM -- DAY FOR NIGHT, with L to R: Brett Bearslee, Robert Joseph Reid, Mark Sawicki, Susan Reno.

Well, night shooting is to be avoided as much as humanly possible. Night shooting completely screws up your schedule because you must give the cast and crew what's called *turnaround*, meaning they get twelve hours off after working for twelve hours (your standard shooting day). If you work the cast and crew until 3:00 AM, then give them another hour to drive home, you can't start shooting again until 4:00 PM the next day, which kills the whole day and puts you back into night shooting. On TV they almost never shoot anything at night. On "Hercules" and "Xena" all of the night exteriors were actually shot in a studio during the day, and lit to look like night. In seven years of working on those shows I never legitimately shot a scene at night, although I had many scenes that took place at night. But night shooting is such a schedule-killer that they simply didn't do it. In the old days in Hollywood they almost never really shot at night, either. And if you're shooting on an interior it's very easy to fake nighttime—you just cover the windows with blue *gels*, which are sheets or rolls of colored plastic, turn the lamps on in the room, then light the scene as though these lamps were the *sources*, or what's supposed to be causing the illumination.

Scene 17 was outside Phil's house day for night. Phil steps outside from the last scene, looks in the window and sees his family engrossed in watching TV, then Phil lights a cigarette and walks away, and we stay looking at his family through the window. Shooting exterior day for night scenes can be very difficult because it's hard to make it believable. Frequently it will just look like daytime slightly underexposed. To achieve good-looking, believable day for night on an exterior, you really must block out all of the direct sunlight. If it's a gray, cloudy day, that will help a lot. If it's not gray and cloudy, as it generally isn't in LA, you must then put up a big *silk*, which is a huge piece of parachute silk strung between metal poles, that will block out the sunlight—but only in a specific, confined area. This scene in front of the house was too wide of a shot for a silk to do the job, but since we knew it was coming we had made sure to have a lot of extra *duvatine*, which is long rolls of black velvet, and we put up a big black tent all over the front of the house, then lit inside it, and it works perfectly.

Scene 18 turned out to be an interesting situation. My initial concept was that Phil would leave his house in Scene 17, then we'd pick him up in Scene 18 walking up the sidewalk past several other houses on his block, all of which would have the TV on to the same channel as his family, and we could see the flickering, blue TV light coming from the windows of all the houses. Since I absolutely knew for a fact that I couldn't afford to get into all of those houses and set up the flickering TV lighting, I decided it would be done in post production as a *special effect*, meaning the shot would have some elements created in post-production, if not the entire shot. I felt that it would be an interesting effect and would be worth the extra cost. As it turned out, the house we were able to rent for our location was on it's own separate piece of property behind a tall wooden fence, and there were no houses next to it. I then decided—since I truly did not want to spend anymore money—that Scene 18 would not include Phil's house, but would instead be a block of very similar suburban houses. Well, I looked and looked for that location in LA and never found it (either of the first two neighborhoods where I grew up in Detroit would have been perfect, with twelve houses a block, twelve blocks a mile, but LA hasn't got neighborhoods like that). And everything I found that might pass for it, like a long 1950s apartment building with a lot of windows, was nowhere near all the rest of the locations and therefore entirely impractical from a logical shooting standpoint—in any shooting day you want all of your locations to be as close together as possible, and this building wouldn't be close to any other location on any day. Therefore, I subsequently chose a location one block from my main location that wasn't really a very good location—it had a few nondescript buildings—however, I could get the angle I wanted, and since I had my actor in his proper outfit and haircut, which I knew I would undoubtedly never have again (he died his hair blue the day after the shoot ended), I got the shot knowing I would use it as a *plate* for a special effect. This story continues in the "Special Effects" chapter in the Post-Production section.

Scene 19 was my biggest production ordeal. Although there were many other scenes that were just as complicated, this was the scene with the most extras (thirty-five), and since it was period film, all of the extras had to be dressed and have their hair done, which meant extra makeup and wardrobe personnel. Also, it was an actual night exterior, meaning call time was 4:00 PM and we then shot all night long until 4:00 AM. In scheduling this is referred to as a *day/night shoot*, because it begins in the day and goes on into the night. Obviously, if the scene is big enough and it takes place at night, you've got to shoot it at night. I needed extra lighting equipment, extra grips, extra trucks, and extra food. In the northern San Fernando Valley in the summer it was blazing hot in the day and very chilly at night, which often makes for cold, unhappy extras. It was a tough night, but we got our last shot just as the sun began to rise.

Scene 20 was the biggest, most complicated interior scene in the film. All of the main characters of the story would be seen at the same time together. After this they would all separate out into their own little groups. When I say *various* in the breakdown I meant that there were hunks of this wide shot that would fall between other scenes, so it made more sense to get them all at once, as you generally do in movies, since you generally work by the lighting setups. This is called block shooting, where you get everything from a lighting setup at the same time. You try as hard as you can to light an entire set only once if I can help it. From there on out we will do increasingly smaller lighting setups, of five people at one table, or two people on one side of the table. You shoot from the biggest lighting setups to the smallest lighting setups.

Since all of act two of *If I Had a Hammer*, which is an hour long, took place at this club in the course of one evening, this confined the shooting to mostly one interior location where I controlled the lighting and the sound. We shot in an abandoned hardware store in Tujunga, and even though it was extremely hot inside, it was an ideal situation because it was confined and it was controlled.

The Schedule:

Generally, the 1st Assistant Director or the production manager will do the breakdown and the *schedule*, which is the order in which you'll shoot the scenes. On both of my last two indie films, *Running Time* and *If I Had a Hammer*, I did the breakdown and schedules myself. My co-producer, Jane Goe, did the *budgets*.

If I Had Hammer had a particularly difficult schedule to work out. That I was able to cram as much shooting as I did into three weeks I still think is a well-planned, low-budget production triumph. I may not be Stanley Kubrick, but I sure can whip up a mean low-budget film schedule. I shot a 117-minute movie in nineteen days, meaning about six and half minutes of edited footage a day, which is exactly like the average TV schedule. There are a hundred film crews in the U.S. shooting at that speed every day, there's no reason you too can't shoot like that just because you're low-budget and independent.

To shoot a movie without having seriously considered what order to shoot it in is utter foolishness. You absolutely never want to go back to a lighting setup, or have to return to a location because you forgot something. There are too many people involved, and too much equipment, and too many vehicles, no matter how small of a film. *When you go somewhere, you must make sure to get everything you need.*

This can only be accomplished logically by first breaking the script down, then scheduling it. It's also the only way to make a serious, believable budget. Unless you honestly know how long it will take to shoot the film, how can you honestly know for how long you'll need the actors, crew, and equipment?

The schedule is its own little puzzle. There are, however, a few dictums to start off this puzzle construction: shoot the exteriors first, then the interiors. The reason for this is very simple, if you intend to shoot exteriors and it's raining, you can always move inside instead, that is, if you still have interiors left to shoot. These are called *cover sets.*

Your next consideration is how much time will you be spending at each location? As I've stated and restated, you want to base your story around one or two main locations. If you've indeed done this, the idea is to now shoot every other scene in your script, inexorably moving toward your main location, the one that's free, or yours for an extended period of time, where you won't get thrown out, and you can take some time finishing the bulk of your movie.

The rest of the scheduling is usually based on the actors, who are generally the most expensive items on a movie set. Keep in mind that one actor getting SAG-minimum is more expensive than the camera rental. If you're shooting with non-SAG actors then you have a lot more latitude. On *Hammer* I was paying the actors $500 a week instead of the SAG rate of nearly $600 a day. And that's if you can even get the SAG actors to work for SAG-minimum (which also includes an extra 10% for agent's fees, plus health and welfare benefits). If you have a "name" actor, whoever they are will undoubtedly want more than the minimum, so you want to get them in and out as quickly as possible.

When you've got someone like Anthony Quinn in the film, as I once did, while they're there all you and everybody else is trying to do is to get their scenes done and get them out of there. You may even have to go back to places you've already shot just to get your name actor in and out. But if an actor is costing thousands of dollars a day, you'd better figure out how to make very quick use of their services.

Other scheduling considerations are special or extra equipment. For that legitimate night exterior of the folk club in *Hammer*, for instance, I needed a lot of extra lighting equipment, extra grips to move the lights around, extra trucks with which to haul the equipment, extra art department people to dress the club exterior (it was really a playhouse), extra wardrobe, hair, and makeup people for all the *dress extras*, meaning extras that are wearing costumes as opposed to wearing their own clothes. On a basic scheduling level, you always want to be getting special, expensive equipment for the minimum amount of time. I had quite a few scenes to shoot on that real night exterior of the club, but I made sure to get all of them in that one night. It was an expensive deal to pull off for a low-budget movie, but I think it was worth it because it gave the film some production value.

Also, try not to leave the hardest stunts and gags for last, because if you screw them up you'll still have a chance to do them again and fix them. Once you wrap and send everybody home, it's difficult to impossible to get people back again.

The Budget:

There are two kinds of movie budgets: the kind that were copied off of other budgets where you can't trust any of the numbers, or the ones where you researched all of the costs yourself and you honestly believe the totals. I opt for the latter since these films have frequently involved a lot of my own money.

This is also when you have to make some concrete decisions that you will be stuck with forever, like 35mm, 16mm, or DV; and Screen Actor's Guild actors or not. If it's a $150,000 movie it will absolutely not have a union (IATSE) crew or Teamsters. But it could have SAG actors, as my film *Running Time* did; or it could be in 35mm, as my film *If I Had a Hammer* was. To have both SAG actors and 35mm at this budget—which I've never pulled off—you would have to be very wise in your story selection, and very frugal in other ways, and you might be able to shoot for two weeks. Well, shooting an entire feature film in two weeks is a real production feat, but possible. They used to shoot B features in five days all the time. You'd just have to be exceptionally prepared. To shoot for three weeks, I think you'd need to go up to $200,000. And get this, if you do shoot with a SAG cast, you have to put up the entire amount of money the actors will earn *in advance*. This can be done through a *payroll company*, which is a company that handles the writing of all payroll checks (a big payroll company is Cast & Crew, who have cut nearly every check I've ever received for film work). For a small percentage they handle all of the payroll, including deductions and tax forms. It's worth it, and if you're shooting with a SAG cast, I believe it's mandatory.

There is a lot to be said for shooting with professional SAG actors. First and foremost, SAG actors are generally of a higher quality because they are experienced enough to have gotten into SAG in the first place. Also, and this is a big consideration, if you intend to try and lure some kind of "name" actor into your film, they will definitely be a SAG member, and you can't just have one SAG member in your cast—it's either an all-SAG cast or an all non-SAG cast. At a $150,000-$200,000 budget you can't really afford any "name" actors anyway and still have money to shoot a movie. Maybe you can get some old-time TV actor, like Bob Denver or Adam West, to come in for a day or two for cheap—but it won't be all *that* cheap. If you fly a SAG actor anywhere it has to be first-class, they stay at first-class hotels, they also get *per diem*, which is a daily stipend of cash to do with what they'd like (DGA directors also get per diem, and I always buy CDs with the money). However, having some kind of name can't hurt you, that's for sure. It may end up being your main or only salable element. Sales-wise, having Bruce Campbell in *Running Time* was a darn good thing for that film. I used a young, non-SAG cast in *Hammer* and I couldn't get it released.

SAG has a category called *SAG experimental or deferred*, where you can pay the actors a lot less (if they'll take it)—although all of the SAG rules still apply—but you can't make any kind of distribution deals until you pay the difference between SAG experimental and SAG minimum, which will be at least $10,000, no matter what you do (I spent just over $40,000 on the actors in *Running Time* for two weeks, and it's a pretty small cast). My feeling has always been to go with SAG actors or don't go with SAG actors, but don't get caught in the middle. When you go to make a distribution deal, which won't easy, having some multi-thousand dollar bill with SAG hanging over your head definitely won't put you in a position of strength. Although to go SAG and to not get a name is probably not worth it at this budget.

If you do use SAG actors then you are subject to the rules of SAG, which aren't all that easy to follow, and if you fail to follow their rules, you'll get fined. If you don't break on time for lunch, you get *meal penalties*; if you don't give the actors the full twelve hours of turnaround, you get *forced-call* penalties; if you go into overtime, you very quickly go to paying time-and-a-half, then double-time, then *Golden Time*, which is double-time and a half (how does a Teamster begin a bedtime story? Once upon a Golden Time . . .). If you don't fill out all of the SAG paperwork properly you'll get fined, and none of these fines are cheap. And it's all of those unplanned costs that will kill your budget. But if you've planned your film well, and you anticipate all of the possible places you could be fined and don't break those rules, it's certainly worth using SAG actors. So, if you're going to use SAG actors you really must study the SAG rule book, as well as assigning someone to the task of filling out their daily paperwork (this is usually the responsibility of the 2nd A.D.).

Meanwhile, there are several types of good budgeting software, and this is a place where the aid of a computer can be extremely helpful. Some of these programs have all of the union scales of pay built in (which it updates yearly from an internet download). So, when you type into the actor's category that an actor is being paid SAG-minimum, plus 10% agent's fee, for two days, it automatically puts in the rate, adds on the health and welfare benefits, and gives you a total. If you change two days to three days, it adds in the extra amount and alters the total. This is very handy because the budget just keeps changing as you prepare it, and the software keeps changing the totals for you.

Regarding payment for the producer, director, or the writer, I say make it as little as possible, or preferably none. Their remuneration should be in general partnership points, or ownership points, and they shouldn't be taking cash out of the budget, if possible.

Assistant Directors:

The 1st Assistant Director (1st AD) prepares the breakdown, the budget and the schedule in pre-production, then basically runs the set during production. A good 1st AD, just like a good director, should never get angry or have to yell at anyone. If both the director and the 1st AD are prepared, and working in unison, there's no reason anyone should be yelling at anyone else. The 1st AD wrangles the actors and the extras (the 2nd AD helps wrangle the extras, too, if they're not off doing paperwork), and makes sure that the necessary actors for each scene are on the set when they should be, and then makes sure that they don't leave before they ought to. The 1st AD is the person who calls for quiet, tells the sound to roll, then tells the camera to roll. The director usually calls "Action," although there are times when the director and the monitor are situated far enough away from where the scene is actually being shot that it's just easier to ask the 1st AD to call action. The director, however, always calls "Cut." If the director has decided that they have the take, and tells the script supervisor to "Print it," then the

1ˢᵗ AD will get everyone moving to the next setup, often saying things like, "The camera's in the wrong place." At the end of the day, after the last setup is gotten, it's the 1ˢᵗ AD's job to call an end to the working day by saying, "That's a wrap for today."

If you can find an experienced assistant director who will work with you for a low-rate or at least a reasonable rate, you really should hire them. A good or bad 1ˢᵗ AD can be the difference between a good and a bad production.

35mm, 16mm, or Digital Video:

This is the time when you must decide whether you're shooting in 35mm, 16mm, or DV. There are advantages and disadvantages to all of them. I'm skipping super-8 because I think it's completely impractical—you can't make a high-enough-quality video transfer off it and it's too small to blow-up to 35mm very well or at all (and we've tried and it looks terrible).

35mm is still the industry standard, as it has been for over one hundred years. This is what they show in movie theaters, and if that's your goal, as it is mine, than 35mm is the best choice. The camera is about twice as much money to rent as a 16mm camera. Also, the film runs through the camera over twice as fast as 16mm (a foot of 16mm film is forty frames long, and a foot of 35mm is sixteen frames long, although both are still running at twenty-four frames a second), meaning you'll need twice as much film stock, and you will have double the cost of processing and video transfer, or printing, should you decide to go that route. You'll also require more lights since 35mm needs more exposure. But 35mm still looks far superior to everything else, and if the photographic look of your film really matters to you, and I think it should, 35mm is the way to go.

I shot with an *Arriflex 35BL-3* with *Zeiss lenses* on *Lunatics*, and it was a good, solid, perfectly reliable camera. I've mainly used Arriflex cameras and Zeiss lenses, both 16mm and 35mm, in my life and have always found both of them to be sturdy and reliable. We used *Arriflex 35BL-4s* on the "Hercules" TV movies, and they too were top-notch cameras (if I had the money, I think I'd buy a used Arri 35BL-3 or 4). On "Xena" we used *Moviecam* cameras, which gave us some trouble at first (the gates were out of whack and kept scratching the film), but that eventually got straightened out. The Moviecam seemed like a well-balanced, solid camera. I used *Panavision* equipment on *Hammer*, and the first camera we had broke down and had to be replaced, which I must say they were very good about doing (of course, we were shooting in LA). I couldn't afford the good Panavision lenses, and I found that the cheaper ones didn't look as good as the Zeiss Lenses I was accustomed to. However, way in Panavision's favor, they were very eager to work with us and make a deal, and I'd rent from them again in a second if I could afford their top-end gear. But their low-end gear wasn't great. If I had been out on location and the camera had broken down, I'd probably still be holding a grudge against them.

16mm can look pretty darn good, too, although it has a quarter of the *grain particles*, meaning the little dots that make up the picture, of 35mm, so it looks 75% less sharp than 35mm (it's a geometric decrease), and it becomes quite apparent when you project it on a screen of any size. However, if you go straight to video off the 16mm negative it can look terrific (as I think it did with *Running Time*), and this is how many commercials are shot. Also, a 16mm camera is smaller and cheaper to rent. There is also a lot of unused 16mm equipment sitting around at colleges, universities, and production houses, that can potentially be borrowed, or gotten at very low rental fees. The main sound 16mm camera on *Evil Dead*, an *Arriflex-16BL* (BL stands for blimped lens, which means there's a covering over the lens housing to quiet the camera's motor noise) was borrowed from Wayne State University in Detroit. For *Thou Shalt Not Kill . . . Except* I found a complete Arri-16BL package, with a whole set of lenses, extra magazines, and a smaller, *MOS* (meaning silent), multi-speed camera, the *Arri-S*, and I think I paid $150 a week for all of it. And that was twenty years ago, and I can assure you that all of that 16mm equipment isn't getting any newer.

On *Running Time* I rented an *Arriflex 16SR-2*, which is another well-made, durable, dependable camera from Arriflex. There is also the *Arriflex 16SR-3*, the newer version of the SR-2, which is what we used on the first season of "Xena," and those are really nice cameras, too.

Another important fact to keep in mind when choosing which format you'll use is, a single 35mm *film print*, the actual item that runs through the projector at the theater, costs almost $4,000, whereas a single 16mm film print costs about $1,500, and this comes into play if you're going to be sending out prints to film festivals.

If you're considering shooting 16mm, then blowing it up to 35mm, which I've done twice, on *Thou Shalt Not Kill . . . Except* and *Running Time*, it's a weird process that never exactly works quite right, although it does work. You get a severe contrast build-up, and if you didn't frame everything exactly right the faults become much more obvious in 35mm. Depending on how you do it, it will cost between $5,500 and $40,000. I'll go into this further in the post production section under "35mm Blow-ups." Of my four independent features, I've shot two in 35mm, and two in 16mm (both of the TV movies I've directed, *Hercules in the Maze of the Minotaur* and *Alien Apocalypse*, were shot in 35mm). The choice really depends on how much money you have when you actually begin shooting the film. I prefer 35mm, but I've been perfectly happy with 16mm.

By the way, to get any reputable camera rental house to rent to you, you'll need insurance. There are several companies that specialize in movie *production insurance* and they can be found in the LA 411 Book which is an invaluable tool to a film production. The insurance rate is based on your budget and will be at most a couple thousand dollars.

Another thing to keep in mind is that the only accepted archivable standard in movies right now (or ever) is motion picture film, either 35mm or 16mm, because it has been in constant use for over one hundred years. No video format has stuck around long enough so that it can trusted to still be here in fifty, let alone a hundred years.

As an example, I did a top-quality, $6,000 video transfer of *Running Time* in 1997, and I still think it looks pretty darn good. But the format to which I transferred, D-2, doesn't exist anymore. Now the top end of video is *Digital Beta*. When I tell someone in the film business now that my video master is on D-2, they look at me as though I'd said it was hieroglyphics scratched on papyrus. I have duped the D-2 to Digital Beta and no one knows the difference, but it wouldn't surprise me at all if Digital Beta is no longer the top-end format in a few years. Whatever that new format may be, if I can't make a dupe from D-2, I can always go back to my film negative and transfer it again. But that's because I have a film negative to go back to.

The Digital Video Feature:

Nevertheless, should you decide to be a rebel and shoot a feature film on digital video (which includes HD) anyway, then try to push the envelope on the system and be one of the forerunners of getting paid feature film prices by the distributors, I think you need to take a few things into consideration.

The first thing filmmakers need to do is to treat DV like it's film, meaning that just because the cameras are small and light doesn't mean you have to hand-hold the entire film. In fact, you shouldn't. I think it's very important to do locked-off shots and smooth camera moves. So far, everyone seems to be treating digital video like it's home video, not like it's film and it's a *real* movie. Just because the way of recording the image has changed doesn't mean that all the known techniques then go out the window.

And just because you're shooting on DV doesn't mean you shouldn't put every bit as much love and care into the lighting, costumes, makeup, and everything else. When filmmakers start to do this, maybe the distributors will begin to accept their films as real movies and actually buy them.

Right now, however, the only DV features to actually get sold are *Star Wars* movies, where it doesn't matter what they shoot it on, or quirky films with all-star casts, like *The Anniversary Party*, where they really didn't need to shoot on DV, but just did it to be hip.

When To Begin Shooting:

This is an important point: if a movie ultimately costs $150,000, that doesn't mean you have to have the full amount to begin shooting. If you create your budget properly, with believable, well-researched numbers, you'll know exactly how much money you'll *really* need to go ahead and shoot and get the film "in the can." Many people misunderstand this term. If a film is "in the can," that doesn't mean it's finished, that means it's entirely shot, but hasn't gone through post-production yet, which will still cost approximately a third of that $150,000. It depends on how you do your post, which we'll get to. The point is, you can go shoot your film before you actually have all the money. We went and shot *Evil Dead* with only $90,000 of the $150,000 proposed budget raised, and ended up staying eleven weeks on a six-week schedule. I shot *Thou Shalt Not Kill . . . Except* with about $20,000 of a proposed $150,000 budget, and two weeks into shooting I was entirely out of money and couldn't feed my crew lunch, nor could I pay any of the lab bills, so they wouldn't let me see my dailies. But I just kept shooting anyway because I had purchased all of the film stock in advance, so I had film, I had a camera, and nothing was going to stop me come hell or high water.

So how much money it takes to actually start shooting a movie is entirely dependent on how desperate and intense you are. I was so desperate and intense that I went and shot a period war movie with about one-tenth of what I minimally needed to do the job. That the film got finished at all is a bloody miracle—it's also had the best release of any of my four movies so far, so go figure.

A Really, Really Cheap Movie: *An Aside*

But you can still shoot in digital video, and you can even use a little home camera if you want, and if your film is good they can show it at festivals. You just can't make many (or any) legitimate distribution deals with it. On the other hand, you can also shoot silent 16mm with a Bolex, as my friend Paul is doing now (I have a Bolex, too, by the way), basically treating it as though it were super-8, and just shooting it a scene at a time on weekends, and you can make a whole feature film for *really, really* cheap. The main differences are, in video you've got sound, using a Bolex you don't (but if you make sure to stay far enough away from people or behind them so you don't see their lips, you can *loop*, or replace the dialog, later). On video you don't have a negative; on 16mm you do.

Paul has cleverly devised a story for his film that not only stars himself, but is frequently just him by himself, and he knows he can always get himself to show up. And even if he can't get someone to run the camera for him, he can always put it on run-lock and do *everything* himself. It is possible. And Paul's about 70% through shooting his film. It's taken him seven years already, but he doesn't seem to be in a hurry.

I was Paul's camera operator for the act one LA section of his film, and we shot about thirty-five rolls of black and white 16mm film with Paul's Bolex. It was just Paul and I, that's it. Paul had observed that his apartment had beautiful lighting between 3:00 PM to 5:00 PM. So we only shot at that time of the day and it took a few weeks to get the entire scene, but neither one of us was working, the lighting was consistent, and we had a lot of fun. And it looks terrific, with cool beams of smoky light slanting through the windows—to achieve this effect we each smoked a cigarette—in high-contrast black and white. I have no doubt it will cut together very well, too.

And he'll have a negative that can be blown-up to 35mm or transferred to any digital format he wishes. And if the film is any good, he'll be able to sell it.

As a note, it's approximately $35 for a 100-foot roll of 16mm film (which gives you two and a half minutes). It costs about $35 more to get the film processed, then another $35 to have the film either printed to 16mm positive *workprint* (without sound), the film that can be shown on a projector, or it can be transferred to video for about the same price. So, it's about $100 dollars to shoot two and a half minutes of footage and have something to look at. If you shot 100 rolls you'd have 250 minutes of footage, out of which you could theoretically cut 90 minutes, which is a slim but rational *shooting ratio* of almost three-to-one, meaning how much footage you shoot compared with how much you end up using. Well, that only comes to ten-thousand bucks. If you spread that out over seven years, as Paul has, that's less than $1,500 a year, which is nothing more than an inexpensive hobby. You could easily spend more money collecting comic books, working on old cars, or just drinking beer.

Yes, you still have to edit and do post sound, but that can be weaseled for cheap, too, if you're of a mind and not in a hurry. I've never made my own movie like this, but I would eventually like to, and that's why I bought a Bolex. A *Bolex camera*, by the way, is an MOS camera that doesn't need batteries, it winds up like a clock. This is what all the wildlife photographers used for many years. It's a somewhat difficult camera to operate, and due to that there are literally thousands of Bolexes sitting around collecting dust. I found Paul's Bolex, with three lenses, for $150. I then bought one myself, and the best deal I could find on the internet was a Bolex and five lenses, one of which is a big zoom lens with an electric motor, for $1,000.

A Small Crew:

If you're in Los Angeles or New York City you can find experienced crew members who are non-union. If you're not located in one of those two cities, or you just want to spend even less money, you can always put a small crew together from college students, whom I've found are quite easy to recruit and are both eager enough and pliable enough to do the jobs with just a little coaching. And if they're getting minimum wage, what the heck have they got to complain about, it's more fun than working at McDonald's. Obviously, kids are more available in the summer than any other time, which is why I made both *Running Time* and *Hammer* in the summer, not to mention the weather is more consistent and dependable.

As a general note in planning, I ended up shooting *Thou Shalt Not Kill . . . Except* in the fall in Michigan. Some days were absolutely gorgeous, others it poured rain down on our heads. Since the film is mainly exteriors, this wasn't a great decision, but I shot that film when and where I had to shoot it, given the circumstances. But trying to edit footage that was shot on a rainy day together with footage that was shot on a sunny day was nearly impossible, and generally ends up looking bogus.

Regarding both your crew and your budget, it's a wise idea to not pay anyone less than minimum wage. You can get fairly cheap *workman's com-*

pensation insurance—which is a good thing to have and insures everyone on the set—through the state as long as everyone is at least getting minimum wage. It's also a perfectly good wage to pay most everyone in the crew, except for perhaps your department heads, like the director of photography, the art director, and the costume designer, should you have one. On another level, people simply work better when they're being paid, plain and simple. Ultimately, free help isn't worth the cost.

Here's my theory on hiring the crew, and generally just working with other people. There are a lot of places where you want creativity shown in the making of a film: the acting, the photography, the art direction, the costumes, makeup, and hair, to name a few. Once I've made my choice as to who I'm hiring as my department heads—the DP is the head of the camera department, either the production designer or the art director is the head of the art department, the costume designer is the head of the wardrobe department—I let them know exactly what I want, as best as I can, then I let them do their jobs. Now I try to stay out of people's hair. If you hired them, that was your creative decision, now let them be creative doing what they do best.

On the set of *If I Had a Hammer*, inside the folk club that was really a vacant hardware store.

Having previously worked as a 2nd unit director, with a crew less than a quarter of the size of the main unit crew—I had sixteen people on my crew, the main unit crew had about seventy-five people—I must say that I personally much prefer a small crew to a large crew. Here's the difference, a big crew can generally handle anything you throw at them with just about any amount of lead time. A small crew can handle anything you throw at them, too, as long as they've had sufficient pre-production time to prepare for everything. Preparation is one of the things you can afford to do a lot of on a low-budget movie because it doesn't cost much or, if you work it right, anything. On *Running Time* I did not pay the cast and crew anything for pre-production, and on *Hammer* I paid a few people for one or two weeks of pre-production, strictly because there was so much art direction, and so many costumes, but not most of the crew, and none of the cast. On a SAG film you are supposed to pay for rehearsal time, but if you work around the actor's schedules, they'll come in for an hour or two or three here and there for free because they know it's in their own best interest.

It's infinitely easier moving around sixteen people than it is fifty to seventy-five people. And things just move faster, too. My 2nd unit crew could kick the main unit's butt any day of the week. And, always keep in mind, the less people to pay the better on a low-budget movie.

Rehearsal:

Rehearsals are invaluable, and the more you can schedule the better. The difference between shooting a scene you've already rehearsed and played around with, as opposed to shooting a scene completely cold, is huge. Just because you've written a line of dialog down on paper doesn't necessarily mean that there's an actor living who can deliver it. A line can sound just fine in your head, but once you hear an actor speak the line it's an illuminating experience. As I've previously mentioned, any line over three sentences long, to me anyway, becomes unbearable when I hear an actor trying to deliver it. My script for *Lunatics* was initially loaded with speeches. After the first rehearsal I began cutting them, and as the rehearsals continued, my cutting continued. By the time we shot the film, not a single speech remained.

My rehearsals are strictly between myself and the actors, and have nothing to do with the rest of the crew. However, if I wasn't the writer, I'd definitely have the writer there, too. Any other personnel present will just make the actors nervous and defeat the purpose of the rehearsal, which is to get the actors and you comfortable with the dialog and the scenes. I don't even want the other actors that aren't in this specific scene present. I want the rehearsal to be as intimate as I can make it, which is generally the two or three lead actors and myself. I have the other actors, the second-leads, and the day players, come in separately at a different time.

For *Lunatics*, which was shot in 1989, I wasn't entirely sure how I was going to block all of the actor's movements in my long act two, where it's just the two actors in an apartment for thirty minutes. I knew I wanted them to end up at certain places at certain times, but I wasn't all that clear how they would get there. I took a hint from my favorite director, William Wyler, and the technique he often employed, which is at first to not give any direction to the actors and just let them do anything they want to do, while making sure to keep your eyes open, and the script and a pen in hand. This is where you can run wild and try anything you or the actors want. Good things will come out of this and you should be prepared to note them all down. The second the scene begins to feel stale or awkward, then give the actors your ideas and see if that doesn't liven things back up a bit. It's a useful technique and it does work.

As a basic note, I'm not an acting teacher and it's not my place to try and teach the actors how to act. I hired them because I thought they could act, and were appropriate for the parts. It's my job to get the actors to clearly understand what I want, and it's their job to give it to me.

So, any rehearsals you can schedule will be priceless. Particularly since there's usually very little time on the set to work with the scenes.

Scouting Locations:

On both *Running Time* and *Hammer* my co-producer, Jane, and I spent months scouting the locations. She and I have driven around almost every square inch of LA looking for just the right alleys, just the right side streets, and just the right storefronts. It is imperative that you find the best locations possible, then really scope them out, and walk through all of your setups. Issues you hadn't thought of will make themselves known—the ceilings are too low and it will be hard to light, the sound is hollow, the factory next door makes too much noise, at lunch time the alley is full of people buying food from a vendor truck, etc. If you know who your director of photography (DP) will be, drag them along, too. They'll bring up issues you've never thought about, like where will the sun be when you shoot, or can you put lights out on the sidewalk aiming back through the windows, or will you need another permit? Where will all the trucks and equipment go? And if you know who your 1st AD or your art director will be, of course bring them, too.

On *Running Time* I needed a very specific type of alley—one that came to a dead end that had a door right near the dead end, so the characters would be stuck having to run up the long alley with nowhere else to go. So Jane and I looked and looked, mainly in downtown LA, up one alley and down another, until we found just what we were looking for. We spoke to the owner of the business with the door we wanted to come out of and he had no problem with our plan. We told him our shooting date and he agreed. Terrific! All our problems were solved. We showed up on the specified date with our crew and cast, went to set up the shot and the door wouldn't open. It was bolted with an old rusty lock that hadn't been opened in many years, nor could anyone find the key. As far as those folks were concerned, we could just go away, which would have cost me about ten thousand dollars to not shoot and send everyone home. We offered to bring in a locksmith and change the lock for them for free, but they weren't interested. Luckily for us, we were doing bullet hits (called *squibs*) that day in the alley, and to do any sort of pyrotechnics in LA you must have a licensed pyrotechnician, as well as a city fire marshal. The owner of the business with the locked door was getting annoyed with us and was ready to tell us to get lost. The fire marshal stepped up at that moment and told the business owner that he was in serious violation of city fire codes—this was an official fire exit and they couldn't open the door or even find the key—and if he didn't want to get a big expensive fine he'd better let us bring in a locksmith and change the lock at our expense. He agreed and all went well thereafter.

The point of this story is, even if you've found a location and the owner has agreed to let you use it, still find out if everything works the way you'll need it to work on the day of shooting. Jane and I still kick ourselves when we remember having not tried to open that door in advance.

You should always take a still camera and photograph all the possible locations for later reference. There's no need to use a Polaroid camera for this since the film is so expensive. Use a digital camera or a 35mm still camera.

Casting:

Next to what story you choose to tell, which actors you cast is the second biggest decision you will make.

As John Huston once said, no matter how much time he had put in on the script and the production before casting, which was sometimes years, the minute he cast Humphrey Bogart in the lead it became a Bogart picture. You may have poured your heart into your script, but it's the actors who will carry it. The actors are who the audience will be looking at for the entire movie, and will either care about or not care about. If we the audience don't care about your characters, your movie won't be any good. Even if you've written a good script, if you cast it wrong, you blew it before you've even started shooting.

I like casting because I like actors, who tend to be funny, goofy, upbeat, outspoken people. I particularly like actors with commanding or interesting voices and unique faces, who are not necessarily attractive. Unless I'm casting the leads of a love story, I'm generally not drawn to attractiveness in actors. I know many other directors are, but I think that the good-looking actors are frequently not the best actors. Many have gotten by on their looks, not their talent. I particularly like actors with strong and distinctive voices, which is really an actor's main tool. Over the years I've ended up casting a lot of theater actors and voice talent, who are actors that generally just do voices and don't appear on camera. I like actors who can really act, and do voices and imitations, and cry or burp on command. Trained actors. Not models trying to act, and not wannabe actors. And once you've cast an actor in a part, listen to what they have to say about their characters because they'll start thinking about them a lot now, and some of their ideas will absolutely be useful—probably not all, but some.

If you're in a major city you can probably find an actual casting agent to assist you. I've liked all the casting agents I've ever worked with and have found them all to be incredibly helpful, while their services come quite cheap—some of them just get their payment from the actors and don't want anything from you. Even if they do want some money, it's usually not very much, and it's worth it. The *casting agents* know where all the actors are hiding, and which are the good ones. A city of at least a hundred thousand people probably has a casting agent lurking somewhere, doing the casting for the local commercials. If you're making a feature film they will more than likely be eager to help you because they want to get all the actors they know into the best projects around, and a feature film is always a good project.

You can also hook up with a local theater group and cast through them, as I did once. Don't just use their actors, though, get the call out to everyone in the area. This can be done with fliers posted at all the other theater groups or an ad in the local paper. Give yourself enough time casting before you shoot so that if you don't find everybody you're looking for right away, you can still schedule more casting sessions.

On *Hammer* I cast all of my major roles in the course of two very full days, where we saw about 120 actors. But I didn't find anybody for one of the roles, that of an angry, Bob Dylan-like folk singer. So, although I only had the casting facility for the two days, I had actors continue to audition for this one part for several more weeks by coming to my apartment. I ended up seeing over thirty actor/singers for this part. Either they could sing and not act, or they could act and not sing. One kid, who really had a great look and was terrific guitarist and singer, couldn't get angry under any circumstances. I tried working with him and let him come back two more times, but there wasn't an iota of anger in him. The fellow that finally got the part, David Zink, is also a terrific singer/guitarist and a very nice guy, and isn't really an actor, either, but he was certainly able to tap into some kind of anger somewhere inside himself. While he was auditioning he took the cigarette from his mouth, flicked it on the floor, and smashed it out on my living room carpet (when I moved two years later the burn was still there). It was such an audacious thing to do, combined with his obvious musical abilities, I gave him the part. He's very good in the film, too (I was then able to say my cast went from A to Zink).

Standard operating procedure during a casting session, by the way, is to videotape all of the auditions so that you can go back and review them later.

When I first moved to Hollywood in 1976, one of my first jobs was working at a huge casting facility, where they ran cattle call casting sessions for commercials. My job was to set up the video equipment and to run it all day long, which meant turning the machine on, then turning it off. I only lasted a few weeks in this job, as it was exceedingly dull and mind-numbing, but I did pick up at least one vital piece of information—try to make the actors feel at ease. While I worked there I never saw any of the agency people, or the directors, or the producers, make the slightest attempt at making the actors feel at ease, and therefore they got pretty crummy auditions, not that it really mattered for what they were casting (dog food and Mexican food commercials during my short tenure). But it's not very difficult to calm the actors down a bit. As each actor entered the room where they would be auditioning, Jane and I would stand, introduce ourselves, and all the other people in the room, shake their hands, then talk and joke with them for a brief minute before they started. I think it means a lot, and I think you get much better performances if the actors aren't scared stiff, as they usually are.

Two very important points about casting are: don't cast actors just because they're your friends, and don't cast actors because you think you might be able to have sex with them. These are both bogus reasons for casting. Choose the best actors for the part and you'll be much happier, even if you don't get laid. In all seriousness, sex comes and goes, but the movie will be around forever.

The Shot List or Storyboards: What Does a Director Do?

Before I move into the next section, which is production, I would be seriously remiss if I didn't discuss the director's responsibilities during pre-production. To do this I must then explain exactly what a director does.

A good director will supervise every aspect of the upcoming production, being involved with the hiring of all the crew members, as well as being involved with all of the casting. The main thing that the director does is to impart their vision of the script to everyone else around them, and everyone else really needs and wants to know this information. So, even though I have this section at the end of pre-production, it should really occur much sooner, like right near the beginning of pre-production, soon after the script is locked.

However, to be able to impart their vision to others, the director must first have a vision to begin with. By doing the shot list or storyboards the director is not only making their vision a lot more concrete and palpable to everyone else, they are also, and much more importantly, making their own vision much more concrete and palpable to themselves. Directors who don't do either shot lists or storyboards are lazy and a pain to everyone around them. All the department heads need this information to do their jobs well and if you deny it to them, you're a thoughtless director who doesn't know how to make the best use of a crew.

Here's a terrifically important point to all beginning directors—just assume that if you don't ask for it, you're not going to get it. Just because you see a flagpole in your vision of two people standing and talking, if you haven't said so to the art director and it's not really at the location, then it won't be there on the day you shoot. This is the reason that most inept directors throw hysterical tirades, because they saw something in their heads that they did not impart to anyone else, and now they're about to shoot and it's not going to look the way they imagined it. However, if the director drew a storyboard of the shot and had added in a flagpole—a line with a square on the end—then showed it to the art director, they would then undoubtedly get a flagpole, if possible. Every department wants to do a good job, but, for the most part, they can only do as good a job as the director lets them. No one can read the director's mind. If the director doesn't communicate their ideas, they will not end up on the screen.

I storyboarded every single thing I ever directed, up to the second season of "Xena," when scripts began coming at me later and later until I simply didn't have time. Then, even when I did have the time, I just didn't do it anymore, and I don't really need to anymore, either. However, when I realized that I was actually going to make this last TV movie I made for Sci-Fi Network, *Alien Apocalypse*, which has more digital effects than any film I've ever made before (130 FX as it turned out), and there was time to do it, I storyboarded the whole film again, and I'm very glad I did. Everyone knew exactly what I was going to try and get every day, and that's what I got (I actually came in at 17 days on an 18-day shoot).

Meanwhile, you don't have to be able to draw to do storyboards. Stick people work just fine (Sam Raimi draws great stick figure storyboards, and his monsters always get Xs for eyes). *Storyboards* are drawings that convey the composition you have in mind, and are a way to see what the cutting will look like before you've actually shot it, as well as a way to count how many shots you think you need to construct your scene. Being a good artist has nothing to do with it, as my storyboards clearly confirm.

Another important piece of information for directors to keep in mind is that, in a twelve hour shooting day, it's nearly impossible to get more than twenty-four setups, which would be about thirty minutes each, and that's fast. By the time you get the camera where it now goes, block the actors, light the scene, then get the actors back from hair and makeup, then shoot a few times, it'll be at least thirty minutes, take my word for it. So, if you have fifteen days of shooting, let's say, at twenty-four setups a day, that's three-hundred and sixty setups in total. If you're shooting a one-hundred page script, that's 3.6 shots per page, which isn't very much. So, if you sit down and storyboard or shot list a two-page scene and get twenty or more storyboards, that's too much, it mathematically doesn't work, and you'd better rethink your approach. Or shorten your script.

Terms and Concepts:

We need to go over some terms and concepts first before we go any farther into the shot list.

Film editing is primarily based on the concept of *overlapping action*. The editor makes many of the cuts based on matching the actions between one shot and the next shot. An actor will start to bring a cigarette to their mouth in the wide shot, then complete the action in the close-up. That's why you shoot the whole scene in a wide shot, then you shoot the whole scene again in one person's close-up, then you shoot the whole scene again in the other person's close-up. The scene now overlaps itself entirely three times and it gives you a lot choices in the editing, and the more choices you have in editing the better.

There are basically three distances from which to shoot a scene: wide, medium, or close, and the variations within those distances. An *extreme close-up* would be just a person's mouth and eyes, or just their eyes or just their mouth. A *close-up* means that a human face fills the frame, from chin to forehead (and is sometimes referred to as a *choker*). A *medium close-up* is from the mid-chest to the top of the head. A *medium shot* is from the waist up (and sometimes referred to as a *cowboy*—that way you could see the six-guns on his belt). A *long shot* is from the feet up. An *extreme long shot*, or a *wide shot*, makes the whole person a figure within the frame against the background. One can also add to these descriptions, *high angle*, meaning the camera is high and looking down, or *low angle*, where the camera is low looking up.

The camera itself can also be moved around, too. The terms for this are: *pan*, meaning the camera is being swiveled horizontally from a fixed point; *track* or *dolly*, meaning the camera is on a wheeled platform called a dolly (or a wheelchair or a shopping cart) and is being pushed along. Another way to move the camera is by simply having the cameraman walk along with it, which is called *hand-held*. You can also *tilt up* or *tilt down*, which is exactly what it sounds like, and is often mistakenly referred to as panning up or panning down but a pan is really a horizontal move. If one had a camera crane (which is also called a *camera boom*, but I find that confusing because the microphone is also on a boom), then one could *crane up* or *crane down* or *boom up* or *boom down*, depending on whether you call the crane a crane or a boom. On a low-budget movie you probably won't have a one anyway, so call it whatever you'd like.

On a real movie dolly (the most common movie dollies are made by Fisher or Chapman) you can also hydraulically boom up or boom down about four of five feet, which I've found very handy and make use of with some regularity.

A shot list is just a numbered list of descriptions of the shots that you intend to get, like this:

```
1. Wide shot of house, a car pulls up the drive-
way, right to left.
2. Medium close-up of the car's driver, an an-
gry man, pulling into frame, right to left. He
```

stops the car, turns off the engine, then gets
out of the car. We pan right to left as we follow the driver out of the car to the front door
of the house, where he goes inside and slams
the door.
3. Medium close-up of the woman in profile in
the passenger seat, right to left, looking off
camera left. She slowly opens her door and gets
out of the car, exiting frame, right to left.

That's a whole scene I've just described, and those are entirely understandable directions as to how to shoot it. We begin with a wide shot of
a house and car pulls up the driveway, right to left. The reason I state the
screen direction is because the scene will continue in that same screen direction and I want to know that.

Screen Direction:

Cuts in a movie are frequently (but not always) made based on which way
things are moving across the screen, which is either right to left, or left to
right. If something starts going in one direction it needs to continue going
in that same direction to make a smooth cut. If someone walks into frame
going right to left in a wide shot, then they should step into frame right
to left in their close-up. This may seem obvious, but it becomes a constant
issue on a movie set. This idea of screen direction is of primary importance
and is incessantly being discussed on the set by the director, the cameraman, the actors, and the script supervisor. But, if you are a prepared director
and have done your homework, it doesn't have to be a constant discussion.
I always work it out in advance and it stays that way.

Never be confused by reality, which ultimately means nothing on film.
The screen direction is what's important in a movie. As long as the action
is going in the same direction, it will cut, no matter what the reality is. So
decide what direction things are going in advance and just stick to it. I also
change screen directions all the time just to keep things varied, but I decide
it in advance.

So, getting back to the first shot on the shot list, just how wide is the
wide shot of this house anyway? It doesn't have to be too wide to express
that it's a house. Perhaps you want the house to fill most of the frame. Then

again, maybe you want to be wide enough to put the house at the bottom of the screen and have sky above it. You will have to choose your exact framing when the cameraman sets up the camera and you choose a lens. If you've drawn a storyboard, then everyone will already know just how wide you mean, otherwise, if you've just done a shot list and stated it's a "wide shot," you can choose the exact framing when you get there. But, by having a shot list you absolutely do know for a fact that you intend to get a wide shot of the house with the car pulling in, right to left, no matter what the framing is. What if you get there and the driveway is on the other side and the car can only go left to right? Well, then you did a crummy job of location scouting. You should have been there previously and already know which side the driveway is on, and have a photograph to prove it.

The second shot is a medium close-up of the angry driver pulling into frame, right to left. Since the car pulled into the driveway right to left in the wide shot, the car must now pull into frame going the same direction of right to left in the closer shot if you want it to cut together smoothly. The cut between these two shots would probably occur by allowing the car to drive all the way up the driveway in the long shot, then cutting in while the car is slowing down, but hasn't stopped yet. You'd then cut into the medium close-up of the driver pulling forward into frame a bit and stop-ping—the action was started in the wide shot and completed in the closer shot, and this is called *matching action*. You could let the car drive all the way up the driveway in the wide shot and come to a complete stop, then cut in, which would work, but it wouldn't be as smooth of a cut (which in and of itself can be an effect). You end up with a much smoother cut by matching the action and cutting into it, which is what most editors would do under the circumstances.

We are now looking at the angry driver in a profile medium close-up, and he's facing right to left, meaning his nose is pointing to the left, toward the house. The woman in the passenger seat would be visible behind the driver, but possibly out of focus. As indicated in the shot list, the driver gets out of the car and the camera pans right to left to follow him to the front door of the house. Since it's a pan the camera is in a stationary spot on the driveway and the driver will walk past the camera and away toward the front door where I would think he'd get to a medium long shot, from his knees to above his head, when he goes inside.

The third shot is a medium close-up of the woman in the passenger seat in profile looking right to left. So we're inside the car, basically in the driver's seat, looking at the woman in profile, from chest to head, and she's looking right to left. This is the key to shooting this scene properly—if she turns to look at the man, which side of the lens is she looking and why? *The answer is always based on which way would the other person be looking back at her from the last shot?* Since the driver exited the car right to left, and the woman is still in the car, he'd have to look left to right to see her. Therefore, she needs to be looking right to left to see him.

This is another key aspect of screen direction, in close-ups, meaning separate shots, to have people look like they're actually seeing each other and speaking to each other, *they must be looking in opposite directions.* The man at the front door of the house would be looking left to right to see

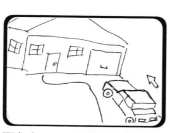

Wide shot - car up driveway R to L

Couple pulls up and stops, R to L
He exits car, pan with him R to L

He walks to front door, looks back,
L to R

She looks back at him, R to L

Alternate version:
Reverse over-the-shoulder shot

the woman in the car, and she would be looking right to left to see him, no matter where they *really* are, or *really* need to look to actually see each other, which doesn't matter. In a movie reality means nothing, screen direction means everything.

Coverage:

Now let's change the scene. How about, once they've pulled up the driveway they then have a conversation while sitting in the car. If that's the case, then you'll need more *coverage*, meaning more shots, because the moment the driver turns to the passenger, from all the angles we have we'd be looking at the back of his head. But if you *rack focus*, meaning shift the plane of focus, to the passenger at the point the man turns to her, this has now become an *over-the-shoulder shot*, meaning the view is over one person's shoulder aiming toward another person's face. If you then got one more shot, the *reverse over-the-shoulder* shot of the passenger with the driver facing the lens, you now have a sufficient amount of coverage to shoot this scene because you can now cut back and forth between to the two over-the-shoulder shots. *Over-the-shoulder shots are always over the opposite shoulders*, so you'd be over the driver's *left* shoulder and the passenger's *right* shoulder.

This next piece of advice is optional, but very common. If the two characters have more than a few lines each it's a wise idea to also get both close-ups and over-the-shoulders or medium close-ups, too. That way you then have four shots covering all the dialog, the two over-the-shoulder shots, and the two close-ups. What's particularly useful about also having close-ups as well as over-the-shoulder shots, is that A. close-ups are more dramatic, and B. they exclude the other person, as well as both people's hands.

Matching Action:

Which brings us to another variation of matching action. Whatever actions an actor makes in one angle need to be repeated exactly in the other angle. A character smoking a cigarette while speaking is a very good example—the actor must puff on the cigarette in exactly the same spots that they puffed on it in the previous angle, that way when you cut between the two angles the cigarette will be in the proper place at the proper time. If you just let the actors do whatever they want with a cigarette and don't pay attention, the cigarette will never be in the same place at the same time, the two angles will not cut together, and you will be screwed. I learned this lesson the hard way by having two actors smoking in a dialog scene in *Thou Shalt Not Kill . . . Except* with no one paying any attention to when they puffed. Well, they never hit their cigarettes twice at the same time. When it came time to edit the scene, my primary concern became those silly cigarettes, not the performances. Personally, I'd rather be paying attention to the performances than the cigarettes.

So, returning to having both over-the-shoulder shots and two close-ups, should one of the actors, or both, not be matching their actions, and the driver, let's say, puts his hand on the steering wheel in one of the over-the-shoulder shots, but doesn't do that same action on the other over-the-shoulder shot—and these mistakes happen often because it's really hard to do exactly the same performance twice—you can always cut into either close-up, which is only a face and contains no hands, and easily get past the problem.

Yet another aspect of matching action is matching the speed of actor's entrances and exits. For example, if you have a character run out of frame, and you want to cut directly to them entering frame, they still must be running. It doesn't matter that logically they would have stopped running somewhere in between, that's reality; this is movies. If you try to cut from them running out of frame, to them walking into frame, it will make for a bad cut.

Cutaways:

When I was about to start shooting my second film, *Lunatics: A Love Story*, I called the editor, Kaye Davis, and asked her if she had any advice for me. She simply said, "Get cutaways," which I think is darn good advice, and I only wish I had gotten more. In fact, now that I think about it, I *always* wish I had gotten more cutaways.

A *cutaway* is a shot in a scene that doesn't include the actors who are featured or speaking. It can be other characters reacting, hands fiddling with things, tight shots (called *inserts*) of interesting props, a waving cigarette, anything you can think of that gets you off the main action. That way if you need to edit out some lines and bridge the scene, or just to editorially perk it up, you have something else to cut to.

In *Lunatics* the art department put these terrific china John and Jackie Kennedy bookends on the set and I fell in love with them. I made sure to get a clear shot of them, and gosh darn if I didn't find an appropriate spot for it in the final film.

The 180-Degree Line:

Two people sit facing each other, a boy on the left, and a girl on the right. The boy is facing left to right, the girl is facing right to left. Since movies and TV only see the world on a 180 degree plane, which means it's a flat view, the other 180 degrees that makes up reality are across this imaginary line, which runs straight through the middle of the boy's and girl's heads, in this instance. If you cross the 180-degree line, the girl would now be on the left side facing left to right, and the boy would now be on the right facing right to left. They would have flopped in their relationship to one another without having actually moved. To cross the line is considered confusing to the audience and is generally avoided, if possible (even if it's done all the time these days). In this instance it in fact would be confusing and is therefore a bad cut. In film terms, *flopped* is when the image is turned over vertically so that right becomes left, and *flipped* is upside-down.

Nevertheless, any experienced director will tell you that the line has to be crossed with regularity, otherwise things have a tendency to look too flat. Not to mention that actors keep moving around, as does the camera, and so the position of the line keeps changing.

There's no big problem with crossing the line as long as you know you're doing it. However, if you cross the line by mistake it will look like a mistake.

Here's an example: let's go back to the first shot on the shot list, which is a wide shot of house, a car pulls up the driveway and stops. Inside the car, if you'll recall, is a man with his back to us on the left in the driver's seat, and a woman with her back to us on the right in the passenger seat. If we cut all the way around 180-degrees, we could shoot straight through the windshield and see both the man and the woman in a *two-shot* (which is a shot of two people), the man now on the right, the woman now on the left. Quite frankly, there's nothing wrong with that cut and it wouldn't be any kind of a problem, even though you've crossed the line and cut 180-degrees. As long as the viewer knows where they are and isn't confused, there's no problem.

But if you were concerned about making that 180-degree cut, you could always cut to shot #2 first, the medium close-up of the driver in profile, then cut to the front shot of the two people through the windshield. To cut from the side shot to the front shot is only a 90-degree cut and perfectly acceptable.

A 180-degree cut you see frequently these days (and I've done it) is following a character from behind, then cutting right around in front of them. There's no problem with that cut either because we know exactly where we are and we're never confused.

180-DEGREE LINE

Boy and Girl on bench

OVERHEAD

Cutting over the
180-Degree Line

CUTTING 180-DEGREES

Car pulls up driveway

Cut 180-degrees to the view
through the windshield.

Or go to profile
side-angle first

Geography:

One of the main jobs of a film director is to establish the geography of a scene. If you cover your scene in a wide master shot (which runs the entire length of the scene), this is occasionally referred to as a *geography shot*. If you don't shoot a master shot and only shoot close-ups, the viewer won't know where they are, nor will the viewer know where the actors are in regard to one another (which can be an interesting effect, if that's what you're after). The second a viewer becomes confused, on some level you've lost their attention, and have failed as a good storyteller. So it's important to keep the geography straight—just where is everybody? That's the reason for the master shot.

Jump Cuts:

Jump cuts, or cuts that don't cut together smoothly, were once considered bad form and were to be avoided at all costs. Now you see jump cuts all the time in most everything and they're considered hip. Just like crossing the 180-degree line—if it's on purpose, it's probably fine; if it's by mistake, it's bad.

If you're shooting the wide shot of the car pulling into the driveway and stopping, then you cut the camera, have the actors get out of the car and begin speaking beside it, then start shooting again from the same camera position with the same lens, when you then try to cut those two pieces of film together, that'll be a jump cut. Before the cut the people were in the car, after the cut they're out of the car—how did they get there? It will look like they just magically appeared there, and that's bad cutting. But you could do this on purpose now, that is if you meant something by it.

Jump cuts have been used as an effect since 1958 when Jean-Luc Godard first intentionally did them in *Breathless*. They didn't really catch on, though, until the 1970s. Jumps cuts are now employed constantly, almost always to show the same thing, which is a character killing time. This was first done by Martin Scorsese in *Taxi Driver*. You set up a wide shot of a room, lock off the camera, meaning it's not moving at all, then have the character pace around the room, sit on every chair and couch, as well as stop moving in different places. Then, in editing, you remove sections, so the character is sitting in one chair—cut—they're on the couch—cut—they're looking out the window—cut—they're in an other chair, etc. This effect is now in nearly everything, including commercials (which, in my opinion, is a sure-fire gauge for that which is no longer hip).

An old rule of filmmaking is that you need at least a 20 millimeter change in your lens to make a decent cut. This rule came from a time when cameras were huge and didn't get moved all that often. They would shoot their wide master shot from a camera position, then cut, not move the camera, change lenses, and begin shooting their coverage. If you shot your master with a 28mm lens, then switched to a 50mm lens, that's a 22mm difference and it will cut fine. If you started on a 28mm lens, then switched to a 35mm lens, which is only a 7mm difference, you'll get a jump cut. You need a minimum 20mm change for a good cut.

But there's an exception to this rule. You can cut from a 35mm lens to a 50mm lens, which is only a 15mm difference, and it still works. There's actually a reason for this, too. All the lenses from the lowest numbers up to 35mm are considered *wide-angle lenses*; all the lens from 50mm up through the high numbers are considered *long lenses*. A wide-angle lens gives you a wider, more panoramic view than your eyes can see. A long lens, or a *telephoto lens*, as they were once called, sees closer-in than your eyes can see (the human view of the world is about 40mm). Therefore, there is enough of a visual difference between a 35mm lens, the last of the wide-angle lenses, and a 50mm lens, the first of the long lenses, to create a big enough visual difference for a decent cut.

But cameras are much smaller now and a lot easier to move, so you shouldn't run into this problem very often if you move the camera when you change lenses. If you do change lenses without moving the camera, though, which occurs regularly, that's called *cutting down the line*. This is not a reference to the 180-degree line, it's the line of view that the camera is looking down. By just changing lenses and not moving the camera, you are staying on the same axis and simply moving down the line of view.

Ignoring the one exception, it's still a wise idea to have at least a 20mm difference between your lenses.

An old adage in filmmaking is, "Change the angle, change the size." What this means is that instead of just cutting down the line and staying on the same axis, if you veer one way or the other, you've changed the angle, too, and that makes for a better cut.

Lenses:

As I just mentioned, any lens from a 35mm down is a wide-angle lens, any lens from a 50mm up is a long lens. What's the difference? A wide-angle lens shows you more than your eyes can see by distorting the image and stretching it. The widest lenses are called *fish-eye lenses*, which are any lenses below 10mm, and they severely distort the image. The closer the subject gets to a wide-angle lens, the more distorted they become. Unless you want someone to look funky and slightly monstrous, you never shoot a close-up with a wide-angle lens (I shot all of the evil Manson character played by Sam Raimi in *Thou Shalt Not Kill . . . Except* with wide-angle lenses because I wanted him to look funky and monstrous).

In a standard lens package, the wide-angle lenses you would get would be: 18mm, 25mm, and 35mm; and the long lenses you'd get would be: 50mm, and 85mm, and possibly 100mm. There are many more lenses than this, but they cost extra to rent. However, if you really intend to make use of a lens, then it's absolutely worth the extra expense.

All of these lenses are known as *prime lenses*.

The Director of Photography (DP):

The Director of Photography (DP), also known as the *Cinematographer* (or *Lighting Cameraman* in England), is the head of the camera and lighting departments. The actual look of the film is their responsibility, as well as their palette, so to speak. The DP creates the look of a film with the choice of a specific film stock, the type of lights and where they are set, which gels are on the lights, and which filters are on the lens. Before you start shooting, the director must convey to the DP their overall vision of the look of the film, like: it's all in shades of burnished gold; or it's all in soft pastels; or it's very sharp and colorful; or it's really dark and moody, etc. Achieving this look is the job of the DP, as well as making sure that the camera equipment and lighting equipment have all arrived at each set and location, and have then been set up in their proper places, as per the director's instructions.

Lighting:

Lighting is the domain of the DP, but that doesn't mean that the film's director can't make suggestions any time they'd like. Nevertheless, one director in any department is more than enough. I generally do have a few ideas for lighting—like having a big backlight with smoky beams the first time we see the monster in "Hercules," or having the stage lights in *Hammer* constantly changing colors—and I bring them all up in pre-production. During shooting, my only question regarding the lighting is, "When will it be done?"

If you can't afford a DP and are doing the lighting yourself (as I did on *Thou Shalt Not Kill . . . Except*), here's a crash course.

There are three kinds of lights: a key light, a fill light, and a backlight. The *key light* is the main source of illumination; the *fill light* is a soft, general, overall illumination that decreases contrast; and a *backlight*, or *kicker*, lights the subject from behind, giving them a glowing edge that separates them from the background and adds dimension.

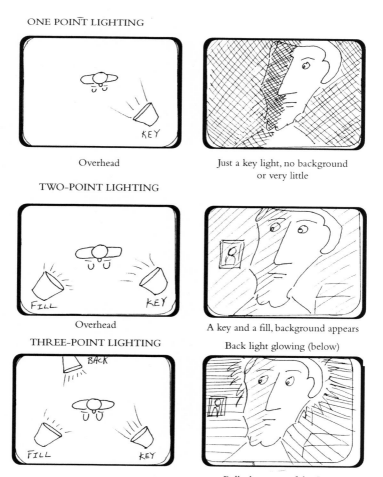

ONE POINT LIGHTING

Overhead

Just a key light, no background
or very little

TWO-POINT LIGHTING

Overhead

A key and a fill, background appears

THREE-POINT LIGHTING

Back light glowing (below)

Pulls them out of the BG

There are also three basic lighting setups:

One-point lighting, which has one lighting source. This was part of my scheme when I took over the lighting on *Evil Dead*—if possible, light the whole scene with one well-placed light. It's not only very quick to set up, it's also very dramatic and interesting-looking, and one light throws a single sharp shadow, which always looks better than multiple shadows.

Two-point lighting, like a menu in a Chinese restaurant, it's any of two of the three lighting positions—a key and a fill, or a key and a backlight, or a fill and a backlight. Adding a second source of illumination adds dimension to the subjects, and makes the background more visible.

Three-point lighting makes use of all three lighting positions at the same time, a key, a fill, and a backlight. This is the standard lighting setup for most scenes.

Many DPs, though not all, try to find a *source,* or rationale, for where the light is supposed to be coming from. If it's a daytime interior scene, and there's a window on the set, the DP will probably use that as the source. There would then be a beam of light coming in through the window, and all other subsequent lighting on that set or location would be *keyed,* meaning where you place the key light, from that same direction. Other DPs don't bother themselves with finding a source, and just light for how it looks.

To achieve a soft fill light you aim a light away from the scene into a white card, or a piece of foam-core, and reflect the light back onto the set.

When shooting outside, it's always wise to try and use the sun as a back light. Then with either the use of lights or *reflectors* (also known as *shiny boards*), which reflect sunlight back at the scene, you control the key light. If you use the sun as a backlight and don't put in a key light, you'll just have silhouettes.

Depth-of-Field and Exposures:

An interesting aspect of wide-angle lenses is that the wider the lens, the longer the *depth-of-field* it has, meaning how much of the shot is in focus. Using a 25mm lens in a well-lit area, you can have someone with their nose almost touching the *front element* (which is the front piece of glass in the lens), and someone else fifty feet behind them, and they'll both be in focus. If you are going to be shooting a lot of hand-held shots, where it's difficult for an assistant camera-person to keep changing the focus, use a wide-angle lens and you won't have focus problems. Also, the wider the lens, the less bumpiness you'll see in camera moves. On *Thou Shalt Not Kill . . . Except*, I shot over half the film hand-held with a 9mm lens (which would be an 18mm lens in 35mm—just for the sake of confusion the lenses for 16mm cameras are gauged at half of what they would be on 35mm cameras). There are a number of shots in the film when I am running as fast as I can with the camera and it looks pretty darn smooth.

Whereas, the longer the lens, the less depth-of-field, and the shorter the plane of focus, and also the bumpier it looks when the camera moves. That means if anyone moves, or the camera moves, you must *follow focus* with the subject or you'll lose focus. Then why bother with long lenses? Because they look really terrific and are much better for close-ups and beauty shots. By throwing the background out of focus, you are forcing the viewer to only look at that which is in focus. Also, long lenses flatten the picture, which interestingly makes people look more attractive. As a rule, I try not to let women ever get too close to a wide-angle lens, and always shoot their close-ups with the longest lens that's easily used—keeping in mind that the longer the lens, the farther back you have to place the camera. It's never all that hard, though, to switch from the 50mm to the 75mm lens for a woman's close-up, or the attractive male, for that matter, and this will always help them look even better.

Depth-of-field is also achieved by the *exposure*, or how much light is illuminating the scene by coming in through the end of the lens and exposing the film. The exposure, which is controlled by the *iris* or *aperture*, is calibrated in *f-stops* or *t-stops,* which are, for all practical purposes, the same thing as f-stops (one is a mechanical calibration, the other a mathematical calculation). I pause here for an anecdote:

Evil Dead was supposed to be a six-week shoot, but within three or four weeks we all knew it was going to go over schedule (we ended up shooting for eleven weeks). It became very clear quite soon, however, that Sam would need more than the allotted six weeks. Since the cameraman, Tim Philo, who had to leave at the end of six weeks, had personally borrowed the main camera, an Arri-BL, from Wayne State University, he intended to take it with him when he left. We still had an Arri-S, a smaller, a multi-speed camera, which is not in the same league as the BL. So Sam began pestering Tim a week before he was to leave that he really needed to leave the Arri-BL, "as a backup camera in case the other camera breaks down." Sam's reasoning was that should such a thing occur, he could not be left with no camera at all. Sam Raimi, being the most persistent person I've ever met, eventually wore Tim down and he relented, under the strict condition that the BL would now be the backup camera. Sam happily agreed. As Tim got in his car to leave, Sam turned to me and said, "Load the BL." I loaded the BL, got it all set up, put on the lens Sam requested, took a light reading with the *light meter*, which is calibrated in f-stops, went to set the exposure on the lens and found that it was calibrated in t-stops. I was twenty-one years old and had never heard of a t-stop in my life. Neither had Sam, Bruce, or Rob Tapert. I quickly tore through the American Cinematographer's Manual we had with us, and it's not in there. With Sam and Rob glaring at me, I finally called my buddy, Sheldon Lettich (who has since gone on to write and direct *Double Impact* and *Lionheart*), in LA and he explained that there was basically no difference, it was a technical thing. We continued to shoot, and all went well.

Meanwhile, the f-stops from the darkest to the brightest, meaning the iris is most-open to most-closed, are: 1.0, 1.2, 1.5, 1.8, 2, 2.2, 2.5, 2.8, 3.2, 3.5, 4, 4.5, 5, 5.6, 6.3, 7, 8, 9, 10, 11, 12.7, 14, 16, 18, 20, 22, 25, 29, and 32.

So, quite simply, the more light you have, the more focus you have. In the bright daytime sunshine, you get infinite depth-of-field with a wide-angle lens, but things will look far away. If you put on a long lens, things become close-up—or you've *zoomed-in*—but now you've lost some depth-of-field.

In the films *Citizen Kane* and *The Little Foxes*, the brilliant cinematographer Gregg Toland created some astonishing effects with extreme depth-of-field lighting. This is achieved by using very bright lights to get a high f-stop, somewhere between f-16 and f-32, then using slightly wide-angle lenses for long depth-of-field, but not too much distortion. Now you can have someone in a tight close-up in the foreground, like Joseph Cotton busily typing his opera review in *Citizen Kane*, and someone else across a long room behind them that's still in focus.

This effect can also be achieved in a much simpler fashion with the use of a *split-diopter*, which allows you to split the frame in half and set one focus for one side, and another focus for the other side. The one drawback is that it causes a fuzzy line between the two halves of the screen, but this can be hidden by the clever placement of a tree or the edge of a building.

Another point about the exposure is that low exposures (1.2 through 3.5) increase the grain and decrease the sharpness of the picture, whereas high exposures (from 4 all the way up) decrease the grain, and increase the sharpness. If you intend to blow-up to 35mm, this is important because the less unintentional grain and the sharper it is, the better it will look, so you want to try to keep your exposure high, if possible.

PART FOUR:
PRODUCTION

Okay, you've got the money, cast and crew, as well as all your equipment and all your locations, and you've done your shot list or storyboards. You're hot as a pistol, and you're ready to go shoot your movie. Now keep in mind the old filmmaking expression: "It's hard to make a good movie, and it's hard to make a bad movie," meaning it's just hard to make a movie.

Good Direction, Part One:
How Many Shots Does a Scene Need?

Here's how I start my approach to every scene I direct: Will one shot cover the whole scene? If not, why?

On both *Running Time* and *Hammer*, I was spending approximately $10,000 a day to shoot the film. That's all in cast, crew, film stock, rentals, everything. Now, if I can only legitimately plan on getting twenty-four shots a day—and that's if I'm moving quickly—that means each setup is costing about $420 each on a $150,000 movie. (On "Xena" and "Hercules," a single day of shooting cost about $120,000, which came to $5,000 a setup). So, any extra shots I add to my shot list will cost me $420 each, plain and simple. The question is, why get any more shots than are needed?

I try to get exactly what I think I need and no more. On a low-budget movie, that's how you have to work. I can think of an endless amount of shots to possibly get for every scene if time were not of the essence; but since it is, the job now is to figure out what I absolutely need and no more.

Let's imagine another scene: A man sits at a table in the kitchen and a woman enters, sits down, they talk for a page, then they both leave the way she came in. If you were to cover this scene in one shot, it could begin on the man at the table in a medium shot; he turns and sees the door open; we pan over to pick up the woman entering in a medium long shot, then pan with her back over to the table where she sits down; and we end up in a medium two-shot of both characters talking. When they're done, they both stand, and we pan with them back over to the door as they exit.

If that doesn't seem exciting enough, once we pan the woman over to the table and end up in a medium two-shot, we could potentially then do a slow dolly forward, called a *push-in or track-in*, tightening up the two-shot as they speak. To make that work even better we'd want to intentionally start the shot wider at the beginning, like a long shot, so that we'd have more room to dolly in at the end. Either shot is perfectly fine if it's not a very dramatic scene, and you're absolutely sure you won't ever need to cut anything out of it. Both of these examples are called *oners*, meaning they're one single shot that covers the whole scene with no other coverage. What this means is that however the oner turns out, that's what the scene will be because there is no editing involved as there's nothing to cut to.

However, if the characters are talking for more than a page of dialog, I don't think you want to leave yourself without coverage. Here's an interesting fact: An edited dialog scene generally moves faster than an unedited dialog scene, even if it's the exact same dialog. Why? Because editors usually cut out almost all of the actors' pauses. By getting no coverage, you're

Man at table, looks R, pan L to R

Woman enters, pan with her R to L

She sits in a med. 2-shot, track
with her back to door

Where we end in a med. close-up,
she looks back R to L

He looks back at her
in close-up, L to R

leaving the pacing of the scene up to the actors. With coverage, you can change the scene's pace whenever you want. If the scene is only covered in a oner, you're stuck.

But oners are exciting and I like them (*Running Time* is like one big oner). I've done quite a few oners myself, and I've rarely gotten screwed by them, although I'm always highly wary when I'm shooting them. I'll generally have the actors speed up a bit if I know it's only to be covered in a oner. The most famous oner is the first shot of Orson Welles's *Touch of Evil*, which goes on for five minutes while we follow a car with a ticking bomb in the trunk as it crosses the border from Mexico to the U.S., then explodes. Another famous oner is the shot in Joseph Lewis's *Gun Crazy* where the camera is in the backseat of a car as the two robbers pull up in front of a bank, get out of the car, go into the bank and rob it—which we only hear, we don't see—then they come running out of the bank, get back in the car and drive away, and it's all been in one long, uncut shot. But since we don't go into the bank with them, on a production level this relieved them from paying for the bank location. Joseph Lewis took his restriction and made it an asset.

JOHN HUSTON'S SHOT

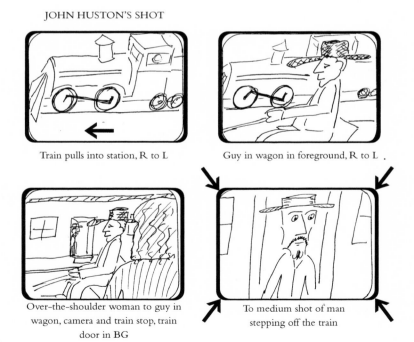

Train pulls into station, R to L

Guy in wagon in foreground, R to L .

Over-the-shoulder woman to guy in wagon, camera and train stop, train door in BG

To medium shot of man stepping off the train

I personally like shots that transform into other shots without cuts. In his autobiography, "An Open Book," John Huston gave a good example of what he considered an excellent shot: We are tracking with a train as it pulls into a station. A wagon pulls up in the foreground going the same direction, driven by one of the story's characters, and we follow it to the platform where we track past another person who stands waiting in the foreground. So now we are over the shoulder of this foreground person and facing the character in the wagon. Then a passenger gets off the train behind the wagon driver, and we rack focus or push in to the passenger. This shot transformed four times without a cut.

On "Xena" I did a shot I'm quite proud of. Xena is standing on a beach at the edge of a lake staring out at the water. Xena's face is in tight close-up to the left of the screen as she narrows her eyes and remembers. At this point in the script it said we flashback to when Xena was a young girl running along this same beach with her younger brother. Most directors would have done a dissolve and gone to the flashback, but since I'm always searching for a different way of doing things, I did a hard rack focus off of Xena's face as the actors playing young Xena and her brother ran into frame behind Xena. Then I panned off of Xena's out-of-focus face and followed the boy and the girl over to the edge of the lake. This way I was able to go into a flashback without a cut, which I think is pretty nifty.

Lucy Lawless in "Xena:
Warrior Princess," episode:
Fins, Femmes & Gems.

Another approach to coverage is beginning the scene with an interesting shot that gets the actors to where they will speak, then it goes into coverage. Basically, you shoot your master shot as though it were a oner until you can bring it to where it goes into coverage. This is how most directors cover a lot of their scenes, and I do, too. An interesting opening shot draws the viewer in, then the actors and the dialog carry the rest of the scene.

This is a good way to go because I think it's important to have at least one interesting shot per scene. As an example, let's use the two people in the kitchen again. The man is sitting at the kitchen table slicing vegetables. What if we started in tight on a close-up of the knife cutting the vegetables, then quickly pull back to a medium-long shot of the man turning and looking at the door, pan to the door as it opens and the woman enters. Follow her back to the table where she sits down, then shoot the rest of the scene in a two-shot with the intention of getting coverage. Now we are

Close-up chopping vegetables
Dolly back to...

Med. shot man, he looks right,
pan L to R, to...

Woman enters, pan R to L, to...

Med. two-shot at table,
push in to...

Tight two-shot

owed (as 1ˢᵗ ADs like to say) two close-ups or two over-the-shoulder shots. This would be *standard coverage* for a scene, meaning a wide shot and two close-ups or a wide shot and two over-the-shoulder shots.

A time-saving variation of standard coverage is to do the whole wide shot opening exactly the same, but instead of stopping in a two-shot when you follow the woman back to the table, she stops in an over-the-shoulder shot facing the man. Now you are only owed the one shot—the reverse over-the shoulder. If you're in a hurry and don't want to do just a oner, this is a wise approach.

Keep in mind, however, if there are too many interesting shots per scene—particularly when it's a dialog-driven scene—it becomes ostentatious and keeps pointing out that there's a director at work. Maybe that's what you want, but I find it distracting from what the scene is really about: the actors and the dialog. Very often these days you'll see dialog scenes covered by having the camera constantly circling the actors, which I also find annoying. Another common contemporary mode of dialog coverage is doing slow dolly moves on the wide shot, then on all of the close-ups, too. This scheme sort of annoys me, particularly when there's so much dialog that the slow dolly moves keep creeping toward the 180-degree line, which you just know the director will not cross. (I saw a short film years ago where a young filmmaker tracked across the line to a jump cut and I burst out laughing.) So if the dialog isn't over by the time the camera gets to the line, they must cut away, reset the camera back to its starting point and start the slow move again. (Slow camera moves in New Zealand, by the way, are euphemistically referred to as "Mickey Rooneys" because they're "little creeps." Mickey Rooney shot the "Black Stallion" TV series down there.) A slight variation on this scheme is what Robert Altman did all the way through *Gosford Park*, where the camera basically never stops moving. It would slowly track one way or the other while the actors spoke, and when the camera got to the line, it would just start back in the other direction. I consider this kind of coverage flaccid and uninteresting.

Here's my theory: If it's actually an interesting scene, you can cover it in a static oner, and it will still be an interesting scene. If it's not a good scene, it doesn't matter how you cover it; nothing will make it a good scene, so you might as well amuse yourself. I've done all the things that I say annoy me just to keep myself interested while shooting less-than-great dialog scenes.

Another approach I'm a fan of is called a *dolly-edit* or a *sequence-shot*. This is where your master is a somewhat complicated moving oner that comes to a stop on several occasions where it then needs reverse coverage. Let's use the kitchen scene again: We start in tight on the knife and the vegetables, pull back to a medium shot of the man; he turns, and we pan to the woman entering to follow her back to the man where we stop in the woman's over-the-shoulder shot facing the man—now we're owed the reverse over-the shoulder shot facing the woman. We follow the woman as she crosses back to the door where she stops and turns back to the man; the camera moves in to a close-up for her several more lines back to the man (who is now off-camera), and then she leaves. Now we're also owed a close-up of the man saying his lines back to her while she was at the door. With a dolly-edit your master becomes far more useful and a lot more interesting than staying out on a static wide shot. But unlike a oner, you have to make sure to get the missing reverse shots, or your coverage is incomplete.

Camera Moves:

I have read quite a few books on filmmaking, and most of them try to convince you that you shouldn't be doing any camera moves unless you absolutely have to, like following someone while they're walking. They use terms like "uninflected"—meaning not visible—as the proper way to shoot. To this I say, nonsense.

Camera moves can be visually exciting and often are the best thing about a movie. But too much of a good thing can quickly become a bad thing. If you're doing camera moves all the time, then it's difficult to have them mean anything after a while.

Well-placed camera moves, however, can be a thing of beauty. Alfred Hitchcock did many stunning camera moves, like the high wide shot of a fancy dress party in *Notorious* (1946) that slowly moves all the way down to an extreme close-up of a key in Ingrid Bergman's hand. Or as the mad killer rapist is in the midst of assaulting a woman in *Frenzy* (1972), the camera (discreetly) pulls back out of the office, down the stairs and out the front door all the way across the street, looking back at the quiet, normal office building.

As a young man I thought crane shots were the most awesome camera moves there were. That is until I actually got to work with a camera crane. This piece of equipment is one of the biggest time-suckers available. They're expensive, and you have to pay for the crane crew (generally two guys), and they're awkward as hell to move around. Also, the crew can't set up the crane until they have the camera to put on the end of it, so you can't have the crane all set up and waiting while you shoot other shots. You must stop shooting, give them your camera (unless you have two cameras) and wait around for at least an hour as they balance the crane, putting the camera, the operator and the 2nd AC on one end and lead weights on the other end. The process is grueling, and I can't bear it.

Here's another bad part about using a crane: being up high often makes everything down below look cheap. Suddenly twenty-five extras look like five people, and any sets that aren't built that well look exactly like what they are—poorly-built sets.

Some directors like to start their scenes up in a tree, or anywhere high, then crane down to the actors. This has been done so many times—and I've done it too—it's a wearisome visual cliché at this late date that won't impress anyone anymore, which doesn't mean you shouldn't do it. This is called *starting off the action*, which is a good idea but doesn't have to be from high off a crane. You can start the shot on anything that excludes the actors—a picture on the wall, a statue, a shadow, a hand gesturing, a cigarette butt being stubbed out on the floor, whatever—and if the previous scene was also people talking, it makes for a better transition than going from a group of people to a group of people. Starting off the action helps bridge the transition from one scene to another and adds some visual interest to the scene.

You can also achieve the same feeling of vertical movement gotten from a crane by use of the hydraulic dolly head, which is standard on any real dolly. By use of items called *risers*—tall stacks of metal that fit on the dolly head and raise the height of the camera—you can get the lens up eight or ten feet, which is pretty high. You can achieve the same visual effect as a crane with a lot less hassle and expense. Another piece of equipment that fits on the dolly head and allows you to stick the camera out away from the dolly (to go through a window for instance) is called a *ubangi,* which is actually the name of an African tribe who ritualistically mutilated and extended out their lower lips. There is also a piece of equipment called a *jib-arm,* which fits on the dolly and allows you to make crane-like moves without the hassle of a crane, although you can't get anywhere nearly as high as with an actual crane.

Another very common camera move, and Steven Spielberg's trademark, is the *push.* It's where the camera moves in or pushes from a long or medium shot of a character to a close-up—generally at the end of a scene or at a dramatic high point during the scene—and is often accompanied by a short piece of highly dramatic music called a *sting. Dun-dun-dun!* Nearly every act end going to a commercial break on "Xena" ended with a push on Xena looking concerned while the composer, Joe LoDuca (who scored all four of my independent films and both TV movies), supplied the sting. A thing to keep in mind when doing a push is that if you intend to *inter-*

cut—go back and forth to other characters also reacting to whatever it is they're reacting to, as you frequently do—those shots should be pushing, too, at the same speed. Moving shots and static shots frequently do not intercut well. It's done all the time these days, and it usually looks sloppy to me, as if a mistake. When I do a push I either mean to stick with it all the way, or I have my intercuts pushing, too, and I think it looks more elegant that way. I think all camera moves look better if you really mean them. It's much easier, though, to cut into slow camera moves rather than into fast ones, particularly if what you're cutting to is another slow camera move.

My friend Sam Raimi did some brilliant camera moves in *Evil Dead*, and we had very little money. We bolted a 16-mm Arri-S with a 7.5-mm fisheye lens to a two-foot board, and Sam ran like hell, nearly hitting every tree and stump intentionally and turning the camera sideways and upside down. It's the invisible monster's POV, which Sam called "the force," and the story was conceived with those camera moves in mind. He had already made a short pilot version called *Within the Woods* with the same camera moves in super-8, and they were just as good.

My point is that intelligently used camera moves can be more than just coverage; they can be an integral part of the story. Just like the shark POVs in *Jaws*. Every time it cuts underwater, it's scary. But just moving the camera because you can is not the same thing. Your intentions mean everything.

Also, too much handheld camera work is a bad idea because it makes the audience feel seasick. Handheld can be used for effect, but for the most part it's ugly, thoughtless and annoying. You simply cannot create pleasing montage handheld. When all of the camera work is handheld, it all looks sloppy and arbitrary. This may be fine for documentary, but it's a lousy idea for a feature.

There's a movement out of Scandinavia called Dogma 95 that, aside from stressing the drama of personal relationships over special effects, gunfire, and explosions—which I think is a very wise position—also says that you can't use a tripod, a dolly or a Steadi-cam—which I think is plain stupidity. This, I believe, precludes them from creating beautiful montage or making a great movie.

Cuts:

The average movie has between 500 and 1,500 cuts in it. Some of the big Hollywood action extravaganzas have upward of 2,500 cuts in them. A good director is always thinking about where each shot will cut and what it will be cutting to. This is the big difference between a well-directed feature and a documentary (good or bad). In a documentary, you shoot anything and everything and basically direct it—meaning figure out how it all goes together—in the editing. With the well-directed feature, on the other hand, how it will all go together is predetermined by the director.

The difference between well-conceived montage and random footage that was somehow assembled in the editing room is the world, and it's where all the possibilities for visual artistry lie.

Walk and Talks:

Sooner or later in most screenplays, there will be a scene when the characters are walking and talking, and these scenes are appropriately called *walk and talks*. Every "Xena" and "Hercules" episode had a couple of walk and talks, and there really aren't all that many ways to photograph people walking and talking.

The most obvious way to do a walk and talk is to follow along with the characters as they are, yes, walking and talking. This can be achieved either by doing a dolly shot, a handheld shot or, very frequently these days, a *Steadi-cam* shot. A Steadi-cam is a brand name of a piece of handheld equipment that steadies out the movement of the camera by use of a gyroscope. I like them a lot, and they're very handy; but they are also an extra expense and not *necessary* by any means. The only time I've used one on a low-budget feature was *Running Time*, where it was absolutely necessary because the camera never stopped moving. But I didn't have one on my last film, *Hammer*, and I didn't miss it either.

I really like dolly shots, and I think they're very pleasing to look at. For any kind of crew at all, setting up as much dolly track as you need is no big deal. A good crew can set up track nearly anywhere—in the mud, in the water, over most any surface—but for places where you can't set up dolly track, a Steadi-cam is the perfect piece of equipment. There have been quite a few spectacular Steadi-cam shots, like the one through the entire Copacabana Club in *Goodfellas*. Stanley Kubrick makes really terrific use of the Steadi-cam all over *The Shining* and *Full Metal Jacket*.

A very common and visually pleasing way to cover a walk and talk is with a long lens. You start to get an interesting effect with 75- to 100-mm lenses, but the effect is much more apparent with lenses 150 mm or higher. You can hold characters in frame for a long time as they walk and talk by following focus with them. The longest lens I've ever used was for a walk and talk, and it was a 300-mm lens with a *doubler*—a piece of glass that doubles the length of the lens—so in this case it went up to 600 mm. I was able to get Xena and another character walking along with time for them to spew three full pages of dialog while keeping an interesting-looking shot going without cutting. The two characters step into frame in a long shot, just below their feet to just above their heads, then begin walking toward us. But they barely grow any bigger in frame *for the next three entire minutes*, which is a long time on film, because they're so compressed by the lens. Meanwhile, the 1ˢᵗ assistant cameraman was in living hell constantly racking the focus to keep the characters sharp. It's a cool trick but kind of hard to do, and the 300-mm lens is expensive to rent. Nevertheless, I think it's worth the time and money if it's going to be three or four minutes of a movie, which is a lot. A beautiful example of a long-lens shot is Omar Sharif's entrance riding up on a camel through the heat haze in the desert in *Lawrence of Arabia*.

Yet another, even simpler, way of covering a walk and talk is to just set the camera up somewhere and let the characters walk past it. Let them grow bigger and bigger in frame, then either let them exit frame or pan with them and watch them walk away.

As a general rule, however, you try to spend as little time as possible looking at people's backs. On TV they're really against looking at people's backs. This rule, too, can be broken though. In Akira Kurosawa's film *Yojimbo*, Toshiro Mifune gives an amazing performance with his back, twitching, flexing and hunching it the whole film. David Lean played Alec Guinness's big final speech in *The Bridge on the River Kwai* on his back (where he drops his stick in the water), and it almost caused the two of them to get into a fist fight even though they were good friends.

Good Direction, Part Two: Talking to the Actors

I believe it's much more important to talk to the actors than to the camera crew. You can talk to the camera people while the actors are away in hair and makeup, but when the actors are on the set, they come first. (I end up talking to the DP all day long anyway, because his chair is right next to mine with the script supervisor on the other side—these are the only three people, by the way, who really need to see the video monitor and watch the scenes as they actually transpire.)

Marlon Brando, in his autobiography "Songs My Mother Taught Me," expressed a deep resentment for directors who preferred talking to the DP over the actors, and I understand where he's coming from. The viewers are not looking at a camera, they're looking at the actors. As the director, you should try to set up the ideal situation for the actors to feel sufficiently uninhibited and will give you their very best interpretation of the scene. If you're too busy gabbing with the DP to pay attention to the actors, you're making a mistake.

Actors want and need direction. Actors need to know that what they're doing is what the director is looking for, and if it's not, what they need to do to change it. On a very basic level, the actors need to know the director is there with them and that they're not out there all by themselves looking foolish. If you like what an actor is doing, tell them so. If you think your reading a line for the actor will help, then do it. If you need to act the whole scene out for them, then do that. Frequently, I will tell actors which words I want them to stress in a line. Do whatever you need to do to communicate your ideas. Some actors need more direction, some less. Lucy Lawless would frequently wave me away, indicating she had as much direction as she needed. Fine with me. And the direction she felt she needed she followed precisely.

The actors at Warner Brothers in the 1930s and 40s used to regularly make fun of the great director Michael Curtiz (*Casablanca, Mildred Pierce*) because he always acted out the scenes for the actors with his very thick Hungarian accent. That may have seemed silly to Cagney and Bogart, but Curtiz managed to communicate his ideas and consistently got strong performances.

The main directorial approach of my favorite director, William Wyler, was to be consistently disappointed with the actors' performances and to let them know it, and this seemed to make them try harder and harder. He took Charlton Heston aside early in the shooting on *Ben-Hur* and said, "Chuck, you're just not good enough." Heston asked what could he do? Wyler shook his head in disappointment and said, "I don't know," and walked away. Charlton Heston got the Best Actor Oscar for that performance. When Wyler was directing Laurence Olivier in his first big film, *Wuthering Heights* (which made Olivier a star), Wyler would say to him, "Larry, you've got to be kidding. This isn't some London music hall. Do it again." After most takes with most actors, apparently Wyler would just shake his head in weary disappointment and mutter, "Again." This method of Wyler's got his films nominated for over twice as many Oscars as the next two most nominated directors combined.

Alfred Hitchcock was of the ilk of director who didn't much like talking to actors (as is true of many directors), and his films are not noted for their strong performances. He was, however, smart enough always to cast top-notch actors who generally could handle their own performances without his help. But you can't depend on actors handling everything themselves unless you're casting the very best actors.

The two most constant pieces of direction I impart to the actors are: let's pick up the pace a little bit—or—could you bring it (your performance) down a little bit? For the benefit of inexperienced actors, I have often added, "You're not playing to the back row; I have camera up your nose." Another one of my favorite pieces of direction is, "More energy," which helps combat fatigue.

After a take on "Hercules" when I was shooting with Anthony Quinn, I asked him for a reaction to a certain line. He said he'd already reacted to that line on the previous take. I said that I hadn't seen it, and he replied, "Look harder." I rewound the videotape, watched the scene again and, by golly, he sure had. It was the tiniest twitch of his eyebrow, but it was there, and it said everything that needed to be said.

Having a camera right in an actor's face is very intimate, and the slightest movements can be seen very clearly. As far as film performances go, bigger is generally not better; subtle is better. As they say, less is more. Watch what Marlon Brando does with his eyebrows in *The Godfather*. Yes, if the part is Hannibal Lecter or Charles Manson, a bombastic performance may be the way to go, but most parts are just not that big. Most parts are just regular people who react to things in regular ways.

As a rule I don't often go back and watch video replays on the set, but occasionally I do; and when I do, I'm always glad they're there. Actors like looking at the video replays sometimes, too, which is okay with me. But watching the video replays can become a time-sucker, so be careful and don't make a habit of it if you can help it.

Directorial Transitions:

I am a big fan of interesting *transitions*, which are the shots that get you from one scene to the next. The standard forms of transition in films are: a *cut*, meaning you just go straight to the next scene; a *dissolve*, where the two scenes superimpose over each other for a moment as one scene goes out and the other scene comes in; a *fade-out* to black, where the scene goes to black; *fade-in* from black, where the scene appears from black. These transitions are often indicated in the script, although directors can add or eliminate them where they see fit.

To accommodate dissolves or fades in editing, directors must remember to shoot extra footage at the beginning or end of the shots they intend to dissolve or fade into or out of. If you don't remember to shoot extra footage at the beginning and end of the shot, you won't be able to make your transitions later. At the *head* or beginning of the shot, wait a few extra seconds after you roll before saying action; and at the *tail* or end, count slowly in your head to about four or five before saying cut. Always tell the camera operator in advance that this shot contains a dissolve or a fade and needs extra head and tail, so they don't start rolling late or cut early.

A technique many directors (including myself) often use for interesting dissolves is to make sure the character you're dissolving out on is all the way over to one side of the frame, then make sure whomever you're dissolving in on is over on the other side of the frame. It's a simple effect that always looks good.

Directors can also dream up their own clever transitions. These may be, by far, the best ones. Let's face it, we've all seen a million dissolves and fades.

David Lean did one of my favorite transitions in *Lawrence of Arabia*. The American reporter (Arthur Kennedy) steps up to a bearded man and asks if he knows Prince Feisal (Alec Guinness). The man says yes, then Kennedy hands him his business card, and the man looks down at it. We cut to an insert of the card, then cut wide, and it's Prince Feisal looking down at the card while sitting with the reporter. In *The Bridge on the River Kwai*, the doctor (James Donald) squints up at the sun. We cut to a shot of the sun,

Photo #1:
The doctor looks up, cut to . . .

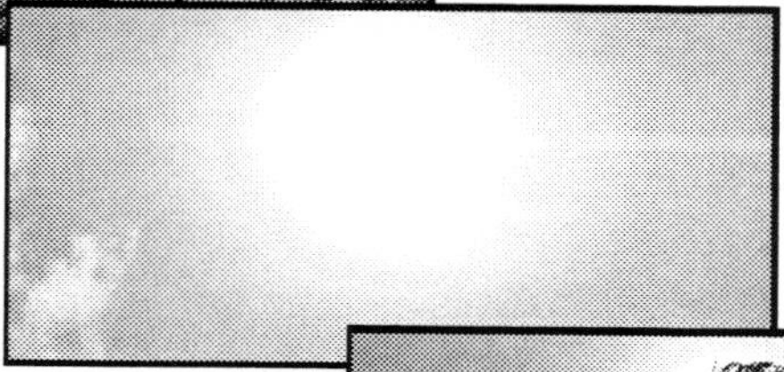

Photo #2: The blazing sun . .

Photo #3: . . . The escaped prisoner steps into frame, low-angle.

then the escaped prisoner (William Holden) steps into the frame at a very low angle. I think David Lean paid attention to his transitions because he began his career as an editor.

In one of my "Xena" episodes, Xena (Lucy Lawless) looks at an ornate knife left behind by the bad guys, then disgustedly throws it at the ground. We cut to an insert of the knife sticking into the ground, then the camera quickly pulls back to reveal we are now in the bad guy's camp watching them throw knives into the dirt.

1. Two-shot of Xena and Joxer (Ted Raimi) inspecting a Scythian knife, cut to . . .

2. MCU Xena throws the knife, cut to . . .

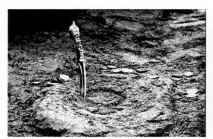

3. Close-up of the knife sticking into the ground, pull back fast to . . .

4. . . . Scythian soldiers pull the knife out of the ground. From X:WP episode "In Sickness & In Hell."

In another "Xena" episode, there is an angry king holding a sword. After saying his last line, he slashes the sword down out of frame. It cuts to a tight close-up of a piece of cheese being sliced by Gabrielle (Renée O'Connor), then pulls back, and we're now in a cave. (see next page)

There is the old standard transition of tracking behind a dark or light object, then coming out from behind a similar dark or light object in a different scene. I used this several times in *Running Time* to hide cuts. I also used it in the "Xena" episode where Lucy Lawless plays three different parts. We're tracking along with Lucy as Xena, then we go behind a dark pillar and come out on Lucy as the princess. Another possible transition is

1. Warlord pulls his sword.

2. He swings the sword down out of frame, cut to . . .

3. Close-up of knife cutting cheese, pull back fast to . . .

4. Three-shot of Princess, Gabrielle (Renee O'Connor) and Joxer. From X: WP epsiode "For Him the Bell Tolls."

the *whip pan*, where the camera pans so fast it blurs. I used these to hide cuts quite a few times in *Running Time*, too.

Check out George Roy Hill's brilliant film version of *Slaughterhouse-Five*, which is teeming with imaginative transitions.

There are also *wipes*, which are conceptually like dissolves in that one scene takes over from the next scene, but it's usually done with a sharp or fuzzy vertical line moving across the screen (or horizontal lines moving up or down the screen). A wipe can be in any design you can think of and are willing to pay for, like curtains opening or airplane propellers spinning. I was a big fan of wipes on "Xena," and I did them constantly. I think I've done every sort of wipe you can do: vertical, horizontal, sharp-edged, fuzzy-edged, saw-toothed. I used them in *Hammer*, too, in what I believe is a somewhat ironic fashion. George Lucas uses them in *Star Wars*. I think that wipes indicate a lighthearted tone—like an old-time Saturday morning serial. One form of a wipe is an *iris*—where the picture becomes a shrinking circle and disappears—indicating nostalgia for the old days or silent movies. There is a brilliant iris in *The Magnificent Ambersons* at the end of the haunting, almost surreal scene of everyone riding in Morgan's new car in the snow, which is juxtaposed with Georgie and Lucy whizzing past in a horse-drawn sleigh and hollering, "Get a horse!" The sleigh overturns, throwing Lucy and Georgie into a pillow of snow where they have their first kiss. Georgie and Lucy are rescued by the family in the car, which promptly gets stuck. As Georgie pushes the car, exhaust fumes sputtering in his face, everyone begins to sing, "I'm the Man Who Broke the Bank at Monte Carlo." As the car drives away, the picture irises down to just the car on a hilltop, which is in fact a miniature.

The Proper Order in Which to Shoot:

This is by far the best order to shoot a scene: At *call time*, which is when you intend to start shooting (not when people should be showing up), have all of the actors in the scene and all the crew report to the location or set. The actors should be coming out of wardrobe and makeup and may not be finished yet, which is fine. Actors, hair, makeup and wardrobe are the first ones on the set, along with *craft service* (the coffee and donuts, etc.). Now, without discussing cameras or shots, *block* the scene—meaning arrange the actors, in front of the crew, in the positions you want them so everyone knows what's going on, particularly the DP, the camera operator and the 1ˢᵗ AD. The actors probably have some suggestions that you can heed or not heed as you feel fit. Once the scene is blocked, and the actors are completely sure of what they'll be doing, send them back to wardrobe and makeup to finish up. Now, and only now, the camera will be set in its proper position, and the lighting commences. If all is running smoothly when the actors return in a few minutes, the lighting should be done, and you can immediately shoot the scene. This is by far the most logical order in which to shoot and will save you a lot of time in the long run. Block it, get rid of the actors, set the camera, light the scene, get the actors back, shoot it, *then immediately block the next scene*—this is the key to keeping things moving. This way the cast and crew won't have a chance to disperse and will immediately get to work on the next shot.

To my own thinking, once the director says "Print it," *attrition* immediately sets in, meaning the system wears down to a stop due to friction, like an engine with no oil. The cast and crew will immediately erupt into chatter and try to disperse, which the director and the 1ˢᵗ AD cannot allow. The lubricant in this case is simply clear direction. If you immediately block the next scene and get the crew to start setting it up and lighting it, all is well and you won't allow attrition to set in. Keep the machine lubricated. If you are trying to get twenty-four setups a day, and you let everybody go get a cup of coffee and have a smoke between every shot, you're not getting twenty-four setups.

On a more basic level of shooting order, you shoot the wide shots first then the closer shots. On the wide shot, you can see all of the actors' movements; then on the closer shots, you can pin them down to stay on their *marks*, which are either pieces of colored tape on the floor or small colored sandbags called *toebags*. Each character gets a different color toebag or different color tape. Then you keep moving from the largest lighting setups down to the smallest, from seeing the whole room down to the individual close-ups.

There are crews, however (like the one I just worked with in Bulgaria making *Alien Apocalypse*), who can't work with the aforementioned system. The hair and makeup departments were so overwhelmed everyday that I set up the camera with doubles, and when enough actors finally arrived, I shot. Luckily the leads were always ready first, so then we'd just wait for the other actors.

The Philosophy of the Director: Whose Vision Is It?

Obviously, different directors work in different ways. I've spent a great deal of my life working on film crews with other directors, and most of the directors I've had the pleasure to watch in action seemed to me to be unprepared, insecure and in a panic all the time. I believe that the director is the leader, the captain of the ship, and should act like it. If the director knows what s/he wants, everybody else will see that and respect it. If the director is unsure and waffling, everyone will see that, too, but they won't respect it. If the captain isn't respected, you can bet it will be a poorly run ship.

You don't get respect by yelling and acting like a tyrant or a *prima donna*. You get respect by being prepared and looking like you know what you're doing. I *know* that I've read the script more times than anyone else on the set (whether I wrote it or not); I've thought about the blocking and shooting of this scene far more than anyone else, and I can prove it because I have a shot list or storyboards. I don't need to yell because I'm the only one who really knows what's going on. There's power in the position, and if you're honestly prepared, there's nothing to fear.

Regarding performance, I'm interested in everything the actors have to say. I don't always take their suggestions, but I'm always happy to listen to them.

Regarding camera placement, on the other hand, I don't want to hear what anyone else has to say about it. I absolutely believe that where the camera goes is entirely the director's domain, if they care to make it so. Many, many directors think that the DP and the camera operator get a say-so in the camera placement, but I completely disagree. As Alfred Hitchcock once said, "You *never* put the camera somewhere because the cameraman thinks it's a good idea." Let's face facts: the DP and the camera operator haven't got the slightest clue which shots this shot we're about to shoot is cutting to or from, and that's critical in choosing the angle. The DP and the operator frequently just want to make this shot more fun for themselves. Well, whether the DP and the operator are having a sufficient amount of fun means nothing to me. Creating good *montage*—which is French for editing—is what I'm after, and the DP and operator can't help me with that. What they can help me with is the *composition,* the arrangement of the elements within the frame, and where the best spot is to put the camera to get the shot I want. But if I say we're starting in a close-up here and ending in a long shot there, I don't want to hear any other possibilities as to how this scene might possibly be shot. I agree that every scene can be shot many different ways; but when *I'm* the director, we're doing it *my* way. All directors must set their own parameters, but this is assuredly the quickest way to work as it involves the least discussion. Discussion takes time, and time is money.

So I say choose all of your shots in advance, then do your damnedest to get every one of them when you're shooting. Just getting the shots *you* want will be more than enough of a chore, so you don't need to be getting the shots anyone else wants, too.

If this is how you want to direct then you must speak to the DP and the operator (who are frequently the same person on a low-budget film) early on to convey your philosophy. I'm the director, and I choose the shots. If the DP doesn't like it, then don't hire him. Always remember: it's *your* movie.

Just to show I'm a good sport, however, I discuss which lens to use with the DP. Once I see what the lens looks like on the camera, I can always change it and frequently do.

As I've already said, many directors don't work this way. Some directors even let the DP choose all of the shots, which I can't imagine. Choosing the shots and angles to me is so much a part of the job of directing a movie that, if I couldn't do it, I wouldn't want to direct (though on commercials, the advertising agency does all the storyboards).

Once I've discussed my overall vision of how I see the film with the DP, however, I let him do all the lighting. It's the DP's job, and I don't get in his way. What I want most from a DP is to light the scene quickly and not waste my precious time.

Also, once the actors come out of wardrobe and makeup, I immediately want to run the scene and then shoot it. I do not want to sit around waiting for the lighting to be finished. Unless you are trying to shoot some giant setup, like a ballroom or big conference room or something, the average scene should take about fifteen or twenty minutes to light. If the DP is taking thirty minutes or more to light simple scenes, then your schedule just went down the toilet, and you will not be getting your twenty-four setups a day. Are you going to give someone on the crew that you hired and are paying the power to blow your schedule and force you to not get all the shots you need? I won't. The DP works for me—s/he is the lieutenant, and I'm the captain.

This is really a key piece of information: I seriously believe that more directors have gotten screwed in the editing room by listening to friendly advice on the set than by any other cause. Don't let this happen to you. Stick to your plan. Remember, a film set is not a democracy—it's a benign dictatorship. Being benign is particularly important on a low-budget film because you're not paying people very much, and they can walk out on you. But it's still a dictatorship, and it should be one person's vision.

Besides, you don't have to be a creep to get your way. As I said, I never raise my voice or get angry on a film set. It's not necessary, and it's not professional. In fact, I'm doing my very best all day long to keep a light, jovial atmosphere on the set so that everybody—particularly the actors—have a comfortable, stress-free place to work. As they say, shit rolls downhill. If the director is tense and freaked-out, the whole cast and crew will also be tense and freaked-out. If the director is happy and light-hearted, the whole cast and crew will be happy and light-hearted, and I think that's a much better environment in which to create quality work. It certainly makes it more fun. And if you can't have fun making movies, than you shouldn't be doing it. I can't tell you how many grueling, miserable shoots I was on when I was a PA, and it's ridiculous. Making movies is fun, honestly. It's just complicated and, if you don't do it properly, it quickly becomes a nightmare.

Of the one hundred or more directors to work on "Xena" and "Hercules" over the course of six and five seasons, respectively, I had one of the best records for coming in on time and on budget, if not the best. I think that twelve hours is a long work day (7:00 AM to 7:00 PM, generally), and no one wants to go into overtime. If you're working with SAG actors, then it's going to cost you a lot of money to go into overtime, and there goes your budget. And don't forget turnaround: the moment you go into overtime, you are no longer starting to shoot the next day when you thought you were, and there goes your schedule. Once things start falling apart on a production, they have a tendency to keep falling apart and get worse. My method for consistently *getting my day*, which is what they call shooting your entire schedule in the time allotted, *is to stick to my plan*. I intend to get these twenty-four shots this day—no more, no less—and I don't want to discuss it. If you have a five to ten minute discussion about the next shot after you finish a shot—as I've seen many directors do—that will add up to several lost hours everyday, and that's a lot of shots you're now not going to get. Is it worth it? I don't think so.

I also feel it's very important to get your first shot off in the morning as quickly as possible. Whether you know it or not, you're setting the pace for the whole day. If it takes two hours to get your first shot, as it frequently does on many productions, once again your schedule is a dead duck. If you're planning on getting twenty-four shots a day, that's thirty minutes each—period. If you blow two hours on the first shot, you'll probably never make it up. And once you start dropping shots to make your day, you'll keep dropping shots. When you get into the editing room, you'll regret it.

When the DP and the camera operator begin to discuss editing, which they inevitably do, they're absolutely wasting time. Pure and simple. As I've said to DPs on a number of occasions when they begin to discuss editing, "Is there a DP cut I haven't heard about?" No, there isn't. The DP and the operator have nothing to do with the editing—they never set foot in an editing room and generally know very little about it—so if they're talking about it, they're simply wasting your valuable time.

Deep down I sincerely believe that anyone who is not helping me to achieve my plan and get my day is sabotaging me, and I'm happy to tell them so. So I say, believe in your plan and stick to it, and you won't go wrong. Ultimately, your plan may just stink, but you're still better off achieving it than not.

Blocking:

Blocking the actors' movements, as I've said, is the first thing you do when shooting a scene. If you've had rehearsals and already worked on the blocking, then all of the actors should have a pretty clear idea as to where to go and what to do. If you haven't had any rehearsals, and this is the very first time you've run the scene (how it always is on TV), then this is kind of a tricky maneuver where things often go haywire.

To have done your shot list or storyboards properly, you must have envisioned the scenes with their blocking already; otherwise, you don't *really* know what shots you intend to get. More than anything else, this is the key thing a director does: envisions or imagines the scenes before they have occurred. Once again I say, if you have a plan, go with your plan. Yes, of course, all the actors want to go off in all different directions, but you can't let them. If you've got nothing but time on your hands—as I hear the Coen brothers and Woody Allen do—sure, go ahead and explore the scene, but I've never had that luxury. That's what I do in rehearsals for free on my films when I'm not spending a thousand dollars or more an hour.

If I give an actor direction to hit a certain mark at a certain line, and s/he says, "I feel like going over there"—somewhere other than I had in mind—I will often politely say, "Please feel like coming over here." I sup-pose if I had $60 million of someone else's money, maybe I'd run a few more rehearsals on the set with more freedom for the actors. But if it's cost-ing me personally a thousand bucks an hour, I say yet again, let's get what I've planned. I've been thinking about it the most—I have a plan and you don't—and I'm the director, so I win.

Another perspective on blocking is simply to keep the actors moving all the time. But actors, like regular human beings, don't just want to keep moving all the time, particularly if they're talking to one another. They generally want to get to a spot where they are face to face to say their lines, and that's generally how scenes are staged and shot. However, just because that's what *they* want to do doesn't mean that's what *you* want them to do. What looks good on film frequently doesn't feel right to the actors on the set. Too bad. If it looks good, and that's how you want it, that's how you should get it.

I keep seeing little time-fillers on Sundance Channel's "Scenes From the Lab," where we watch young, first-time movie directors at work. One of these wannabes said, "I can't tell the actors where to go. They'd laugh at me." Perhaps this young man ought to look into other fields of employ-ment, because part of the job description of a film director is: telling actors where to go and what to do. If you're afraid the actors are going to laugh at you, then a) you're an idiot, and b) you don't understand actors. Actors love and thrive on direction. They don't always follow it, but it gives them something else to think about besides their own internal issues, which is

Figure 1 — Reforming Blocking

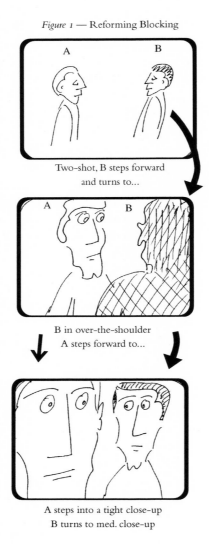

Two-shot, B steps forward
and turns to...

B in over-the-shoulder
A steps forward to...

A steps into a tight close-up
B turns to med. close-up

good. Obviously, too much of anything can be bad, and direction is no exception to the rule. But directors communicating what they have in mind
is crucial to the process and far more important than just letting the actors
do whatever they want.

I like blocking that keeps reforming itself into new compositions (see
figure 1). Two actors are speaking in a profile two-shot, then one of them
steps over to where they are now in an over-the-shoulder shot with the

actor facing the lens. The actor facing the lens walks straight forward past the other actor and into a tight close-up, while the background actor turns to look at the close-up actor's back and is now in a medium close-up over the foreground actor's shoulder. That's one possibility. Orson Welles was an expert at this. Watch the blocking in *The Magnificent Ambersons* because it's incredible. Welles could get the blocking of even a short scene to reform into new compositions three, four, or five different times, and it looks natural every time. It may not have felt natural to the actors on the set, but it looks spectacular on film.

An old-time piece of filmmaking advice is to always have the actors exit the *long frame*. What this means is that it visually looks better if actors cross across the frame on their way out of the shot, where there's more frame to cross than less. For instance, if I'm looking at someone in an over-the-shoulder shot, and she's facing left to right, she would exit out the right side of the frame as opposed to the left as that would make her exit much shorter. This may once again seem obvious, but it is not always obvious when you're shooting, so keep it in mind.

Another noteworthy aspect of blocking with regard to the camera is that movement toward or away from the lens is visually more interesting and three-dimensional than movement going laterally across the screen, which looks flat.

Standard Blocking Configurations:

Since most of the movies ever made are about humans interacting, most every configuration of people talking has been filmed. Many of these groupings are now considered standard blocking configurations. I've already gone over several ways of blocking and covering a scene with two people talking: basically facing each other laterally in profile or facing each other perpendicular to the camera in over-the-shoulder shots, or you can also have them facing away from each other. In any case, there aren't many different ways to approach two people standing there and speaking.

In his book "The Total Filmmaker," Jerry Lewis put forth a two-person coverage scheme that I quite like (see next page). You shoot one over-the-shoulder shot (often sort of wide, or *baggy*, as they say) and two close-ups, using the over-the-shoulder shot as the master. For a simple coverage scheme, I think this is more interesting than a flat profile two-shot along with two over-the-shoulder shots or two close-ups.

JERRY LEWIS' APPROACH

Over-the-shoulder   Close-up

Close-up

Now, what if you have three people standing facing each other talking? Three people will naturally form a triangle, unless they're all standing in a line watching a parade pass by. The triangular, three-person configuration is called the *L-Grouping*. The question is, where does the camera go in regard to this L? The L-Grouping keeps all three actors on one side of the 180-degree line, and you end up with two people speaking to one person. The camera is placed in the crook of the L with person #1 at the top of the L, person #2 at the juncture of the L and person #3 at the bottom (figure 1A). Person #1 is facing left to right while both #2 and #3 are facing right to left. The basic coverage of this grouping is a close-up of #1 (figure 2A) and a two-shot of #2 and #3 (figure 3A). Or, you could cover the same grouping with two over-the-shoulder shots, which are over #1's right shoulder facing the other two (figure 4A) and over #3's left shoulder facing #1 (figure 5A). Adding one more shot to the coverage, you could get three close-ups: #1's close-up is left to right, #2's and #3's close-ups are right to left. Person #2 can turn to person #3 changing *eye-lines*—which is the direction they're looking—from right to left to left to right. Everything will still be correct, and we can see everybody perfectly.

THE L-GROUPING

Figure 1A

A woman speaks to two men

Figure 2A

Close-up of woman, L to R

Figure 3A

Two-shot of men, R to L

Figure 4A

Over-the-shoulder of woman
to the two men, R to L

Figure 5A

Over-the-shoulder of man #3
to woman, L to R

Another way to cover three people speaking is the *A-Grouping* (figure 6A): Person #1 is at the top of the A, and persons #2 and #3 are at the bottom where we're over both of their shoulders. Once again you have the one person at the top speaking to the two people at the bottom. This configuration causes person #1 to split his eye-line, looking right to left to person #2 and left to right to person #3. Now, if you shoot close-ups of #2 and #3, they must be looking in different directions: #2 looks left to right to #1 (figure 7A), and #3 looks right to left to #1 (figure 8A). A simpler way to cover this grouping is to shoot the double over-the-shoulder shot facing #1 (figure 6A) and then from directly behind #1 facing #2 and #3 (figure 9A), which would be the simplest, quickest coverage of a three person grouping. Oddly, I think, you can shoot the double over-the-shoulder shot of characters #2 and #3 (figure 6A) where character #1 has a split eye-line, then come around to the two-shot of characters #2 and #3 and, though both can be facing one way, it will look fine.

THE A-GROUPING

Figure 6A

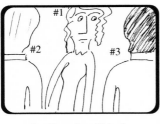

A - Grouping, #1 looks
both L to R and R to L

Figure 7A - A continued

#2 looks L to R

Figure 8A

#3 looks R to L

Figure 9A

From behind #1 to #2 and #3.

If four people are standing and talking to each other, this configuration is called the *H-Grouping*—a person at each end of the H—where you have two people speaking to two people (figure 1H). Now you can cover this scene with two two-shots: #1 and #2 facing left to right (figure 2H) and #3 and #4 facing right to left (figure 3H), or you could get four close-ups, time permitting.

THE H-GROUPING

Figure 1H

Figure 2H

#1 and #2 face L to R

Figure 3H

#3 and #4 face R to L

I'd like to address here a misconception about coverage I've encountered a number of times: Many DPs believe that if you cover one over-the-shoulder shot with a 35-mm lens, then you must cover the other over-the-shoulder shot with a 35-mm lens. This is not true—coverage does not have to match. If a man is talking to a beautiful woman, you can cover him with a 35-mm lens and cover her with a 50- or 75-mm lens, and then you try to get the framing similar by moving the camera back. But both shots do not have to be the same framing, like the coverage of the L-Grouping where you're intercutting between a close-up and a two-shot. And, as Jerry Lewis suggests, just because you get one over-the-shoulder shot doesn't mean you must get the other one.

Eye-Lines:

When you are shooting a close-up, it always looks better to have a *tight eye-line*, meaning you want the actor looking as close to the edge of the lens as possible, as opposed to a *loose eye-line*. Usually you achieve this by squishing the other actor in beside the camera, or *off-camera*. If you can't finagle the off-camera actor into the proper spot because of equipment or you're up against a wall, then you tell the *on-camera* actor which edge of the lens to look at, keeping in mind your screen direction and which way the other actor would be looking back at them. Often you stick a piece of tape on the edge of the lens where you want the actor to look or tell them to look at the camera operator's shoulder.

Loose eye-lines, where the actors are not looking near the edge of the lens, look weak. You see them a lot in old movies, and now they're odd-looking. The exception to this are *profile shots*—the loosest of eye-lines with the actors looking 90 degrees away from the camera—because two profile close-ups will cut just fine as long as the actors are looking in different directions. Profile close-ups are rather arty-looking but fairly common these days, particularly in a long, talky scene.

If one actor is standing and one is sitting, the actor standing will look down out the bottom of frame, and the actor sitting will look up out the top of the frame. In this case it's even more important to jam the other actor into a proper off-camera position so the on-camera actor is looking in the proper place.

As a basic rule when actors are in a profile two-shot, both actors should be playing to the other actor's *outside eye*, meaning the eye nearer to the camera. What this does is open the actors' faces out to the lens a little bit, and it looks much better.

For the most part, you never want anyone looking directly into the lens. But, like most rules in filmmaking, it can be broken. The most obvious use of looking into the lens is for comedy, when Woody Allen or Groucho Marx makes comments directly to the audience. As Zeppo and a girl begin to sing a song in *Horse Feathers*, Groucho looks into the lens and says, "Look, I'm stuck here. You can go get more popcorn."

But there are other uses for looking straight into the lens. If you're using point-of-view (POV) shots—going from a close-up of an actor to a shot of what she's seeing—if the actor sees someone in this setup, than that person should look directly back into the lens to see the actor, which can be disconcerting to the audience. I used this technique in "Xena" when Joxer

(Ted Raimi) is being dragged to the chopping block to be decapitated, and people keep stepping into his path to accuse him of various deeds. When I asked Ted to look straight into the lens, he became nervous and said this just isn't done. I said, "Do it anyway." Perhaps a year later Ted told me that when we were shooting, he had no idea why I had him look into the lens and felt he was breaking a sacred rule. But when he saw the episode, and the other characters are playing back to him directly into the lens, he finally understood and liked it.

When you are shooting two people having a phone conversation in different locations, they should still be facing in opposite directions as though they were looking at each other and speaking in the same room without being on the phone.

Composition:

As a friend of mine once said, "No, *composition* is next to Godliness." How you compose your shots—the *mise-en-scene* as they say in French (and also, in fact, their term for the director)—is directly connected to your relationship with the camera operator and the DP. If you've drawn a storyboard, it will tell the tale to some extent. If not, you then have to give the camera crew the position for the camera, decide on a lens and then see what it looks like. It's no big deal to change lenses, and don't let anyone act like it is (which ACs sometimes do). If you need to change lenses a third time, do it.

But composition is a personal thing. Do you prefer close-ups that are centered or off to one side? Do you like medium close-ups or tight close-ups? Do you like objects down at the bottom of the frame? Or do you like half the screen really tight and the other half far away? Composition is all preference.

Besides watching good films to develop a sense of composition (like *The Magnificent Ambersons* or Ridley Scott's first film, *The Duellists*), you can also study classical paintings.

Zoom Lenses:

Some directors and DPs won't use zoom lenses at all, and I think that's silly. A zoom lens is a tool just like all of the other gadgets on a film shoot. A *zoom lens* can optically change from wide angle to telephoto, or the other way around, at the push of a button or the turn of a dial. If you don't like the look of zooms, they can be hidden within dolly moves. But a zoom lens will allow you start tighter and end wider, or vice versa, than you would otherwise be able to do. You *zoom in* or *zoom back*. I've heard a zoom back amusingly called a *mooz*.

Through a wonderful twist of fate, I ended up talking to the brilliant cinematographer, Vilmos Zsigmond (Oscar winner for *Close Encounters of the Third Kind*), for about two hours one day. I asked him how had he accomplished the amazing follow-shots of characters in canoes shooting rapids in *Deliverance*? Mr. Zsigmond smiled and said, "Zooms." I said that they didn't look like zooms, and he nodded proudly, "I know."

Zooms can be used as an effect, too. A *snap zoom* moves in or pulls back very quickly in a blur and is effective for revealing things. Stanley Kubrick liked zooms and used them very artfully. In *Full Metal Jacket*, when the soldiers are being shot at by an unseen sniper, they hide behind a wall with a hole in it. From the sniper's POV, it snap zooms to the hole where we can see one of the soldiers through it, who then gets shot.

There is also the effect of using a zoom and a dolly at the same time, which is sometimes called a *zolly*. This was first done by Alfred Hitchcock in *Vertigo* to give the dizzying effect of being up too high. By craning down while simultaneously zooming back from telephoto to wide angle, it alters the depth-of-field and makes the ground look like it's getting farther and farther away even though the framing isn't changing. Another beautiful use of this effect is in *Jaws* where Chief Brody (Roy Scheider) is sitting on the beach watching the swimmers. When he thinks he sees a shark in the water, the camera rapidly dollies back while zooming in, thus compressing the depth-of-field and causing the background to rush up behind him.

The drawback to a zoom lens, though, is that it has a lot of glass in it, meaning it has many *elements*, or individual lenses, within it. Every time the light passes through another piece of glass, it loses a minute amount of sharpness. Also, it takes more light to get an exposure through a zoom lens, so they are not terribly useful in low-light situations.

Zoom lenses also cost extra to rent, so if you don't plan on using it, don't rent it.

The Producer:

I am the producer of my own films now. I've worked with a co-producer on my last two films—Jane Goe—but legitimately she worked for me, not the other way around. She was really the production manager (who is also now often called a *line producer*); but since credits don't cost any more whether they say "production manager" or "producer," and it made Jane happier and gave her more clout with the cast and crew, she and I are both credited as producers.

But I'm actually the producer because I'm the one who put the deal together and raised the money—a key part of the producer's job—and she had nothing to do with that.

Until pre-production started and we actually began to pay some of the crew members, the only people working on my films were Jane and I. We scouted all of the locations together, then set up the rental deals on them. We met with all the various crew members together and hired them. Together, we did all the casting (with a wonderful casting director, Donise Hardy). I handle the technical issues on my own, like which lab to use and which post facilities to work with.

Since Jane could not be any nicer nor more intelligent about what we're doing and has no interest in being a director nor in altering my vision at all, she's an absolute joy to work with. However, since she's no longer particularly enamored with the film business, I may not be able to get her assistance anymore.

Still, it's important to have someone to work with during the long, lonely days, weeks and months of setting up a production.

Once pre-production begins, however, Jane is the producer, and I'm the director. All money issues are delegated to her; all artistic issues are delegated to me. I simply won't discuss money with anyone but her. If anyone in the cast or crew has a money problem and comes to me, I immediately send them to her.

Also, I use her as my hatchet-person. If I decide that someone needs to be fired (and we fired six people in three weeks on *Hammer*), I tell Jane, and she does the firing.

Firing Crew Members:

Down in New Zealand, where we made "Xena" and "Hercules," they have a somewhat socialistic system making it nearly impossible to fire anyone. Once you get a job down there, almost any job, it's yours for life or until the job ends. Well, I think that's a bad system. If someone isn't doing his job, or not doing it well, I say get rid of him. A film crew needs to be a well-oiled machine that runs smoothly. Anything that's clogging the works must be removed posthaste.

By the third day of shooting *If I Had a Hammer*, it was apparent to me the production designer and his two teenage sons would not have anything ready when it was actually needed. Time and again in those first three days, the crew would show up at a location ready to shoot, and the art department would be within an hour or two of finishing up but not ready. So the whole cast and crew would have to sit and wait until they were done. This is an unacceptable situation. Even on a very low-budget film, you're still spending $1,000 an hour to shoot. Sitting around waiting for the art department to finish a job that should have been done that morning or the day before is a terrible waste of money. So I clandestinely met with the art director—my friend, Gary Marvis, who was the number two person in the art department on this film (when there is no production designer, the art director is the department head)—and asked if he could deliver what was needed on time with the people he had, or with possibly a few more people I'd hire for him, and he said yes. Then I went to Jane and told her to immediately fire the production designer and his two sons, which she did. There's no point in hesitating once you've made your decision; just get it done and move on.

Well, the art director was as good as his word, and my life improved 100% by no longer waiting on the art department. This maneuver ended up saving me thousands of dollars and made sticking to my schedule possible. Had that production designer and his sons remained and continued to be as unprepared as they were (which I knew would only get worse, not better), it probably would have cost me an extra $20,000 to $50,000. As it was, I came in exactly on schedule and on budget (and Gary Marvis ended up being credited as co-production designer).

It's a tense, uncomfortable situation having to fire people, but sometimes it has to be done. You simply can't let anything stand in the way of your production—certainly not if you've gotten all the way to actually shooting. The shooting part of a film is insanely crucial and very short compared with everything else. If things start to go wrong, you can't let them stay that way.

I also fired the 2nd assistant cameraperson on *Hammer*, who was a very cute, utterly obstreperous girl who couldn't get her job done on time and was always making me wait. Everybody else would be ready to shoot, and she'd still be messing around. Getting rid of her probably saved me at least an hour a day, not to mention it eliminated the bad vibes she was emanating.

The first DP I hired on *Running Time* got progressively more obnoxious and argumentative every day he was onboard, and this was before pre-production even began. He finally lipped off to Jane, which I think is unacceptable behavior from a DP to a producer, so I told him to get lost. I then hired a longtime friend of mine, Kurt Rauf, who had just made the switch from *gaffer* (the head electrician) to DP and needed the break. He did such a good job that I hired him again for my next film, where he also did a fine job.

It is very important that everybody involved in the production is making the same movie as you and on the same schedule. Since there are so many creative types involved in film production, often you'll get crew members who want to use *your* film to express *their* vision. If their vision and your vision are not the same, *they are wrong.* Either you get them onboard helping to bring your vision to the screen, or you get rid of them.

Location Sound:

I think it's very important to get a good, clean, usable *production soundtrack,* meaning the sound recorded during production. (A lot of sound is added during post-production, and that's a different job entirely.) If you have a clean, usable production track, you will save a lot of money later in post-production doing *looping*—or dialog replacement, also known as ADR ("automated dialog replacement")—and the real sound always looks better, too. Synch sound is just better than looped dialog, even if it's not a perfect track. As hard as you try, looping always looks a little bit *rubbery,* meaning it's not exactly in synch, and is ever so slightly off-putting to the audience. There is a reality to the production track that you'll never exactly reproduce with looping.

You can also save money in post by having your *production sound mixer,* or *sound recordist,* pick up any uncertain dialog "wild." *Wild sound* is recorded on the set or location between shots or after the shooting is done. Since the camera was always moving on *Running Time,* and we were frequently not looking right at people's faces while they spoke, putting dialog back in was not all that hard. I made sure to have the sound mixer pick up all the dialog wild for every scene, just in case. There are several good reasons to do this: The wild sound will have exactly the same ambiance as the production track because you're on the same set and recording with the same microphone; also, the actors can reproduce their pacing and inflections much more exactly having just done it for real a few moments before. I ended up using quite a bit of the wild sound on *Running Time* and, subsequently, did very little looping.

It's also important that the production sound mixer always gets *room tone*, which is the sound of your set or location without anyone speaking. This is done immediately after the take. Experienced sound recordists will always do this on their own, but inexperienced sound recordists might forget—don't allow them to. Room tone is important, and you'll need it later. You use room tone during post-production to fill the holes and smooth out the rough spots in your production track. Since every room has its own unique sound, this process must be repeated on every new set and location. If you forget to pick up room tone, it can be stolen in post from between two lines of a dialog—if, in fact, there's a long enough pause between two lines to take it from. All in all, you're better off getting it when you shoot.

Here's a good example of the need for room tone: On *Hammer* I had a long dialog scene in an old car (it's listed in the breakdown as a Cadillac, but it ended up being a 1964 Chrysler 300). Old cars are notorious for having loud engines and bad mufflers, and this car was no exception. As I've mentioned, you can get past this problem by towing the car so the engine isn't actually on. Since I wasn't able to afford that, I had to shoot in the car with the engine running. Each different direction that we shot in that car, the tone of the noisy engine and the loud muffler sounded different, and cutting between them made it *very* noticeable. Luckily, the sound man had gotten a wild track of the car driving with no one speaking—the same thing as room tone but in a car. By taking this wild track, putting it on an endless loop and letting it run under all the other shots, it smoothed out all differences in the other sound. It added more noise to the track, too, but that's how it's done.

A good production sound mixer also should always have their ears open for interesting sounds occurring naturally around them and record them for you. You never know what might be useful in post.

Production sound mixers make a big deal out of not letting actors step on each other's lines, which is overlapping each other and something regular humans do all the time. The sound mixer will explain it's impossible to edit the sound if there are overlaps. Well, that just isn't true. Yes, it's more difficult, but not impossible by any means. Why this annoys me is because it slightly inhibits the actors and makes them self-conscious, and nobody on the set should be allowed to do that, particularly when I'm doing everything within my means to make them feel free and uninhibited.

Firstly, if you're shooting a oner with no coverage, the actors stepping on each other's lines means nothing at all—if there's no editing, then there's no possibility of a problem. Secondly, if you're in a wide shot when the actors step on each other's lines, it could make it difficult to cut to a close-up at exactly that moment but, once again, not impossible. Here's a quick solution: don't cut in at exactly that moment. You have twenty-four choices a second of where to cut, so don't choose that one; cut in right after it.

The one place it's a better idea not to overlap is when shooting close-ups because the other actors generally are not on microphone then, and their sound isn't very good. Also, it does make the cutting more difficult, but not impossible. A good editor will always figure out where to cut. I say, let the actors do whatever they please on wide shots, but don't let them overlap on close-ups.

The Gaffer and the Grips:

If you are shooting in a lot of various locations, it's important to have an experienced *gaffer*. The gaffer is the head electrician and is in charge of *tying-in*, which is getting you the power you need to shoot out of the electrical lines. In practical locations like office buildings and restaurants, you are going to want to pull your power from the building—this is trickier than plugging in a power strip. Even on the smallest films I made in super-8 as a kid, with those cheesy clamp-on lights, we used to blow the circuit-breakers and fuses all the time. With real, multi-1000s-watt movie lights, pulling power out of electrical outlets is impossible. A gaffer knows how to wire into the main electric box to pull out the power in large amounts and not blow anything. The standard lights used on movies these days are *HMI lights*, which are very bright and give off *daylight* being 5400 degrees Kelvin and more to the blue side. Quartz lights emit *incandescent* or *tungsten* light—like light bulbs—that is much more orange and 3200 degrees Kelvin. (If you'd like to know more about the Kelvin thermodynamic scale, go look it up.) HMI lights have these really heavy power packs connected to them, called *ballasts,* that pull a lot of power, and you can't plug them into normal outlets. Thus the need for the gaffer.

On both *Thou Shalt Not Kill . . . Except* and *Running Time,* however, I didn't have a gaffer or a *key grip*—the head of the *grips* who are the burly guys that haul around the lights and lay the dolly track. (The grip that pushes the dolly, by the way, is the *dolly grip.*) On both those films I didn't have a dolly. It was because I couldn't afford it on *Thou Shalt Not Kill . . .*

Except, so if I wanted to move the camera, I used a wheelchair with sheets of plywood on the ground, or I shot handheld. On *Running Time* it was because I had a Steadi-cam instead. Just having a Steadi-cam and no dolly or track saved quite a few paid grip positions and reduced the number of trucks as well. All you need is one extra person who generally is the owner of the Steadi-Cam. On *Running Time* this same guy was also the full-time camera operator even when it wasn't on the Steadi-cam, so the entire camera crew consisted of: the DP, the operator/Steadi-cam operator, the 1st AC, and an assistant called a *clapper/loader* who loads the camera's magazines and runs the *slate*, formerly known as the *clapboard*. The slate now is usually an electronic item called a *smart slate*. This is frequently owned by the sound mixer because it's electronically connected to the sound recorder, running a series of numbers called *time code,* which is what keeps the sound and the picture in synchronous orbit.

Dailies:

Dailies may seem like a post-production issue as they are the source of what you'll use for the editing, but they are actually a production issue since you begin to get dailies the day after you start shooting (if you're near a lab, that is). If you haven't specified just what you want to the lab and the transfer house—if you're using one—they won't know what to give you. If you start getting the wrong thing, it will be hard to change, cost extra money and give you big headaches in post.

So you must decide how you intend to edit your film before you start to shoot. If you're going to cut the way most people do now, you'll be editing digitally on a system such as Avid or Final Cut Pro. To do that you will need your film processed by a film laboratory, then transferred at a film-to-video (known as *telecine*) transfer house to videotape that comes with a corresponding floppy disk fed into the editing system. For the most part the labs that do the processing do not also do the video transfers—these are two separate processes—but the lab still needs to know the film is immediately going in for video transfer, and they will set up the reels accordingly.

There are film labs and video transfer facilities in several major cities, but Los Angeles is just teeming with them. I've used many of the labs in LA, and I've always had the best results and the friendliest relations with Deluxe Laboratories—although there are many places to choose from, and don't feel you must deal with LA companies either. There are reputable film labs and facilities in many other places, like New York and San Francisco, but also Chicago, Detroit, Toronto, Vancouver, Portland, Miami, Austin and a lot of other places, too.

You get your film processed at the lab, then transferred to DVD or videotape for input into the hard drives of your digital editing system. On the Avid and the other digital editing systems I've used, the picture comes off of three-quarter-inch videotapes or Beta-SP tapes, which is the form of professional Beta videotape below Digital Beta and quite a bit cheaper. VHS is insufficient for this purpose, although it's much handier for watching dailies. If the transfer house makes you both three-quarter or Beta-SP transfers and VHS copies, it's more money. Instead, you can just have your editor make VHS dubs when they load the dailies into the hard drives, which is what I do.

I don't think it's a good idea to watch your dailies on the set while you're shooting. I think the director and the DP (and the producer, if they care to) should watch dailies either after the shooting day is over or before it begins. It's only important that the director and the DP see the dailies. Directors need to know if they've got the shots they think they've got, and DPs need to know if what they're doing with the lights, filters and exposures is actually working. I watch the dailies at night, after the day's shooting, often fighting to stay awake.

But there's also another choice: Have the lab print your film to *workprint*, which is positive film stock (as opposed to negative), then cut on film the old-fashioned way. I cut all my short films, as well as my first two feature films, on actual film. Steven Spielberg apparently still cuts on film. I think it's harder to do it properly that way—and it takes more people—and therefore, not the wisest idea on a low-budget film.

Then again, you have my wacky friend Paul who has had all of his 16-mm film printed to workprint and cuts with rewinds, a viewer, and a guillotine tape-splicer. As I said, I cut several 16-mm short films this way, and I really enjoyed it. But this is only feasible if you don't have much sound footage, which Paul doesn't. As soon as you need to be in synch and running at *sound speed*, which is a constant 24 frames-per-second, this system is impractical.

Unruly, Unprepared, or Inexperienced Actors:

I haven't dealt with very many obnoxious, unruly actors who wouldn't do what I asked them to—a few, but they generally seemed crazy as opposed to malicious. The most unruly actor I've ever directed was Anthony Quinn, who seemed to take a perverse joy in busting a director's balls. The first day I worked with him he wouldn't do anything I asked him to do. In fact, he wouldn't even listen to what I had in mind—he'd just state what it was he'd be doing and made it clear it was simply my job to shoot it.

Well, I didn't appreciate the situation. This was my first TV movie, and I wanted to do it my way. I spent a great deal of time lying in bed at night, when I should have been sleeping, thinking of ways to get my good buddy Tony Quinn to do what I wanted him to do.

My solution, which I'm still quite proud of and pleased to share with you, was to shoot the order of his scenes backward, meaning I began with his close-up and worked my way out to the wide shot. What this did was cause Mr. Quinn to be stuck on the mark I gave him, which is where we shot his close-up. Then I'd shoot the other actor's close-up, getting them stuck on my mark, too. When I pulled back to shoot the wide shot then, both actors had to get back to those same marks or it wouldn't cut, and I'd be forced to reshoot both of the close-ups—which no one was willing to do, particularly not Mr. Quinn who really just wanted to get the hell out of there. I also believe it appealed to Mr. Quinn's vanity to begin each of his scenes with his close-up. It also made better use of his talents, I think. Really good actors are much more fun to watch in close-up than in a wider shot since you get to see all the nuances they perform with their face. And regarding Anthony Quinn—who was over eighty when I worked with him—he used up his energy very quickly, so it was much better getting his close-up first. There was no point in wasting his limited energy in wide shots when we'd certainly be spending much more time in his close-ups. This method worked brilliantly, and I just wish I'd figured it out sooner.

It should always be kept in mind that in the finished cut film you spend significantly more time in the close-ups than you do in the wide shots. Basically, once an editor cuts from the wide shot into the close-ups, they stay there, only rarely going back for a brief second to reestablish where we are. Therefore, it's more important to get good close-ups than complete wide shots that play all the way through the scene.

Another variation on this theme is the insecure actor—an actor who's in a panic because he thinks he can't act the part. I had this problem with the lead actor in *Thou Shalt Not Kill . . . Except*, who was a last-minute replacement for Bruce Campbell. The actor was tall, handsome, gay, and cast as a tough marine sergeant. I couldn't care less what an actor's sexual orientation is, but in this case it was getting in the way of his performance. He kept saying things like, "I never played with guns as a kid." The final straw that broke this actor's back was having to chop wood with an ax. After he had tried about twenty times, missing the log each time and sending it flying, he finally broke down and began to cry. Okay, now what do you do?

I took the actor aside away from everyone else and explained I didn't really need him chopping all that wood; all I really needed from him was one single believable chop, with a good beginning and a good ending, and I'd get the rest later. Regarding his appropriateness for the part: Since I'm the one who cast him, obviously I thought he could handle the part, and that's all that was important in this circumstance. He didn't have to believe in himself, just believe in me. I'd make sure to make him look as good as I could.

So he did one good chop, then turned and played all of the dialog in the rest of the scene perfectly. Once he was gone I went in tighter on the stump where the chopping occurred and shot a series of logs being split. In the final film the actor takes his one good chop, then it cuts in to a series of quick cuts of logs being split, and finally it cuts wide to him removing his hands from the embedded ax and doing his dialog. It's not perfect, but it works all right. And the actor made it through the remainder of the scene while doing a fine job, which was the most important thing.

The one thing you don't want to do, generally, is to get aggravated with an actor. A director's aggravation will only make an actor more insecure, and insecure actors are just going to mess up worse than they're already messing up.

This situation came up regularly with the day players on "Xena" and "Hercules." A *day player* is an actor with dialog whose part is small enough to be shot entirely in a day or two. This was frequently the day player's big break—the first time s/he has appeared on camera speaking lines—and often they would be in a royal panic. When a day player goofed up, which was inevitable, I would make sure to laugh loud enough for him to hear so he'd know I wasn't angry but amused. If his panic continued and he still couldn't get the lines out of his mouth, I'd take him aside and, in a light-hearted jovial tone, tell him please not to worry about it. We'd get the line sooner or later, and since I wasn't worried about it, he shouldn't be either. I always add (since most actors don't realize this), "I cast you in the part, and I know you can handle it because I've already seen you do it. So just calm down a little, and you'll be great."

Many actors, I've found, are under the delusion that the casting director cast them in the part. Well, the *casting director* wrangles all of the actors in for the auditions, but the director chooses which actor for which part (producers certainly get their say on this, too). I want actors to know I chose them, and I believe in them. I'm not the slightest bit angry, and there's no problem having to go again until we get it right, which we certainly will. My confidence in them increases their confidence in themselves, then we promptly get the lines. This method always works for me.

On the other hand, I'm not very understanding with actors who don't know their lines. I think it's lazy and incompetent, and it pisses me off. It's the minimum requirement of an actor—know your stinking lines. I don't let this bother me with the lead actors—who generally have an enormous amount of dialog to learn every night and have their own individual methods for getting through their dialog, one way or another, or they wouldn't have gotten to be leading actors—but day players with very little dialog who don't know their lines are yet another story. It's a very different matter being frightened and unable to deliver your lines as opposed to just not knowing them. I will definitely let unprepared actors know their behavior is unprofessional and that they have seriously displeased me, then I'll send them off to a corner to quickly study their scripts. If I haven't shot with them yet and they're not on film, I may just replace them right there. Once you've shot with an actor, of course, you must reshoot all his scenes if you replace him. That's why you make sure to cast properly in the first place.

Here's an interesting little tidbit that I bet isn't in any other book on filmmaking: the way to replace actors immediately when you haven't shot anything with them yet—should they show up totally unprepared, or drunk, or stoned, or having recently had a nervous breakdown—is by their costume size. Have someone get the file of all the actors who read for the part and find ones who are the same size and can wear the costume. Often you can have an actor in shooting a scene the same day because actors are frequently available. If you have a casting director, let that person handle it.

Philosophy, Part Two: Believe in the Process

If you understand the filmmaking process—and truly believe in it—you can move along through the shooting even quicker and, I think, actually do better work, too. Let me explain.

I recently went to the set and watched a few hours of shooting of an HBO TV show, which is about as high-budget as a TV show gets these days. They had six days of shooting per half-hour episode, or about four pages a day. On "Xena" we shot six to seven pages a day, which often contained crazy action and complicated fight scenes. On this show, though, as it is with most things, there were just several people in a room talking to each other. It was, however, quite a long scene of just over four pages. So the lead character enters a room, says a few lines and does a little routine hanging up his coat, then crosses to where the other people are standing. He has a number of lines with these people, then everyone leaves except his wife. They go on to talk for three more minutes. I watched them run this whole scene over and over and over for hours. If there had ever been any energy in the scene, they slowly leeched it out over the course of innumerable rehearsals and takes. In three hours I did not see them complete the master shot, let alone get any of the coverage they would obviously need.

Now admittedly, that four-page scene was all they had to shoot that entire day but, by not trusting the filmmaking process, they were slowly but surely killing the scene and clearly looking at going into severe overtime.

If you know absolutely you will be shooting coverage once the lead character gets to the first group of people—and you like the way he did his entrance, which in this case was a thirty-second routine—*you don't have to keep shooting his entrance.* You got it. He only has to make it up to the first cut, then you can concentrate on the next hunk—his talking to the group of people.

But no, they wanted to get a complete, four-minute long master shot in a single take, which they absolutely knew they didn't need. That's what I mean by not trusting the process. Who the hell is ever going to know or care that you got it all in one long take if it's full of cuts?

Break it up. Each hunk is its own bit of business, and once you've got it and there's a cut, you've got it—move on. If you keep playing this entire four-minute-long scene over and over and over, *you will kill it.*

Drama is an ephemeral, fragile, magical kind of thing, and it needs to be recognized and respected as such. Over-rehearsing and over-running a scene is a bad idea.

How Many Takes?

As many as it takes to get it right, and this is based on whatever you as the director construe *right* to be. Generally, given the time and money constraints of shooting, I'll construe right to be: the actors got the words out of their mouths, and no one got hit in the head with the microphone. That may not sound like an artistic or refined method, but it does work. It keeps things moving, and if you don't keep moving, you're screwed.

Unless things have gone seriously haywire, I rarely shoot more than five takes of anything. Frequently, I stop after three takes. And, unlike many other directors, if I get it in one take, I'll move on. Many directors are far too insecure and nervous to live with just one take. They'll shoot a second take for the sake of safety, which is what they call it—a *safety shot*. If you only shoot one take, someone will ask, what if the film's scratched? Well, the 1st Assistant Cameraperson (1st AC) checks the *film gate*—the area in the camera behind the lens where the film is clawed down into position—with a flashlight and a magnifying glass after every completed shot. If she says the gate is clear, you have to trust her, believe the gate really is clear and move on. Once again, believe in the process. If you think you've got it in one take and the gate is clear, move on. You'll be running film through that camera all day long, and if it's said the gate is clear, it's clear. If you think you got the take, you got it.

An interesting phenomenon I've noticed is that you can get most any line or piece of action within five takes. But if you go past the sixth take, you'll probably keep going to the twelfth. For some reason everything falls apart after the sixth take, then it takes five or six more takes to get it back together again. On a low-budget movie you just don't have time for twelve takes, not to mention all of the film stock you're burning up. If you've got it in three takes, move on. If it takes six, then do it, but don't go past that if humanly possible. And remember, you don't need *two* good takes, just *one*.

If you're shooting in 35 mm, you get to choose which takes will be printed, called *selects*. They just print everything in 16 mm, because it's harder to stop and start the machines. So if I'm shooting 35 mm, I'll invariably choose (as most directors do) the last take we shot—when we finally got it all together—and often one other take that may not be entirely right, but had good parts in it and might be useful in editing.

2nd Unit:

I've never had a 2nd unit on a low-budget feature. We always had a 2nd unit on "Xena" and "Hercules," and it's very handy and a real time-saver. A *2nd unit* crew (and I was a 2nd unit director for about six months) shoots all of the shots that the main unit hasn't got time to get: all of the inserts, the wide establishing shots without actors or with doubles, the beauty shots—like sunsets and beams of light through the trees—as well as most of the fight scenes and stunts, too. Any shot where you can't see the actors' faces is often a 2nd unit shot.

On a low-budget movie, though, you probably can't afford a 2nd unit; I know I never could. That means the main unit is also the 2nd unit, but that doesn't mean you should be shooting both things at the same time. This takes some consideration.

If you are making a film with a lot of inserts, like an action film, you may want to do what I did on *Thou Shalt Not Kill . . . Except*. After *principal photography* was complete, which is the main bulk of shooting with all of the actors, I then got rid of all of the cast and most of the crew and continued to shoot for another two weeks. For all intents and purposes this was a 2nd unit crew, and we picked up a vast number of shots that didn't include the actors. You can also hang onto an actor or two, or just have them come and go as you need them. After six weeks of principal photography on *Evil Dead*, five of us spent the next five weeks working as a 2nd unit picking up several hundred shots from all over the film. The actors came and went during that time, generally for a few days each, and we picked up many shots of them doing dialog, too.

Shooting Inserts:

It's not a great idea having the whole cast and crew stand around while you shoot an insert of a hand picking up a lighter. But if you don't shoot it, who will? You can put inserts off until later, as I just mentioned, but many times it's simply easier to get them while you're there—while the lighting is right, while you have a camera and film and everything else you need to make the shot. (That's what they used to say in the old days in Hollywood: "Let's make this shot.") If there are only a few inserts in the scene, it's probably a better idea to get them during principal photography. If there are a lot, schedule a 2nd unit. I've also had some luck starting my days off quickly during principal by picking up an insert or two right away, with the AD's hand or foot, before the actors were ready.

Any shot that ultimately makes it into the finished movie is important. I really do like inserts, and it's hard finding the time during principal photography to shoot them. The main problem with putting them off until later is, if you can actually pull it together to set up an insert shoot later on, recreating the scene and the lighting is tough—and if it's not set up right, it won't cut in very well. I'd say you're better off not having any inserts than having poorly-done ones.

When you're shooting extremely tight inserts of hands grabbing props or guns firing or a finger pulling a trigger, get the entire action of the movement of the prop or gun moving into frame, performing the action, then moving out of frame. This gives the editor many more choices of where to cut in the insert, and inserts are frequently hard to cut in.

Extras:

Extras, also known as *background players* or *atmosphere,* are the on-camera performers without dialog. If you have assistant directors, or even one AD, it's their job to deal with the extras. But ADs still get their instructions from the director, so you'd better have some idea of what you want to do with the extras. Depending on how many extras you have, they can really clog up the set and slow things down. Therefore, it's probably a better idea to keep the extras off the set until you need them. So, you must make sure you have someplace to put your extras until you need them—preferably out of the sun and with snacks, sodas, water, and bathroom facilities. Keep in mind that extras are people, too, and should be treated as well as you can treat them, even if they act like locusts around craft services.

Anytime you're shooting a dialog scene with extras in it, make sure the extras pantomime their actions and don't actually speak. You need good clean sound for the dialog, and you'll just put the sound of the crowd (called *walla*) back in during post production. The only time you really want to hear the extras speak is in crowd shots that don't include the actors speaking dialog.

Also, it's a good idea to get wild sound with the extras so that you have it when you get into post.

If you have *bits* of action for the extras to perform that don't include any dialog—because once they speak, they're no longer extras; and if it's a SAG shoot, you must now pay them the same as an actor—have your ADs keep their eyes open for extras who seem on the ball and use them to perform the bits. If you're using extras more than one day, you'll see which ones seem intelligent and, when you've got a bit of action, give it to them.

There is a way around turning an extra into an actor with a line, causing them to go from minimum wage to over $500 a day, and that's called an *upgraded extra*. If the extra is delivering a line that's not in the script, meaning the director probably just came up with it on the spot, they only go up to $150 a day. This happened to me a couple of times on "Beverly Hills 90210," when I worked as an extra about fifteen times on the second season (my buddy was the 2ⁿᵈ AD and got me the gigs). During a pool hall scene they chose me to slap Luke Perry five and say, "Good shot, man," although it didn't end up being used. Nevertheless, I got the $150 instead of the regular pay.

A sneaky way to do this, that I'm sure SAG doesn't approve of, is to remove all of the one-line parts before you submit your script to SAG, which you must do if you're working with them, cast extras in the parts, then upgrade them with the lines on the set. By doing this you'll save over $350 per one-line part. (Note: I'm innocent, I've never done this, but an experienced 1ˢᵗ AD told me about it).

When shooting *reaction shots* with extras, which are the shots of them reacting to the main action—gasping at the sight of Godzilla, flinching when someone gets hurt or killed, laughing when someone says something funny—it's not important that they know exactly what they're reacting to, as long as they clearly understand what reaction you want. If you tell an extra to laugh heartily, they don't necessarily need to know what the joke is. If you have a lot of reaction shots to shoot, as I did on *Hammer*, you're better off just telling them the reactions you need, like: laugh, applaud mildly, applaud heartily, look down in shame, now look up and smile. If you bother explaining the motivations for all of these reactions to all of the different extras, you could potentially be there forever. With this approach I was able to shoot over one hundred extra's reaction shots before lunch one day, which might be some sort of record. To pull off this routine, the 1ˢᵗ AD and I spent the better part of the Sunday before figuring out how to get what we needed as quickly as possible. Edith, my 1ˢᵗ AD, turned it all into sort of a rap song on the set: Now we're lookin' right, now we're lookin' left, then we clap real hard, then we smile, then we look away in shame, etc. It all worked great, too, and I used every one of those reaction shots.

On some level you can never have enough reaction shots. Sam Peckinpah, as a good example, always had a lot of wonderful reaction shots of non-actors with interesting faces in his films, which make great cutaways. Check out *The Wild Bunch* which is loaded with terrific reaction shots.

The Script Supervisor or Continuity:

A good *script supervisor* (formerly known as the continuity girl or script girl) is a real joy to have around. A not-so-good script supervisor can be a hindrance, and a bad one can be a saboteur. The main thing a script supervisor does is keep the *script log* or *script notes*. These contain a description of every camera setup, particularly which screen direction everything is going, as well as any notable continuity observations. An example would be: the boy is smoking a cigarette with his right hand, takes a puff at this specific word, then lowers his hand to the top of his beer mug at that word, then keeps it there for the rest of the scene. They also note in the log how long each scene runs (which is why they keep a stopwatch around their neck) and which lens was used in case you need to go back and reshoot or match it for any reason. However, directors ought to keep their own eyes open for continuity issues, too. Two sets of eyes are better than one. There are certain props that are obvious continuity giveaways, like cigarettes, food, and beverages of any kind. There is an old piece of filmmaking wisdom that says: "Don't give actors props if you can help it—they'll just cause continuity problems." As for screen direction issues (often a topic of conversation with the script supervisor): If you've done your homework and chosen your screen directions in advance—and have stuck to the plan—it shouldn't be a problem. If my shot list says it's supposed to be right to left—and I always stick to my shot list—then there's nothing to talk about. However, if it comes to a dispute, as it has a few times, I always go my way.

At the end of each scene, the director tells the script supervisor which takes to print. These takes are called *selects* that the script supervisor marks in the log. They also convey this information to the camera department who then marks it on the camera reports.

Camera Reports:

A *camera report* is a quadruplicate form, generally supplied by the lab, that accompanies the cans of exposed film stock to the lab. This is what the lab uses to decide which processes they will perform on the film. If it's not filled out correctly, you just may get the wrong thing. The 3rd AC on *Running Time*, who filled out the camera reports (and had never worked on a film crew before), had no idea what workprint was and checked that box every day for the first three days. Well, I had no need for workprint since all of my dailies were being transferred to videotape, yet I ended up getting and paying for three days of workprint I didn't need. It certainly wasn't the lab's fault—they were just following the camera reports. I couldn't even dock the 3rd AC's pay because she wasn't earning enough on the entire shoot to pay for her mistake. So I ate the cost and learned a lesson: Don't assign the camera reports to people who don't know what they're doing.

Which Film Stock?

If you decide to shoot on film, either 16 mm or 35 mm, you have to choose which film stock to use. First of all, you can choose black and white or color. I've shot one film in black and white, and I love the way it looks, but distributors inherently don't like black and white and will probably give you trouble because certain international markets absolutely won't buy black and white films. Sometimes, though, you just have to do what you have to do. There are also many choices within the worlds of both color and black and white.

One of the first creative production decisions you will make is what speed film stock you will be using. *Film speed* is rated in *ASA* numbers, such as 25, 40, 64, 100, 120, 200, 250, 500 and 1000. The slower the film stock, the lower the number, meaning the chemicals—known as *emulsion*—are spread on the film more thickly and more light is needed to penetrate it. The faster the speed, the higher the number and the thinner the chemicals, so less light is needed to expose it.

Slow film stocks have deeper, richer colors, less grain, and more *contrast* (meaning the darks are darker, and there's a bigger difference between the dark areas and light areas). Fast film stocks have less saturated colors, more grain, and less contrast. The choice of the film stock will really establish "the look" of your movie. The lighting has a whole lot to do with it, too; but to a great extent, the lighting schemes will be based on which film stock is being exposed. I've used nearly the entire gamut of film stocks on just my four movies.

On *If I Had Hammer* I chose Eastman (Kodak) color negative 5248 35-mm stock, which has an ASA speed of 64 in daylight and 100 indoors. The film is balanced for tungsten or incandescent light—like light bulbs or quartz movie lights—which are rather orange. So when you are outside, you must use an orange filter called an *85 filter*. When you're inside, you don't need it. This is a fairly slow stock not used very often anymore and had to be special-ordered. When I was a kid shooting super-8 films, the stock came in three speeds—40, 64, and 160—and I always enjoyed the look of the super-8 stock Kodachrome 64. It has very rich colors, fine grain, and a lot of contrast. It also reminds me of days gone by, and since *Hammer* was set in 1964, that's what I was looking for. However, to expose slow film stocks, you need more lights and brighter exposures. I was already renting a whole truck full of lighting equipment. If the grips needed to haul a few more lights onto the set, so what? It did make the set even hotter than it already was, which in LA during the summer is already pretty hot, but what the hell. It's generally uncomfortable on a film set anyway. The really old color film stocks used in the late 1930s and the '40s were rated at ASA 5 and 10, and you can just bet those were extremely hot sets to work on. But the old color movies—like *Gone With the Wind*, for instance—have an amazing look to them that I've always admired. I didn't quite achieve that look, but we came close, and *Hammer* certainly doesn't look like most modern movies.

Here's the drawback with slow film stocks in the modern world: the high-contrast makes the video transfer more difficult. In fact you can't really get a good-looking video transfer off of the print (the finished film). You must transfer off of your negative, which is more expensive. Should your film be released on DVD, you'll have to do a transfer off of your negative (or your IP) anyway. (More on that later.)

On *Running Time* I chose Eastman Plus-X black and white negative 7231 16-mm stock, which is rated at ASA 80 in daylight and 64 under tungsten lights. This is the slowest black and white negative film stock Kodak makes and also is special-order now. (All of the Kodak 35-mm film stocks begin with 52, and the 16-mm stocks begin with 72.) You can buy an even slower 16-mm black and white film stock from Kodak, 7276, which is 40 in daylight and 50 under tungsten, but it's *reversal film*. Just like super-8, the film that comes out of the camera is not a negative but a positive image and can be projected, if stupidly you were going to project your original. When using reversal film, you really must go straight to videotape to see your film. There's also an extra step in the lab if you want to make prints, and that involves making an *Inter-negative (IN)*, which is a negative they make off the positive. (Darren Aronofsky's film *Pi* was shot on 7276 reversal stock and looks absolutely gorgeous).

Anyway, I got a very high-contrast look on *Running Time* that's sort of like the old Hollywood film noir pictures, and I think it looks wonderful. Since a great deal of *Running Time* was shot outdoors in LA, where it's usually bright and sunny, getting exposures (meaning enough light) was no big deal. I tested Ilford black and white 16-mm film stock before shooting *Running Time* and didn't think it looked nearly as good as the Kodak stock. I've tested Fuji film stock, too, but never chosen it. Kodak film stock is just good stuff and seemingly the best.

On my film *Lunatics: A Love Story*, I used Eastman color 35-mm negative

5297 film stock, which is ASA 250 in daylight and ASA 80 tungsten. This is the same stock they used on "Xena" and "Hercules," and it's a good-looking film stock with a lot of latitude. It never gets overly contrasted, and the grain is reasonably fine. This is probably the main film stock that most everybody uses now and, unless you do something really special with the lighting or filters, it will look a lot like every other film and TV show out there—which, honestly, all look pretty good these days.

On *Thou Shalt Not Kill . . . Except* I used Eastman color 16-mm negative 7296, which is ASA 320 in daylight and ASA 500 tungsten. This was a radical decision that many people disagreed with at the time. Since I intended to blow up the film to 35 mm later, the accepted wisdom is to shoot a slower, finer-grain stock because the blow-up all of the grain particles will be magnified by 400% (you can fit four frames of 16 mm into one frame of 35 mm). However, I had already done quite a bit of the lighting on *Evil Dead* at that point. We used Eastman 16-mm color negative 7248, being ASA 64 daylight and 100 tungsten, which theoretically ought to look better than the 7296 I chose for *Thou Shalt Not Kill . . . Except*—except that it doesn't. Why is that? Because on *Evil Dead* we didn't have nearly enough lighting equipment or know-how.

Well, since I had even less money for *Thou Shalt Not Kill . . . Except* than we had for *Evil Dead*, I knew that I'd have the very same lighting problems. Here's an important piece of information: grain matters far less than sharpness in a blow-up. If your image isn't perfectly sharp in 16 mm, it will be four times softer in 35 mm, which is awful. Also, less contrast is better for a blow-up and, honestly, a lot of grain can be cool-looking. Anyway, *Thou Shalt Not Kill . . . Except* may not be nearly as influential or successful of a film as *Evil Dead*, but the blow-up of *Thou Shalt Not Kill . . . Except* looks far superior to the blow-up on *Evil Dead*. So I recommend shooting fast film stocks if you don't have a lot of lighting equipment and the people to use it. Just make sure to shoot sharp, well-exposed images.

Screen Formats:

There are four film formats: 1.33:1, 1.66:1, 1.85:1, and 2.35:1. The two numbers for each format represent the width of the image compared to its height. Pretty much all movies from the inception of the technology in the late 1880s up through 1953 were shot at 1.33:1, which is 33% wider than it is tall but, for the most part, looks almost square. Since most TV screens are almost the same dimensions, old movies have always looked fine on TV.

Then in 1953 the first wide-screen film was released, *The Robe*, shot in Cinemascope at 2.35:1, which is two and one-third times as wide as it is tall. To achieve this look *anamorphic lenses* are used: the lens on the camera is concave so that it squishes the image onto the negative, then a convex lens is used on the projector to stretch the image back out to its proper proportions. This system is still in use today and is often seen in high-budget Hollywood films. The only extra expense in shooting this way is the higher rental cost of the anamorphic lenses, which isn't really all that much (they're not twice as much as regular, *flat lenses*). But it does give you a weird, squished negative image that didn't please a lot of DPs and directors, as well as the fact that anything near the sides of the screen looks distorted.

So a compromise wide-screen format was developed that was not so wide you needed anamorphic lenses. This is 1.85:1—almost twice as wide as it is tall—now the most common format in use today and the most often used for feature films (also comparable to the HD format of 1.77:1 or 16x9). It makes the least efficient use of the full-frame negative image as well. To achieve the sense of a wide-screen image, 1.85:1 cuts off the top and bottom edges of the picture, or about 20% of the image. That's a big loss. However, the common wisdom now is you can't shoot anything but 1.85:1 unless you have the money for anamorphic 2.35:1. It is presumed the projectionists of the world are numbskulls who can't figure out how to show anything but those two common formats. Well, that's not true. Since a projectionist may be called upon to show an old movie made before 1953 at any point, they're all prepared and ready to show 1.33:1 whenever it says so on the film cans. I shot *Running Time* at 1.33:1, and no one has ever had any trouble showing it.

Why did I choose 1.33:1? Once I had decided on 16 mm and black and white, it just seemed like the logical next step in going for an old-time look. 1.33:1 makes the best use of the full-frame negative image and fills the whole thing. And just like all of the old movies, it plays perfectly on TV where, as with most films, its main life is and will always be. I also like 1.33:1 because most of the movies I've ever seen in my life were shot that way.

1.85:1 is still a wide-screen format that's not entirely compatible with regular TV. To see the full 1.85:1 image on a TV screen it must be *letterboxed*, which is when there's a black band above and below the image. 2.35:1 needs an even larger letterbox, so even that much more of the TV image is lost. When high definition, wide-screen TV finally takes over, it will correct part of this problem—although 2.35:1 will *still* need a letterbox.

Shooting the Entire Image:

When I'm shooting in 1.85:1, I always make sure to keep the entire full-frame image—everything I can see in the monitor—clear of lights, stands, booms, or people. There's a very good reason for this. Rather than a *pan and scan* version done in post—letting someone in the lab choose only parts of the whole frame to get a squarer image for TV so it won't need to be let-terboxed—you can use the full-frame version instead, and it will look *much* better than a pan and scan version. Therefore, I won't let the boom man get the microphone anywhere into my visible frame on the monitor, and that way I know the mike is *way* the hell away from the 1.85:1 frame line.

Production Assistants:

A *production assistant (PA)*, formerly known as a *gopher*, is the lowest position on a film crew. I've heard it said that a film crew is only as good as its PAs. I've also heard it said that a PA never sits down. Good PAs anticipate where they will be needed next and eagerly join in to help, never waiting to be told what to do, and are loyal and true. I worked as a PA for many years, more than I wanted to actually, and I got pretty good at it. I was the high-est-paid PA in Detroit for a while—$150 a day in the early 1980s, which was darn good money then. PAs ought to be young people, like high school or college students, so you can work the hell out of them. The PAs are the first people on the set in the morning, and the last people to leave. Their job is to do anything that's assigned to them, from stopping traffic to unloading trucks to moving furniture to setting up scaffolding. The PA is never allowed to complain—or sit down.

Car Chases:

Filming car chases is sort of like filming walk and talks—there are only so many ways to do it (although you can certainly try to think of more). There are only three places to shoot a car chase from: in the *picture cars* (which are the cars in the picture), on the street outside with the picture cars going past the camera, or in a *camera car* (the car from which you photograph) cruising along with the picture cars. Generally, most movie car chases are shot from all three positions and then rapidly intercut.

When shooting in the picture cars, the camera is either in the car with the actors or outside the car affixed to the vehicle with a *car mount*, which is a specialized item that can be rented from the camera rental house. Car mounts are slightly tricky to use and, since a very expensive camera is attached to it and hanging out in space from a speeding vehicle, you really need to know how to use it properly. Most camera people using car mounts that I've observed—and I've watched many being from Detroit and having grown up working on car commercials—generally don't trust the car mounts entirely and add several of their own nylon ratchet straps. These work like bungee cords but ratchet down tight and don't stretch. Wide-angle lenses help smooth out the bumpiness of these shots. One of the trickier aspects of shooting in a moving car is finding a place for the director to be to watch the monitor—already in the car you've got the actor or actors, the camera operator, possibly the 1st AC, and the sound recordist. On a number of occasions I have found myself smashed down on the floor of the back seat, or in the trunk with the monitor beside me or on my chest.

When shooting from a camera car—probably just another car, or a pick-up truck works quite well—you have to make sure the sun isn't behind you throwing the camera shadow on the picture car. Also, you have to make sure you're not picking up the camera's reflection in the picture car's windows and finish. If you are getting reflections, the camera can go higher. You also can spray the car with *dulling spray*, an actual item you can buy at an arts and crafts store. If you haven't got dulling spray, any kind of aerosol spray, like bug spray, will work (but remember, you've still got to clean it off).

If you're on the street shooting the cars going past, you can be mounted on a *tripod*—also known as *sticks* or *legs*—and either let the car go through frame or pan with it. A somewhat more provocative angle for cars going past is to be on the *high-hat*, which gets the camera down near the ground. Or you can place the camera on top of some *sand bags* (also known as *shot bags*) to get it even lower, then put on a wide-angle lens and have the cars come as close to the camera as possible.

If you haven't legitimately got a permit to shoot a car chase on the street with cops to enforce your permit, then you must block off the street yourself. This isn't exactly legal, but you can't go tearing around at high speed—potentially with a camera car in the oncoming lane going the wrong way—and just leave it up to fate as to whether another car will drive by. So you must first choose roads with very little traffic, posting production assistants at either end of the road with walkie-talkies, and have them stop any cars trying to come through. As I say, it may not be legal, but it will be a lot safer. I directed the reenactment segments on the first season of "Real Stories of the Highway Patrol," and every segment had a car chase in it. Luckily for us, since we were working with real cops, they'd just hit their flashers and sirens, and all of the other cars would pull over and get out of our way.

Fight Scenes:

On "Hercules" and "Xena" I shot quite a few fight scenes, often two per episode, and I pretty quickly figured out how to do them fast and economically. Minimally, you need to shoot the whole fight scene twice—over-the-shoulder in both directions—and generally handheld to stay mobile. On "Herc" and "Xena" we always ran two cameras in each direction—the inside camera on the over-the-shoulder shot, the outside camera on a close-up—which works as a cutaway and is very handy to have. You can achieve with one camera this same coverage of an over-the-shoulder and a close-up both ways by running the whole fight two times in each direction and changing lenses, generally from a 35 mm to a 75 mm.

If you're working with stunt people who are doubling your actors, it's always better to have an actor fighting a stunt person as opposed to two actors fighting each other, if you can help it. That means when you're over someone's shoulder, it should always be a stunt person.

Or you can break a fight up into little bits and pieces that all need to be shot separately. This way is harder to do, harder to cut and frequently doesn't work at all, but that's how you shoot the specialty fight routines: as separate pieces from the rest of the fight. A shtick I've used twice now is having a guy (Iolaus [Michael Hurst] in a "Hercules" movie, Joxer [Ted Raimi] in a "Xena" episode) do a handstand in front of a bad guy, grab them around the neck with their legs, sit up and punch the hell out of the guy's face with both fists until the bad guy drops and our hero lands on his feet.

A sure-fire cut from a stunt person doing a flip or a spin to the actor landing, is to start tight on the ground and have the actor jump into frame, or just jump up and down in place, so you see the feet land on the ground then quickly tilt up to his face. You can also add a little camera jerk when the actor lands, which is effective.

If you're cutting from a stunt person wiping out on a motorcycle to your actor, let's say, then have the *actor* complete the movement into frame. You may want to have a person or two out of the shot to push them the final couple of inches into frame. This will make for a far better cut.

Alternate Film Speeds or Frame Rates:

If you run film through a camera slower than 24 frames per second, it will look as if everything is going faster when projected and is called *fast-motion*. It is also referred to as *under-cranking,* from the days of silent, hand-cranked cameras, and it means you're turning the crank slower than normal. Fast-motion was used regularly in old movies for comedy scenes and fight scenes. The moment punches begin to be thrown in a pre-1950 movie, invariably everything speeds up. It's silly-looking, and they finally stopped doing it. The frame rate for this was generally 16-18 fps.

Nevertheless, this technique of under-cranking fight scenes is still done regularly, but now they only go down to 20-22 fps, which makes it a lot less noticeable. This is done frequently on any martial arts fight scenes, and we did it constantly on "Xena" and "Hercules."

If you under-crank sufficiently—to one frame a second, for example—you can create the effect of people zooming around like animation and having hours occur in seconds. To keep the frame rate consistent for this sort of an effect, an electronic item called an *intervelometer* is used. It can be set from a few frames a second to a frame a minute (or less), so that sixty minutes then becomes sixty seconds on film. Set at one frame per hour, sixty hours becomes sixty seconds on film, and you can watch flowers bloom or see over two entire days occur in one minute.

On the other hand, you have *slow-motion* or *over-cranking*, which is generally considered to begin at 36 fps. Most shots you see in slow-motion (or *slo-mo*) are shot at 48 fps, which is double the standard frame rate of 24 fps and, subsequently, twice as slow. Suddenly a ten-minute roll of film is only five minutes long.

Many, many movies these days contain slow-motion sequences. Used imaginatively, slow-motion can be a beautiful effect. Used unimaginatively, it makes everything twice as dull.

Using slow-motion to film violence began in 1967, when director Arthur Penn used it for the machine-gun deaths at the end of *Bonnie and Clyde*. In *The Wild Bunch* in 1969, director Sam Peckinpah took slow-motion violence a step further, using it for much longer sequences and for inter-cutting various slow-motion frame rates together with 24 fps to achieve some stunning, unsurpassed effects. By 1972 and *The Godfather*, I felt that Francis Coppola was right on the money by not using slo-mo for Sonny's machine-gun death—it was already a cliché and would have detracted from the brutality of the scene.

Now, however, it's *de rigueur* and expected that if a scene contains violence, it will be shot in slow-motion. I actually made fun of slow-motion violence in a super-8 film I made in 1979 called *Holding It*, where the big shootout finale is all in slo-mo with spurting blood and Sam Raimi and Bruce Campbell also acting as if in slow-motion to increase the effect. Photographing violence in slow-motion, particularly gunplay, is now a severe cinematic cliché.

A director who has always made terrific, and very personal, use of slow-motion is Martin Scorsese. In films like *Taxi Driver* and *Raging Bull*, he uses slow-motion for POV shots where the person looking (often Robert DeNiro) is in regular-motion and only his POVs are in slo-mo—with the sound playing normally and not slowed-down—like when Jake LaMotta sees his wife crossing the Copacabana Club, or when Travis Bickle sees Betsy (Cybill Shepard) cross the street.

Scorsese also made very interesting use of varying frame rates in the boxing scenes of *Raging Bull*, using both slow- and fast-motion, sometimes in the same shot. If you simply change frame rates while the film is running, you will also change the exposure. If you go from 24 fps to 48 fps, the image will become darker because the faster the film moves through the camera, the more light it needs for exposure. If you switch from 24 fps to 12 fps while the film is running, the image will get brighter because each frame is being exposed for twice as long. So, to achieve changing film speeds while the film is running, you need a camera with a special shutter controlled by a laptop computer that simultaneously alters the exposure as it changes the film speed.

Having used slow-motion to film violence, I think regular-motion is more shocking, and slo-mo is more voyeuristic. I am personally very circumspect in my use of slow-motion, and I don't use it very often.

Shooting Action:

Action is most always made up of many shots and, frequently, a lot of complicated shots with special effects in them. (One of the very few exceptions to this statement is my film *Running Time,* which is made up entirely of long, extended takes and has action scenes in it.) When shooting an action scene, you can either plan the scene meticulously, employing the concepts of montage, or you can *run and gun,* as they say—just shooting anything and everything—and hope the editor can make some sense out of it.

I think the run and gun method of shooting action is a bore, whereas I believe the Hitchcock method of montage is endlessly fascinating.

Montage and Alfred Hitchcock:

Montage is French for editing, but it's more than just editing—it's the logic and flow of the images as they are juxtaposed with one another. Some directors have a beautiful sense of montage; others have no sense of it at all. It's all based on how the director covers the scenes with an idea in mind of how it will be edited later. This to me is a very important aspect of filmmaking.

The master of montage was Alfred Hitchcock, who got very specific shots for what he felt the scene called for as opposed to just general coverage. This isn't to say Hitchcock didn't shoot many, many dialog scenes in straight coverage of a wide shot and two over-the-shoulder shots. However, anytime he could find something visual in the scene, he'd shoot it specifically. And as a basic rule in life, anything specific is better than anything general, particularly in film direction.

Alfred Hitchcock

Here's an example: A cop is interrogating a guy in a room, and while they're talking, the cop looks through the window behind the guy to see a priest and a woman step up. The standard way to cover this scene would be in a two-shot of the cop and the guy, a close-up of the cop, a close-up of the guy, and a cutaway shot of the priest and the woman through the window.

Here's how Hitchcock covered the scene in his film *I Confess* where Karl Malden is the cop interrogating the guy: There's a two-shot, then it begins going back and forth between the two over-the-shoulder shots of the cop and the guy. It then oddly cuts to a long-lens over-the-shoulder shot of the guy that's entirely blocking the cop's face—that is, until just one of the cop's eyes moves out from behind the guy's head and he sees . . . Anne Baxter and Montgomery Clift as the priest stepping up outside the window. The cop's eye slides back behind the guy's head, and then it goes back to the over-the-shoulder shots. When I encounter these sequences in Hitchcock's films, it takes my breath away. This is what you can do with film that can't be done in books or on stage: make the visuals so specific to the scene that the visuals are what the scene is really about.

Everyone's favorite example of montage is the shower sequence in *Psycho*, which has seventy shots in forty-five seconds; but that's rather extreme and pretty obvious as well. In *Notorious*, Ingrid Bergman is working as a spy for the U.S. and has married a Nazi (Claude Rains), who has figured out she's a spy and is slowly poisoning her. Hitchcock keeps shooting the scenes with Bergman's teacup way in the foreground of the shots. What's being said doesn't really matter, but what's in the teacup certainly does matter.

The main element of montage, as far as Alfred Hitchcock was concerned, is based on two shots: a close-up of someone looking and a shot of whatever that person is seeing. This is called a *point-of-view shot* or a *POV*. Hitchcock illustrates this concept beautifully in the long sequence in the cornfield leading up to the crop-duster scene in *North by Northwest*, where Cary Grant is just standing there waiting for someone, although he doesn't know for whom. Every time he turns and looks, it then cuts to a car coming past. As this keeps occurring it gets more and more dramatic, yet nothing is actually happening. A car stops, and a guy gets out on the other side of the road. He and Cary Grant stand there and look at each other. Cary Grant comes walking over and just stands there. Finally, the man points at an airplane and says, "Strange, that. Crop-dustin' where there ain't no crops." Then a bus stops, the man gets on, and the bus drives away leaving

Cary Grant alone in the middle of nowhere with a crop-duster dusting crops where there aren't any.

This is all achieved with montage. It is a sequence that's composed of many, many shots with very little dialog. However, since Alfred Hitchcock was an A-director working for MGM with an A-budget, he had as much time as he needed (as well as a 2nd unit and possibly even a 3rd unit) to pick up all those shots.

On a low-budget film it's difficult to do complicated action scenes, because you generally have neither the time nor the money to stage them well nor shoot them properly. As I've already said, the easiest and most logical thing to be shooting on a low-budget is people talking to each other. However, if you need to make an action movie, as I've twice had to, then that's what you must do. Just be prepared to run a 2nd unit after principal photography is over.

Physical or Practical Effects:

Physical or practical effects are special effects performed live on-set, either by the main unit or by the 2nd unit, but not in post-production. Among the most common physical effects are bullet hits, called *squibs*, which are little explosive devices inside a condom filled with fake blood and detonated by an electrical charge. To do squibs properly you need to hire licensed *pyrotechnicians*—people who handle explosives professionally—because they're the only ones who can legally purchase and detonate real squibs. Squibs can be set off by the pyrotechnician or by the actors themselves, using concealed buttons in their hands connected to wires running down their sleeves, which is what we did on *Running Time*.

On *Thou Shalt Not Kill . . . Except*, however, it was much too low-budget to afford a licensed pyrotechnician, so we did the squibs ourselves. Setting off explosives on actors' bodies, no matter how small, obviously can be dangerous, so be very careful. I recommend using a licensed pyrotechnician if you can afford one (and if you're using SAG actors, it's required). If not, though, here's how we did them.

You first cover the area where the bullet will hit the actor with a couple of pieces of thin foam rubber, then put a thin but sturdy piece of wood on top of that, like a piece of paneling or thin plywood (any kind of metal is bad). Next, take a small firecracker (not a big one), pull out the fuse and replace it with a model rocket engine starter—items found in hobby shops that set off homemade rockets. (A single strand of steel wool will work, too, but not consistently). Next—and this is important—squirt a dab of hot glue onto the end of the firecracker with the rocket starter, which will seal it and make the chance of it going off at the right moment (or at all) much higher. On my earlier films I didn't perform this step, and it was always hit or miss whether the squib would fire or not. Attach the firecracker to the piece of wood with thin strips of *gaffer's tape* (known in the civilian world as duct tape), leaving most of the firecracker exposed. You then fill a condom (the thinner the better) with fake blood, tie off the end of the condom, and then affix the blood-filled condom on top of the firecracker once again with thin strips of gaffer's tape. (Note: Our recipe for fake blood is to use a bottle of clear Karo syrup, some red food coloring, then a few drops of blue food coloring for depth.) Attach the two ends of the rocket starter to wires running to a battery (a dry cell will work, but a car battery is better). The moment you touch the two wires to the battery contacts, it will explode, so you may want to put some kind of switch in-between for easier handling.

If you're setting off multiple squibs, you'll probably want to construct a *nail board*—a piece of wood with a row of nails pounded into it. You connect wires to all of the nails and run all the wires to one of the battery contacts. You take all of the various squibs and run all of the positive leads of the rocket starters together, then separately run all of the negative leads together. Take one of these groups of wires and run it to the other battery contact. Take the other group of wires and run them all to one big nail. Now, when you run the big nail along the row of nails on the board, it will set off all of the squibs one by one.

Once again, I repeat, be very careful. And if you blow off your hands or fingers, I had nothing to do with it.

There are many other kinds of physical effects beside squibs. For instance, if you want to see car tires burn rubber on pavement, you put bleach on the tires first. It smells terrible and is undoubtedly highly toxic, but it looks impressive.

Or a bullet shooting out a window. The easiest way to accomplish this is to fire a marble or ball-bearing through the window with a slingshot.

If you are using weapons, as many movies do, you are once again supposed to have a licensed pyrotechnician or armorer on the set at all times, as well as a fire marshal. If you intend to rent movie weapons that fire blanks, the weapons rental houses (the biggest being Stemrich Rentals in LA) demand a licensed pyrotechnician and will only rent to them. However, you can always use real weapons, as I did on *Thou Shalt Not Kill . . . Except.*

Do keep firmly in mind, though, that even with a licensed pyrotechnician on the set, several actors in recent memory—Brandon Lee and John Eric Hexum, specifically—have been killed with movie weapons on film sets. Both of these actors were killed due to negligence. Well, need I say, negligence and weapons do not go together.

First of all on *Thou Shalt Not Kill . . . Except*, I assigned all of the weapons to the 2nd AD, and no one was allowed to touch them without both my permission and hers. (Her name was Ann, so when we needed the weapons, I would say "Annie, get the guns.") I also did not keep any real ammunition with the weapons—they were kept in different places (all of the live ammo was in the trunk of my car). Actors never fired real ammunition, only blanks. You can easily get blanks for all of the pistols but not the rifles. With shotgun shells it's very easy to pry open the cartridge and dump out the buckshot. They will still fire, although a hunk of plastic wadding comes out that can still be dangerous—I saw a cameraman get a hunk of his cheek blown out that way. With most rifles, though, you can't get blanks. And if you intend to use an automatic weapon, which is illegal, they will not fire blanks without a big hunk of orange metal that screws on the end of the barrel and makes the weapon unphotographable. That's why movies use specially rigged fake weapons with very easy to see blanks that have to be rented from special places by licensed individuals.

As a little note, blanks come in two sizes: small charge and large charge. I say always go for the large charge blanks. The human eye can see the fire coming out the end of the barrel with a small charge blank, but it's happening so fast that motion picture cameras frequently don't pick it up. With the large charge blanks you will always see the fire blast on film, and it generally covers three frames.

This is what killed John Eric Hexum, by the way. He put a blank-firing movie pistol loaded with a large charge blank to his temple and pulled the trigger. The fire blast out the end of the barrel blew a hole in the side of his head and killed him. The point is, weapons are dangerous, even weapons rigged just to fire blanks for movies. You can't be too careful with all of them. Nevertheless, weapons are an integral part of many movies and, therefore, I think they need to be discussed.

I did have a scene in *Thou Shalt Not Kill . . . Except*, however, where a car gets shot to pieces, and the only logical way to do it without extensive (and expensive) special effects was to use real bullets. I mention this to people now, and they think I was insane to do it—but it was the only way I could think of. The only person on my set to fire a weapon with real ammunition in it was me. I fired every single shot into that car—perhaps a hundred shots—and the next day my right armpit was so bruised I could barely lift my arm. Nevertheless, no one was injured on my set, and the car was shot to pieces.

I repeat: If you intend to use SAG actors or DGA ADs, then you must have a licensed pyrotechnician. You have no choice. A DGA assistant director would never let you get away with any of the above-mentioned antics.

There are yet many other kinds of physical effects that are performed during shooting. In "Lunatics" I had a scene where a giant, twelve-foot spider is chasing the lead character through the streets of the city. Most of the giant spider effects were achieved with *stop-motion animation,* meaning they were shot frame by frame with a small clay spider and done in post-production. However, to keep things interesting, I also had hunks built of the giant spider to use during shooting. We had a set of giant spider mandibles (the serrated clampers on the mouth) that we mounted on top of a van and shot down through toward the actor, who was running away. The effects guy opened and closed the mandibles by use of a large scissors-like device. I also had the two giant-sized front legs of the spider made and operated with cables. As the lead character leans against a wall, the two huge spider legs step into frame above his head.

In *Alien Apocalypse* there were several cool physical effects: I needed a puff of dust on the horizon when the rocket lands at the beginning, so the pyrotechnician blew up thirty-five bags of cement with dynamite, creating one huge puff of dust. The pyrotechnician also blew up a building supposedly hit by alien rockets and truly blew the hell out of that building for real.

Another common physical effect is getting people to bleed. Although some folks use electric pumps or squirt bottles to get the blood to go through the tube, we found the most dependable and accurate method was to have someone fill his mouth with fake blood and blow it through the tube. This method gives you the most control, and it continually worked fine on *Evil Dead* where I was the main blood-blower. The only drawback to this system is that since fake blood is Karo syrup—which is all sugar—you can just feel your teeth rotting if your mouth is full of it for any length of time.

Hammer was the first film I've ever made without any physical effects in it—no guns, no blood, and no giant spiders. But if you've got physical effects, then you'll want someone in charge who knows what he or she is doing. This is an area where people can get hurt or even killed. Plus everybody is used to seeing properly done physical effects, and there's no point in doing them poorly.

There is an old-fashioned physical effect we used on "Hercules" called *glass paintings* that was much more common in the days of silent films. First you lock down your camera and set up a large sheet of clear glass in front of the lens, and then you have an artist paint onto the glass the elements you want added to your shot. On "Hercules" we went to a hilly park surrounded by foliage so no modern buildings or roads were visible, then added in villages on the glass paintings. I had a few costumed extras walking to or from the villages to add some movement and, hopefully, to take your eye off the painted villages. To pull this effect off, you need a bright exposure and a lot of depth-of-field to keep the painting sharp in the foreground yet keeping the extras in the background sharp, too. When you see the effect, the painted village looks like it's in the background, and the extras look as if they're in the foreground.

I worked on the crew of one of Mariah Carey's very first music videos, in 1991 or 1992, that had a beautiful glass painting in it. We were shooting on the Paramount lot on a New York street. They set up an MOS camera down low on a high-hat at the very end of the street so the street filled the bottom of the frame. Then an artist added in all of the high-rise buildings looming above the street on the sheet of glass, and it looked spectacular. The one big difficulty is that you need a good artist.

In-Camera Special Effects:

I love *in-camera special effects*, which are effects that occur during principal photography (or 2nd unit) but have no post-production elements to them and could just as easily be referred to as plain old trickery. A favorite in-camera effect is *reverse motion*: You have the actors play the scene backward, and you shoot it backward as well; then when you show it forward, people can do impossible things—such as dropping something will have it flying back up into your hands.

There is a scene in *Thou Shalt Not Kill . . . Except* where the Manson-like character (Sam Raimi) is being chased on a motorcycle and rides right into a Y-shaped branch that catches him in the throat, yanking him off the motorcycle. Shooting in reverse motion, the shot began in a close-up of Sam, his neck all the way into the Y-branch and painfully reacting to having been caught. On "action" Sam simply took a step backward, pulled his neck out of the Y-branch, and changed his expression from pain to wide-eyed amazement at seeing the Y-branch coming at him. In forward motion,

Sam was in wide-eyed amazement, his throat goes into the Y-branch, then he reacts in pain. Just to add another visually dramatic element, I began the camera in a close-up and, as Sam stepped backward so did I, pulling back to a medium close-up. In forward motion, it quickly pushed-in from the medium close-up to the close-up.

On "Xena" I had a scene of Aphrodite (Alexandra Tydings) talking to herself in a mirror, and her reflection was not doing or saying the same things as she was (it's her alter ego). The obvious way of doing this effect would be as an *optical effect*, meaning it's done in post-production in the lab, shooting the reflection as a separate piece of film and superimposing it into the mirror frame. But that would be the usual way, which often doesn't interest me. I set it up to be done live, in-camera, with a *double*—another actor who is dressed the same and somewhat resembles the featured actor. I began on a long shot of Aphrodite who then turns, and the camera pans to the mirror where we see her reflected as she walks toward the mirror, finally stepping into an over-the-shoulder shot. Only the shoulder belongs to the double—and the mirror is slightly angled to pick up Aphrodite's real reflection—so now she and her reflection can do different things.

Francis Coppola does some terrific fake reflections in *Peggy Sue Got Married* where he moves past the backs of everybody in a room (all doubles), looking into a mirror to the reflection, which is actually a hole in the set wall aiming at another set just like the one we're on with all of the actual characters looking back. This way Coppola can move the camera all the way through the "mirror" into the "reflection."

A great use of in-camera effects is the *old switcheroo*, which is switching between the actor and the stunt person without cutting. Blake Edwards did this beautifully many times with Inspector Clouseau (Peter Sellers) in the *Pink Panther* movies. In *The Pink Panther Strikes Again*, Clouseau falls down the stairs. The shot begins on a stunt man dressed as Clouseau falling down the stairs and disappearing from view behind a couch, then up stands Peter Sellers brushing himself off saying, "That felt good."

I did a switcheroo in the middle of a fight on "Xena." Xena's having a sword fight with this guy, and she jumps up on a table. He takes a swipe at her feet with his sword. It cuts to Xena's legs standing on the table—waist down to conceal it's a stunt person—and as she jumps away from the sword, she does a back-flip to land behind the table where Lucy Lawless was waiting and popped up.

Here's a cool old-time gag that I used in my "Hercules" TV movie: We are over-the-shoulder of a guy when the evil monster slashes him across the face with his claws. The guy spins around from the over-the-shoulder shot to a close-up revealing horrible bloody cuts across his face. Well, the bloody cut makeup was already there, and turning to the camera at the right moment simply revealed it. This also can be done with arrows already stuck into an actor whose back is to the lens and who reacts as if hit with an arrow, then turns to reveal the arrow stuck into him.

Another variation of this used all the time is to stick a knife or an arrow into a tree or a person, give it a little shake, then quickly pan to it. This is called a *whip pan* (in New Zealand, it's called a *whiz pan*). If you add the sound of the knife or arrow hitting something in the blur of the whip pan, it seems like you just saw it stick into the tree or the person.

On some level I prefer in-camera effects to optical or digital effects because they're just more clever.

Stunts:

If your film has difficult *stunts* or *gags*, as they are called, you'll undoubtedly need professional stuntmen to perform them. You never want to endanger your actors for two reasons: 1. It's not nice. 2. It will slow you down. If a character has a lot of stunts, you can always cast a stunt person in the part, and most of them have SAG cards. I've worked with stuntmen a lot on television, but I've never had any on my low-budget features.

Stunt women and men are, for the most part, the nicest people, and it's their job to make sure the stunt is safe and no one gets hurt. If stunt people tell me something can or can't be done, I believe them. But I don't think there's anything you can pitch at them they won't do. I believe most stunt people would prefer to do all their stunts while on fire.

Stills:

It's imperative that you shoot still photographs during your production since the distributors demand them afterward and, if you don't have them—as we didn't on *Evil Dead* nor *Thou Shalt Not Kill . . . Except*—you then have to set up another still shoot to fake them. I personally have shot the publicity stills for my last two films with my two-and-a-quarter large format camera. After the scene is completed, I move in with my camera and make sure to get several stills of similar angles used in the film. It's not hard to do because the lighting is all set up. You just have to remember to do it.

On *Lunatics* we had an actual still photographer (Mike Ditz) and surprise, surprise, that's the one movie of mine with enough good still photographs.

In addition to shooting with the two-and-a-quarter camera on *Hammer*, I also purchased three cheap 35-mm point-and-shoot cameras and about a hundred rolls of film, then I assigned three PAs the job of shooting anything and everything. This method worked well, and I finally had enough stills without hiring a professional still photographer (but Mike's photos on *Lunatics* are still *way* better).

For both *Running Time* and *Hammer*, I made sure to use the same film stock for the stills that we were using in the movie camera to achieve a similar look.

Comfort and Hydration:

This may sound silly, but I think it's worth mentioning: Make sure to wear comfortable shoes. You'll be running around constantly for over twelve hours, and if you're not wearing comfortable shoes when you get home at night, your feet will kill you, and it will be much harder to work the next day.

Also, it's a very good idea to drink a lot of water all day long. This way you will avoid headaches and stay clear and alert. Be sure not to drink too much coffee because a film set is a bad place to get too wound up. Switch to water as soon as possible.

PART FIVE:
POST-PRODUCTION

Reshoots:

Reshoots (or *Pick-up shooting*) are the film shoots that occur after you've edited the film and can see what's missing or isn't working.

It's hard to set up reshoots. You may have to reassemble all or part of your cast along with some kind of crew, if not your original one, on similar locations or sets. But reshoots need to be done with some regularity, so keep in mind you can go back and fix things—and may have to. Be sure to keep every prop you think you may still need, as well as furniture, costumes, and even hunks of sets. You may want to leave some money in your budget for reshoots, too.

Editing:

As I've already mentioned, you need to decide how you intend to edit before you start shooting so that the lab processes your film correctly and the transfer house does the transfers properly. If you don't think about this in advance, post-production will begin very poorly, and you'll already be in a world of trouble.

If you're editing on a digital editing system, and you've had your dailies processed and transferred correctly, it's perfectly reasonable to begin editing before you've finished shooting. The only time I've ever been able to pull that off, however, was with my last film, *Hammer*. You can't begin editing right away, though—because the editor won't have enough footage to work with—but you can start after about the first week of shooting.

The Editor's Cut or the Assembly:

I picked up a piece of post-production wisdom from working in TV called the *editor's cut*, otherwise known as the *assembly*. On TV, as well as many movies, there are three different cuts: the editor's cut, the director's cut and, finally, the producer's cut.

The idea behind the editor's cut is to let editors put the whole film or show together themselves without any interference. The only stipulation I and many producers have is that the editor should not cut anything out completely; s/he must use all of the scenes and all of the shots. Even still, editors may very well drop a shot here and there if they feel it just doesn't work or won't cut in. I have disagreed on occasion with editors' assessment of "doesn't work" or "won't cut" and had them put the missing shot back in but, admittedly, not very often.

Here's my own observation about editors and editor's cuts: If you leave editors alone to do their own cuts, it's like feeding them speed, and they'll cut madly until they're done. My editor, Kaye Davis, had her cut of *Hammer* done within three weeks of the completion of shooting. The editor of *Alien Apocalypse*, Shawn Paper, had a cut done in less than two weeks.

This gets back to my theory that once you've hired people to do a job, trust them and let them do it.

As I see it, having worked with many different editors over the years, some will stick their necks out and really try to cut the film together in what they believe is the proper fashion. Other editors, however, won't stick their necks out and pretty much just cut off the slates. Then they stick all the shots together in the loosest possible way, waiting for the director to come in and tell them where to really cut. I much prefer the former type of editor to the latter.

Let's face it, no matter what an editor does, you can always change it. Any editor who gives you trouble about changing things is, very simply, a bad editor. It's *your* film, and you get to cut it *your* way. End of story. In Hollywood the editor must do whatever the director asks for—it's a rule of both the Editor's Guild and the Director's Guild. This rule came into being, by the way, in the early 1960s on the TV show "The Twilight Zone," when an editor wouldn't cut a show the way the director wanted. Now they have to.

I edited my first feature film myself, as I had all of my short films previously, and personally I didn't find it to be the very best system. Most editors I've worked with haven't got the slightest problem trying to entirely accommodate the director. I'm certainly willing to listen to their opinions all the time, but I'm still going to do what I think is right. I conceived these shots and, ultimately, I think I know best how they should go together.

You may think that editing the film yourself will keep you in much firmer control—and that may be true, too—but it doesn't mean you'll end up with a better final product. Good editors have a lot of tricks up their sleeves, things you simply will not know if you haven't edited a lot of footage. An experienced editor brings a lot with them to the party.

One of the most important attributes of a top-notch editor is having good taste in knowing just which are the best moments in every scene. A quality editor pulls the very best moments from every take, then figures out how to seamlessly stitch them all together. Obviously, you go over all the footage with the editor and tell her which pieces you like the best, but there are still hundreds more decisions to be made that the editor will make without you. Therefore, it's very important to trust your editor and believe that he's making the right decisions.

Here's an example that illustrates an important point: At the end of *If I Had a Hammer* there is a fast dolly move, then the character Lorraine (Lisa Records) starts to cry, has a whole freak-out scene, then exits. I had two takes of the shot. The first take had a smooth camera move, some of the blocking was off, and the performance was more subdued. The second take had a severely wobbly camera move but was much more charged-up, and the blocking was perfect. I told Kaye to use the first take with the smooth camera move. When I watched the first assembly of the film, she had used the second take. I was shocked and said, "But I asked for the other take." Kaye shook her head. "This take is better. The performance is better." Then I said, "But the camera move—" Kaye cut me off, "—isn't as important as the performance." And, of course, she's right.

Entering and Exiting Frame:

Good editors are constantly finding ways to remove frames here and there to tighten up the scenes. Film does not have to be cut literally if one understands how the human brain comprehends information.

Let's suppose you have two shots to cut together: a medium shot of a person picking up a glass of beer and taking a drink, and a close-up of the glass of beer with the hand coming into frame, grabbing the glass, then removing it from frame. The inexperienced way to cut these two shots together would be to let the person's hand get right near the glass in the medium shot; then cut into the close-up, have the hand enter frame, grab the glass and remove it from frame; then cut back to the medium shot with the glass having just been lifted off the table and letting the person bring the glass to their mouth and drink. Experienced editors would probably have the person just start to reach for the glass and, long before the actor's hand actually got anywhere near the glass, they would cut into the close-up just as the hand grabs the glass (not entering frame). Then just as the person starts to lift the glass off the table (not waiting for it to fully exit frame), they'd cut wide when the glass was already halfway up and let the actor finish the action of bringing the glass to the mouth. By editing this sequence the second way, you would probably save a second or two. That may not seem like a lot, but it quickly adds up over the course of many cuts, and this is where your film's pace comes from.

People and objects do not have to fully leave frame to make a cut. A theory I've heard and accept is that once a person's eyes have left frame, you can cut. This is based on the fact we are mainly looking at actors' eyes, and once their eyes have left our view, we're no longer sure where to look anymore. This goes for entering the frame, too. You don't have to let people fully enter. They can already be a step into frame when you cut to them, with their eyes just about to enter frame.

When characters exit frame left, they must enter the next shot frame right and vice versa. This keeps the screen direction consistent. To exit frame left, you have to be going right to left; to enter frame right, you have to be going right to left as well.

As I mentioned earlier, I like to change screen directions regularly. I think it's a good idea. If I'm inter-cutting between two scenes, I will generally try to have them going in opposite directions to differentiate them. That way, the second you realize it's going a certain way, you know where you are. It's a form of mental geography.

Editing Overlaps:

Also, people do not have to start or finish saying their lines to cut to them or cut away from them. These are called *overlaps*, and editors do them constantly. You'll be on one character's close-up as she says a line, then you hear the first word or two of the other character's line before you cut to him. Before he completely finishes what he's saying, it has already cut back to the other close-up. This is another way to tighten things down and keep the pacing up.

Montage Sequences:

Although montage means editing in French and also refers to the flow of images, a *montage sequence* is a term referring to a scene without dialog— looking frequently, these days, like a music video with a pop, rock or rap song on top of it. A montage sequence is often used to indicate the passage of time: characters falling in love, building an airplane, starting a business, learning to dance or play the violin, etc. Whatever the montage is about is generally something filmmakers don't want to dwell on—they just want to get it out of the way. It always seems to me like the perfect time to go get more popcorn or go to the john.

The classic style of a montage sequence was created by Slavko Vorkapitch in the 1930s. Vorkapitch was known for using the leaves of a calendar blowing away while, in a series of quick cuts and dissolves, the character would either look for a job and not find one, or work her way up to being the head of the company, or drink so much liquor that he became an alcoholic and wound up in the gutter. Soon every studio had its own montage experts who put in similar sequences in many, many films. By the 1950s the montage sequence had become a painful cliché and fell from favor. But they returned in the late sixties and have been around ever since.

I'm entirely in favor of snappy, quick, thirty- to sixty-second montage sequences, that contain nicely composed shots and interesting editing (like when they "go to the mattresses" in *The Godfather*). However, when a montage sequence runs two to three minutes long just to accommodate some dull pop song that nine times out of ten doesn't even fit the scene anyway, I'll either change channels or hit the head.

Remember, every scene in your movie is the most important scene in the movie, and that includes the montage sequences. The minute you start to make decisions that are based on something other than telling your story well, like trying to have a hit song (which is bloody unlikely), you're thinking the wrong way. Besides, you can always dump a song on top of your end titles if you need to.

Editing Digitally or on Film?

My first two feature films were edited on film, and the next three were edited on digital systems. I think digital editing is a quantum leap over editing on film, and I'll never go back.

You will first need a bigger facility to edit on film because you have to store and arrange literally hundreds of boxes of workprint and *mag track*, which is the accompanying soundtrack. In 35 mm this is clear plastic film with a magnetic soundtrack running down it and, in 16 mm, it's called *full-coat* because the entire piece of film is covered with the magnetic soundtrack (magnetic sound is the same exact thing as the tape in a cassette or videotape). Second, you'll need a minimum of two assistants to keep all of that film and soundtrack logged and arranged so it can be found and gotten at. You'll also need an editing machine, like a KEM or a Steenbeck flatbed editor, as well as a moviola—the green, upright, old-fashioned-looking editing machine that the 1st assistant editor will need. Other requirements are several sets of *rewinds*, the items you crank to wind film back and forth on the reels; several *synchronizers*, the items that keep the picture and soundtrack in synch; several *tape splicers*, the items used to stick the film back together with clear tape; as well as a number of *split-reels*, the reels that unscrew at their centers to hold the *cores* of film. This is how film comes from the lab—not on a reel but on a yellow plastic hub.

It's a huge pain in the butt, and I'd say quite a bit more expensive at this juncture in history. I also don't think editing on film is as efficient as digital editing, and it takes longer.

On *Lunatics* for example, which was cut on film, there is a scene between the crazy boy and the crazy girl sitting on the couch in his apartment, where he starts to hallucinate about a mad doctor strangling him and trying to stick a syringe in his eye. I had more coverage of this sequence than any other scene in the film. It's also a tricky sequence because it keeps going in and out of fantasy, and there were a lot of shots to choose from. So Kaye cut the scene and, even though I thought she did a pretty good job, she wasn't satisfied. To recut the scene she had to have the assistant editor *reconstitute* the footage, which means peeling off all of the tape splices, disassembling the scene, then cutting it back into its original shots—a several hour ordeal. Well, Kaye ended up recutting this scene about thirty times, each time taking a somewhat different approach, and each time improving it a little.

Were we using a digital editing system (which didn't yet exist), Kaye could have saved all of her previous cuts of the scene for comparison purposes, and she could begin recutting anytime she wanted since nothing ever has to be reconstituted—it all exists digitally in the hard drives.

From what I hear, Steven Spielberg still cuts on film. Personally, I think he's a stick-in-the-mud. However, since he can afford as many editors, assistants, and as much equipment as his heart desires, it really doesn't matter.

You only need one assistant at the most when you cut digitally, and you don't really *need* any at all. It's just handy because it makes the editor's life easier. You can also use a room the size of a large closet to edit in because you don't need any storage space, just room enough to set up a computer and a row of hard drives (and I have no doubt the number of hard drives will continue to diminish as the technology improves).

Editing on Film MOS:
The *Really, Really* Cheap Method, Part II

This is how I edited a number of my short films, and how my friend Paul is editing his super-low-budget feature: You have all of your 16-mm film printed to workprint; get yourself a set of rewinds, a *viewer* (the illuminated little screen to watch the film) and a tape splicer (*cement splicers* are for negative not workprint)—all of which can easily be borrowed since none of it is used very much anymore—then you can sit there and edit at your leisure for as long as you'd like. If nothing's on rental, or the rental is so cheap it doesn't matter, then there's no pressure, and you can just take your time. I spent about four months cutting my nine-minute short film, *Cleveland Smith Bounty Hunter*, and I enjoyed the process very much. I even had a little bit of synch footage that I cut this way as well. I did all of the sound-cutting this way, too, on a little *sound-head* set up between the rewinds that played the sound. I finally rented a moviola for a weekend—which was a minimal expense—just to make sure all of the sound was in synch. It's a slow process, but it does work, and it can be very enjoyable and rather therapeutic if you're not in a hurry.

A little rental scam my buddies and I have used a number of times is to rent a piece of equipment, like a moviola, on Friday morning and pay for only the one day's rental, then return it on Monday morning having run it non-stop all weekend long.

Special Effects or Visual Effects:

Special effects are difficult to pull off cheaply, so I don't recommend them for low-budget films. They're also not easy to do well and frequently take several tries, thus increasing the costs.

My film *Lunatics* has a fair amount of special effects in it of all varieties: *stop-motion clay animation,* which is when motion is created by shooting frame by frame with clay creatures; *rear-screen projection,* where an image is projected on the back of a large screen which the actors perform in front of; *miniatures,* where buildings and sets are recreated in tiny, table-top versions; *super-impositions*, where images are put on top of one another; *mattes*, where part of the frame is blocked-off and shot separately, as well as various combinations of these effects. We spent about $50,000 on all these special effects, and we had them done by local guys in Detroit, not by Hollywood professionals. We ended up spending more time shooting the effects—which only equal a couple of minutes of film time all together—than we spent on all of the *live-action* shooting (which is all the scenes with the actors). But this was my most expensive film to date, at $650,000, so we had the money to do all of this crazy stuff. If you're making a $150,000 film, though, you do not have the money for special effects, or at least not very many of them, that's for sure.

This was all before the advent of *digital effects* that are created on a computer digitally instead of done optically in the camera and in the lab. Most optical effects are now done digitally. But had we done all our effects as digital effects in *Lunatics*, I don't think we would have saved a penny. Digital effects have not made special effects any cheaper because there's not much difference between having effects technicians sitting behind a camera shooting one frame at a time and having them sit behind a computer creating one frame at a time. There's still an enormous amount of man-hours involved.

In *Hammer* (as I mentioned earlier), I have one special effect done as a digital effect: my lead character walking up a street past many buildings with flickering TV light coming out the windows. The main reason I shot this as a special effect is that it would have cost a lot more money to get into that many houses to do the lighting, as well as all the old cars I'd need to line the streets. So doing this shot as a special effect saved me money, which is a good reason to do a special effect.

While we were shooting the live action, I made sure to get a shot of my lead walking up a street past a number of houses and buildings, none of which were very impressive. My intention was to use this shot as a *plate*, which is either a background or foreground element for a special effect. In the final shot, the only aspect of the plate that remains is the lead character and the sidewalk he's walking on—everything else in the shot was removed and replaced. This was all done digitally. To save money I personally shot all of the other needed elements for the effect, including all of the buildings behind the character, as well as all of the old cars. I originally intended to use my two-and-a-quarter, large format still camera for this, but the effects guy talked me out of it. He said that he would have to degrade the images so much to fit in properly that I was better off shooting with a 35-mm still camera, so that's what I did. And interestingly, I think, I simply had the photographs processed at the drugstore by Kodak and had them transfer the images digitally to a CD, which they'll do at a nominal cost.

We added five buildings to the shot, as well as three old cars on the street, and each one was a separate photograph. The key to shooting all of these photographs, or *elements* as they were now, was to get them all from the same angle I had shot the original plate. The most difficult and time-consuming aspect of this process was the effects person had to create a *traveling matte*—a black outline of the character—for every frame he's walking, and there were over two hundred frames. The traveling matte allowed the character to walk in front of the images of the buildings that were put in behind him. We also added some streetlights for him to walk behind. The flickering TV light in the windows was created by shooting actual flickering TV light off a wall with a home digital camera, then super-imposing it into the windows. It all works pretty well, too, although it is a tad cosmic and doesn't have as much depth as it might. Still, it's pretty impressive in its own weird way, and it only cost me about $1,000 to have it done. It cost twice that much to have the digital images (which were delivered on many CDs because they are very high-resolution images) transferred back to 35 mm. Still, at a cost of a couple of grand, it was cheaper than doing it for real—renting all of the extra lighting equipment and extra personnel to set it all up and run it, as well as getting into that many different houses.

The Music Score:

The music for all four of my feature films was composed and scored by my good friend, Joseph LoDuca, who also did all the *Evil Dead* films and the TV shows "Xena" and "Hercules." Almost every image I've ever shot in my adult life has had Joe's music on it (Joe scored both of my TV movies, the short-lived TV series "Jack of All Trades," and even a fishing documentary I did). Needless to say, I like Joe's music. I think his score for *Thou Shalt Not Kill . . . Except* is the best thing in the film.

Film composers get the final cut of the film transferred to video (either DVD or tape) with time code, which allows them to stay in synch with the picture. The composer watches each scene, decides on the rhythm of the action and the editing, sets a *click-track*—an electronic metronome—and then composes to that beat. With this setup composers don't even need to speak to anyone else—they can just score the picture as they feel appropriate, which is how it's frequently done.

However, that's not how I work with Joe, nor is it how I work with anyone. I particularly enjoy the process of getting Joe going on one of my film scores. First, I want him to know how I envision it, what I'm hearing. That doesn't mean it has to be that way, but it's a starting point. Joe may think my vision is crazy—and he'll tell me so—and the score may very well end up being something entirely different. But both Joe and I want the inspiration to come out of our interaction together on the subject.

As I've said a few times before: If you hire someone, let him do his job. I accept that Joe's opinion on musical matters is much more highly evolved than mine, and I will humbly acquiesce to his opinion. I thought that *Running Time* should have a jazz score. Joe watched the edited film and informed me it was getting a rock & roll score. "But why?" I inquired. "Because," Joe explained, "you don't have any jazzy characters." And so the film got a very cool rock & roll score, not to mention a cool, gutsy rock song on the end titles.

On *Thou Shalt Not Kill . . . Except* I was hearing an orchestral war score—like Jerry Goldsmith's music for *Patton* or Elmer Bernstein's music for *The Great Escape*—and that's exactly what Joe gave me. I really do love that score, too, and it's also very easy to hum.

For *Lunatics: A Love Story* I was hearing a bebop jazz score. Joe wrote a terrific combination bebop/hip-hop score that's wonderfully unique, and it made the film much hipper than I ever suspected it could be.

For *If I Had a Hammer*, which is about folk music and has ten folk songs in it, I had no idea what kind of dramatic score it should have. Joe thought about it for a while and suggested a straightforward jazz score since it would be highly appropriate for setting the 1964 time period yet also wouldn't interfere with the folk music. And as the lead boy really likes rock & roll, while the lead girl prefers folk music, the jazz score didn't "take sides" as Joe put it.

I gave him another particularly difficult problem on this film because the lead character, Phil, is blatantly not musical and is a poor guitarist. What music theme do you give to a non-musical character? But even though he's non-musical, he thinks he's hip. So Joe decided to go with the sound of what Phil thinks of himself, which is a hip, jazzy tune in the vein of Henry Mancini's "Peter Gunn" Theme. It's consistently amusing every time you hear that music with that goofy character, and it gets several laughs I didn't even know were there.

I think music is incredibly important—it sets the emotional landscape of your film—and it's why I highly recommend never showing a rough cut of a film to anyone without at least putting on *temp music* (music borrowed from other films). Music is the glue that holds all of the images together and, without music, it can be a very dry, arid landscape. Joe doesn't like looking at anything with a temp score on it and neither did the great Bernard Herrmann, who scored *Citizen Kane* along with many of Hitchcock's films. I see where they're coming from, too. They want to come at it from their own emotional response to watching the scene, not hearing someone else's musical interpretation.

Another important part of musical scoring is to make sure not to score some parts of the film. A dramatic musical score does not have to be continuous and, in fact, it shouldn't be. Too much music lessens its impact. Other than the front title music, there is no dramatic score in the first thirty minutes of *Running Time*. There is one *source cue*, which is music coming out of a car radio. Source cues can also emanate from store PA systems or boom boxes, or anywhere you might actually hear music. Anyway, for the first thirty minutes of *Running Time*, there's no dramatic score. Suddenly right at the end of act one, the first music *cue*—what each individual piece of music on a film is called—kicks in, and it's very dramatic. So don't be afraid to leave certain scenes without music. The lack of it can be very dramatic, too.

Songs:

It's a big mistake to just drop pop or rock songs on top of your action and call it a score. This is known as a *song score*, by the way, and most times they're terrible. And if you have any intention of using known pop or rock songs, you're kidding yourself. The average run-of-the-mill song that was *not* a big smash hit will cost at least $50,000. And the big music companies do not negotiate lower deals, or at least they never have with me. They don't need low-budget films, which I was informed of several times.

I needed three songs for *Thou Shalt Not Kill . . . Except* to be used as source cues coming from a car radio. Initially I had "You Were On My Mind" by We Five, and God knows what other fantasies in my mind. After talking to all the major music companies, like Warners Special Projects and EMI Music, I realized I could not afford any known songs—they were all way too much money—so I did something I think I'm quite good at: I delegated the responsibility to Joe. I said, "Joe, source cues count as music, too, and I have about $2,500 I can spend on this. Find me something." So Joe used his contacts and dug up the rights to three songs by The Rockets—a Detroit band with former members of both Bob Seger's and Mitch Ryder's bands—for, you got it, $2,500.

At the very end of *Lunatics*, we hear the song "Strangers in the Night." For the rights to the original Frank Sinatra recording, they wanted $75,000. What we did instead was simply to purchase the re-recording rights, called a *cover version*, for $7,500. Then we got a Frank Sinatra sound-alike to re-cord it for another grand. (I still have the cassette tape Joe sent me at the time, entitled "Dueling Sinatras," with three or four Sinatra sound-alikes.) Joe scored it exactly like the original, and you can barely tell the difference.

There are several different music clearance companies whose only job is to secure the rights of songs, like Evan Greenspan and Harry Fox. They're all listed in the LA 411 Book and on LA411.com.

Rough-Cut Screenings or Test Screenings:

Many people believe in *rough-cut screenings* wholeheartedly, but I don't like them. This is where you show an audience your edited but not printed, nor color-timed, nor finally scored film. To expect average people to understand what their looking at, with funky visuals and an incomplete soundtrack, is a huge leap of faith that I personally can't make. To now base crucial editing changes on their reactions seems crazy to me. This may well be purely an egotistical response on my part, but I honestly don't care what other people think. I am no longer trying to please all the people all the time, which is an impossibility anyway. As Bill Cosby once said, "I don't know the secret of success, but I do know the secret for failure: try to please everybody." I cut the film the way the editor and I think is correct, and I can live with that.

However, I do show my films in various early stages to good friends whom I trust. I can make use of intelligent, straightforward comments at this time—just like while I'm writing a script—but not from strangers and certainly not from kids.

They call rough-cut screenings *test screenings* in Hollywood, and they live or die by them. The test screenings are put on by research companies that have everyone in the specially-chosen audience fill out forms, rating all aspects of the movie. Based on this, the film companies then decide how much money to spend on the prints and ads budget. The direct result of the test screenings often is to cause every person involved with the film to go into a blind panic and begin doubting their product.

I've had a few of my filmmaker friends question my practice of not having test screenings. They think I'm quirky and a little nutty. Fine. But I've sat through my films with audiences many times, and I don't mind sitting there. When I know all the decisions were mine and weren't made out of blind panic, I'm comfortable. And that's the bottom line. However, if you're not the producer, then you may very well have to have test screenings and make changes based on them. I've had to do this quite a few times, too, and those are always the changes I regret. All I can suggest you do under those circumstances is to fight the good fight—and don't give up until you have to.

If I make the movie I honestly and truly wanted to make, then it doesn't matter what anyone else thinks. As Ricky Nelson sang, "You can't please everyone, so you've got to please yourself." If your goal is an attempt to appeal to the largest common denominator, however, then you might find test screenings worthwhile. Frequently test screenings will cause filmmakers to shorten and tighten their films at minimum, and that's usually a positive thing in and of itself.

But ultimately, I trust my instincts, as flawed as they may be. And I think my flaws and quirks are undoubtedly what give my movies their personality.

Front and End Titles:

One of my obvious trademarks as a filmmaker is that I always do elaborate front title sequences. My feeling is that once the film has begun, off we go, and it's now my job to be entertaining. I can't tell you how many movies I've seen in my life that have managed to bore me before the front titles were over.

The new hip approach is not to do front titles at all, but instead have them all come at the end with the director's name first (as opposed to last on the front titles). I'm not a fan of this because I like to know who did what while I watch the film, and, without that information, I always feel a tad lost. Therefore, I always do a front title scene on my films. Plus it gives composers a chance to strut their stuff and do a *main title piece* or *overture*.

The standard movie front title sequence is composed of a variety of shots of someone going somewhere, either on foot or by car or both, with the titles printed over the images—or else static shots of the city or town where the story takes place, with titles printed over the images. If you cut these scenes off of most movies and threw them away, it wouldn't matter at all nor affect anything since they're generally utterly extraneous.

Front titles are shown in this order, by the way:

1. The distribution company
2. The production company
3. The director's *possessory credit*, if any, like A Josh Becker Film, or Un Film du Josh Becker
4. The star's names above the title, if you have any
5. The name of the film
6. The lead actors
7. The secondary cast (optional)

Then department heads, which can also contain a special effects supervisor or special makeup effects (if you had such a person) and can also go in any order as long as it ends with the writer, the producer, then the director, such as:

8. The editor
9. The production designer
10. The costume designer
11. The director of photography
12. The co-producers or associate producers
13. The writer or writers
14. The producer
15. The director

I didn't see the first version of *Shaft* until years after it was released, but I always loved the record—"Who's the black private dick that's a sex machine to all the chicks? Shaft. Damn right." Finally seeing the film several years later, this wonderful, Oscar-winning Isaac Hayes song with a terrific beat is laid over the top of twenty generic shots of Richard Roundtree walking through NYC, cut together with no thought to the music. Man, what a bummer.

The king of imaginative title sequences was the great Saul Bass who did many of Hitchcock's films, like *North By Northwest* and *Psycho*, both of which have stunning front title sequences. Bass also did the *fully-animated* (meaning a full-fledged cartoon) front titles for *It's a Mad, Mad, Mad, Mad*

World, along with many of Otto Preminger's films—like *The Man With the Golden Arm* and *Anatomy of a Murder*—all with a brilliant sense of design. Every time I see one of Saul Bass's title sequences, I feel inspired.

Most of these sequences are simple *cell animation,* meaning frame-by-frame animation of artwork on *acetate,* which is clear plastic. This style of animation is easily done now on a computer, and you see it all the time. *North By Northwest* is nothing more than green lines moving diagonally across the screen, crossing other green lines, with the titles following them and finally dissolving into the side of a building. *Psycho* is just black and white lines moving vertically, with the titles moving across the screen and sometimes separating at their centers.

Saul Bass's title sequences are really awe-inspiring, however, and they allowed the brilliant composer, Bernard Herrmann, to write incredible main title pieces. Bass also did the titles for *West Side Story*—done as graffiti painted on a wall—and his titles for *Walk on the Wild Side* were over live-action shots of a black cat slinking down an alley.

Another great title sequence, not by Saul Bass, is in *To Kill a Mockingbird.* We see a cigar box filled with marbles, a knife, crayons, carved dolls, an old pocket watch, and many other things as we hear a child humming. This then transforms into the heart-breaking main musical theme (by Elmer Bernstein). Later in the movie when we see the cigar box again, we magically already know all of its contents.

I've had two very Saul Bass-inspired title sequences, both created by my cousin's wife, Jennifer Grey Berkowitz. In *Running Time* the white titles on a black background act like ticking second hands, and each of the names either ticks up or down across the screen. The *main title,* which is the actual name of the film, does a complete 360-degree turn. In *Lunatics* the multi-colored titles move onto the screen from all directions, with scratchy lines underneath them squirming around. The scratchy lines form the main title then explode off the screen.

One of my favorite front title scenes is on John Ford's *My Darling Clementine,* where all of the titles are on old wooden signs attached to a post that's turning to reveal each name.

In an early super-8 short film I made called *The Blind Waiter,* the titles were printed on restaurant checks spinning on a stainless steel lazy-Susan, which I must say worked quite well. It's not expensive to have a highly imaginative title sequence. I truly feel that once your film has begun, it's your job now to interest the audience, and an imaginative front title scene is a cheap, easy, effective way to begin.

As a note, front title scenes don't often exceed two minutes in length and are sometimes only sixty to ninety seconds.

End title scenes are, for the most part, a *crawl*—meaning the titles scroll across the screen from the bottom to the top—and generally last from two to three minutes, although there have been many Hollywood special effects extravaganzas with so many effects personnel, it occasionally takes five or six minutes to list them all. A standard two to three minute crawl costs about a thousand dollars. You can achieve this much more cheaply by shooting it right off of a computer screen. It will look kind of funky, but this might be okay for your film depending on the subject matter. If you create your titles on a computer, then want them transferred back to film, it's the same as a digital effect and costs $1.25 a frame. I'd say you're better off having a title and optical house shoot them for you on film.

The best end title scene easily goes to Orson Welles's *The Magnificent Ambersons*. Welles speaks each name and position in *voice-over narration*, meaning we hear but don't see him. While we see a beautifully-lit shot of a movie camera, we hear Welles intonem "The film was photographed by Stanley Cortez . . ." then we see a beautifully-lit shot of a moviola and hear, "The film was edited by Robert Wise . . ." finally ending with a boom microphone swinging through a spot of light directly into the lens and hear, "I wrote and directed the film. My name is Orson Welles."

Stock Footage:

I have twice done my front title sequences over *stock footage*, which is footage shot by someone else and purchased (or purloined) by you. I think that nothing sets a time period better than actual images of the day. In *Thou Shalt Not Kill . . . Except* I used actual Vietnam War footage, and in *Hammer* I used black and white newsreel shots of major world events between 1958 and 1964. In both instances I used yellow titles against the stock shots, which I think show up very well. (This is also a tribute to Wayne Fitzgerald who has done the titles for hundreds of movies including *Bonnie and Clyde*. He clearly likes yellow titles, and I agree they look good and show up very well against almost anything yet aren't boring like white titles.)

I've gotten the stock shots from a number of different sources—NBC, ABC, National Geographic, and several different stock footage houses—and it's really expensive, so I've just plain old stolen some of it, too. Yet who are you stealing a stock shot from? You can be pretty sure that any black and white stock shot from about 1970 back is in the *public domain*, meaning it has no ownership rights attached to it anymore. When you buy most stock shots from stock footage houses, you're not buying any kind of rights—you're simply purchasing a copy of it. Well, it's very easy to steal a shot from a DVD or a videotape, particularly if it's already grainy and old-looking, and have it shot back to film just like a digital effect. And if you're shooting on digital video, you don't even have to do that—you can just drop it in.

Some stock footage companies charge by the shot, and some charge by the second. All of the Vietnam footage was by the second, so I purchased sixty seconds worth. Then I had it *double-printed*—each frame was printed twice, making it slow-motion—thus increasing its length to two minutes. Even though I stole all of the stock shots for *Hammer*, I still double-printed it because I like the way it looks.

You must follow your own conscience and do what you think is right and what you can afford, but most of all, what you think you can get away with.

Opticals:

Even though most optical effects have now become digital effects, there are generally still a few actual optical effects that need to be done in a feature film.

On *Hammer*, for instance, I needed a big For Sale sign on the side of a building but, given my low budget, it wasn't practical to actually paint a sign that big. So I shot the building without the sign and had the optical house put it in later, and you'd never know. Luckily for me, though, it's a night shot.

In *Lunatics* I did a camera move all the way through a keyhole, which was an optical effect. This was achieved by doing a dolly shot with a zoom lens on the camera and pushing in on a door, then in tight on the keyhole until it filled the frame. We then set the camera at keyhole height inside the room and continued the dolly move. The effects technician optically continued the camera move into the keyhole until he was entirely within the keyhole. He then created a keyhole-shaped matte and superimposed the interior image on the keyhole, which fades in as we get close. As we push in, the interior image appears in the keyhole, and then we move right through the keyhole into the room.

In *Thou Shalt Not Kill . . . Except* many of the AK-47 rifles I had did not really fire, so I had the muzzle-flashes put in optically. It worked okay but not great. Still, I'd rather see those optical flashes than nothing.

Post-Sound:

Even if you should opt for cutting your picture on film, which I don't recommend, you simply won't cut your sound on film anymore. It's just way too big of a hassle, and it takes about six sound editors, a large room, six sets of rewinds, six splicers, and at least one moviola to run the sound and picture at sound speed to be sure it's actually synching up. It's an enormous ordeal—expensive and no longer worth it.

Cutting the sound digitally, however, takes one person—possibly two—and can be done in a room the size of a closet (which is how we did *Hammer*). It's way quicker, much easier, far less messy, and really does give you superior results.

If you go to a sound facility that has cut sound for films before—and there are many of them around now—they will already have a lot of the sound you need, so you won't have to bother creating it. Back in the old days (I mean the early 1930s up through the early 1990s) to do the *foley*—that is the replacement of all the footsteps along with many other incidental sounds—you had to actually recreate all of these sounds in a studio under a microphone. There was an item called a *foley box*, which was a wooden box split into four sections: one section containing a hunk of cement, another with gravel, another with leaves, another with carpet. As a character in a movie walked along, the *foley artist* would wear shoes similar to the character's and imitate footsteps on the proper surface in the foley box with a microphone down at the feet.

Sound facilities now have every kind of footstep imaginable on CD. They simply feed the sound through a keyboard and play all of the footsteps on two keys with two fingers. It's so much simpler and quicker now it's ridiculous.

You can get every possible type of *presence* or *background sound* (abbreviated to BGs) on CD now, too. These are sounds such as wind, city noise, crickets, chirping birds, howling dogs in the distance, etc. You'll still have to recreate some of the foley sounds yourself because certain sounds are just too specific to your picture to have been pre-recorded, like jingling keys or crunching paper or lighting a match or whatever the case may be.

The actual sound effects editing can be a very creative job with an enormous impact on the film. Although sound is generally edited very literally—encapsulated in the post-sound expression, "See a dog, cut a dog"—it doesn't have to be. Such sound effect editors as Frank Warner, Alan Splet, Walter Murch, and Ben Burtt on films like *Raging Bull, Apocalypse Now, The Elephant Man*, and *Star Wars*, create entire aural landscapes by use of sound effects. *The Elephant Man*'s use of clanking, banging machinery noises not only set a tone of the booming industrial revolution occurring, but also makes everything seem creepy. The boxing scenes of *Raging Bull* are masterpieces of sound editing and mixing. As "Sugar" Ray Robinson is clobbering Jake LaMotta, all of the background sounds fade away to leave only Ray's breathing, which transforms into a lion growling. His fist whooshes through the air, bashes into Jake's nose causing it to explode, then suddenly all of the background sounds come bursting back in. It's very imaginative and exceptionally well-executed.

The *mix* (or *dub*) is when you mix all of the various tracks of sound together onto one or two tracks, depending on whether it's mono or stereo. This process was originally performed on a mixing stage with a screen, projectors, a long mixing board, engineers, and 1st and 2nd mixers. Then, for a while, all the mixing was done on 24-track mixers just like music. Some people are still using that system. On *Hammer* we actually mixed in the computer, which is the best system yet, I think. The software is called Sonic Solutions, and it works great. Instead of having to listen to the scene over and over again, bringing up one track and bringing down another, now you simply put your cursor on the visual representation of the sound (a wavelength). By clicking one way or another, the wavelength gets smaller and quieter or bigger and louder. It's much easier and quicker than the old way.

When you are done mixing the sound, it is then downloaded to either a *DA-88 tape*—actually an 8-mm videotape that records eight discreet (separate) tracks of sound—or a *DAT tape* (digital audiotape), which is already almost a defunct technology.

The Optical Soundtrack:

The *optical soundtrack* is a technological holdover from 1928 when sound first came to movies. It was known then as the Fox System since it was developed by the Fox Film Corporation (prior to becoming 20th Century-Fox). Fox got the technology from the U.S. Navy, by the way. It's a weird old system that seems like it should have already gone the way of IBM punch cards and disappeared. With optical sound, the audio track is converted into squiggly lines that obscure a beam of light and recreate the sound. Oddly, optical sound is still the system that's in use with most film prints—although there are some now that are digital optical but not most. It's a very simple, quick procedure having the sound transferred from tape to optical, and it sounds fine; it just costs a couple of thousand dollars.

Negative Cutting:

After your film is edited and locked, meaning you're not making any more changes, then you must have the negative cut, or *conformed*, so that it exactly matches the cuts in your work picture. If you edited digitally, then the computer spits out an *edit list* or *EDL* when you're done, which is what the negative cutter will use to conform the negative. If you cut your film on workprint, then you have to make an edit list off the *edge numbers*. These are the tiny photographic numbers running along the edge of the film beside the *sprocket-holes*, those square perforations used to claw the film into position.

I cut the negative myself for several of my short films, and it's a touchy, nerve-wracking, time-consuming job that I absolutely believe is best left to professionals.

I had the negative for my first two features cut in Detroit by a wonderful woman named Joan Dietrich, who has since passed away. She charged three dollars a cut (there are between five hundred to fifteen hundred cuts in your average feature film), and it took her a couple of weeks to do a feature. When you got it back, it was perfect, and you knew exactly how much it would cost. My last two films were made in LA and, subsequently, the negatives were cut there, too. Both experiences were quite painful. *Running Time* has thirty cuts in it and should have been the easiest negative cutting job of all time, but it took many extra weeks and came out costing nearly twice what they had originally quoted me. On *Hammer* I went to the largest negative cutting house in LA, and they were really obnoxious creeps that clearly didn't like independent features. As God is my witness, I will never have another negative cut in LA (although I hear the negative cutters at Deluxe Labs are good). Negative conforming is usually about a $3,000 to $5,000 job, by the way.

Negative cutting is a technology over one-hundred years old and, once digital filmmaking takes over, it will go the way of the quill pen. For the time being, however, we're still stuck with it. (As a little historical note, Marilyn Monroe's mother was a negative cutter at CFI labs in Hollywood in the 1930s).

While you are editing your picture, it's very important to keep in mind you cannot cut a shot in half and drop another shot into the middle. In 35 mm, every cut must have at least one frame of excess on either side to accommodate the negative cutting. These extra frames are called *handles*, and without them you will be in trouble. In 16 mm, your handles need to be two frames long. Since the negative cutting is done after the sound mix, your picture must come out to the exact same length as the sound, or it won't be in synch. And once you've made a cut in the negative, that's pretty much it. It's very tricky, and sometimes impossible, to recut a negative. Therefore, you absolutely don't begin cutting the negative until you're 100% sure you're done editing.

Single Strand or A&B Rolls:

There are two ways of cutting the negative: *single strand*—where it's all in one long piece—or *A&B rolls* (also called *checkerboard editing*), which is on at least two pieces of film (the A- and B-rolls and sometimes a C-roll, too, if you have a lot of special effects). To have your negative cut as a single strand, the method used on most movies, all of your dissolves and fades must be shot as optical effects (at extra expense) then cut back into the negative. This will cause all of the dissolves and fades to look slightly different than the picture they're coming from or going to, because now that they're optical effects, they have lost a generation from the original making them somewhat grainier. In many movies you can see every dissolve or fade coming because it becomes slightly grainier the moment before it occurs.

There are, however, a couple of advantages to having your negative cut as a single strand: First of all, it's a lot easier for the lab to handle, and there's less chance for any kind of mistakes; second, you can have dissolves and fades of absolutely any length you'd like. This grain problem can be avoided by having all the dissolves and fades created directly on inter-positive (IP), but then you absolutely must have an IP made, which is expensive (more later).

If you have your negative cut as A&B rolls as I always do (another one of my rebellious quirks I guess), you can only have standard length dissolves and fades—12, 24, 36, 48, or 72 frames—but there's no shift in grain before the dissolve or fade since it's not an optical effect. When the negative is on A&B rolls, it is indeed cut just like a checkerboard with shot #1 on the A-roll, shot #2 on the B-roll, shot #3 back on the A-roll, shot #4 back on the B-roll, etc., going back and forth. With A&B rolls, the lab makes the dissolves and fades on a printing machine that only runs at standard lengths. Lab dissolves look *way* better in my opinion, and since I've never wanted anything but the standard lengths—nor have I ever been able to afford an IP right away—I have A&B rolls cut.

Post Lab Processes:

With your cut negative you now can have the lab make a film print. This is called the *first trial answer print*, and it usually doesn't have the soundtrack on it making it cheaper. The chances, however, of it looking just like you want it to are very slim. Now you must go through the process called . . .

Color Timing:

This is where you and the *color timer* or *colorist*—a specialist who works at the lab—sit and watch your film and, shot by shot, you tell them what color tones you had in mind. Is the shot too bluish, or possibly too reddish? Either way, they can change it. The color timer can even make scenes shot in the daytime look like night by adding more blue. The prints from this process are called *trial answer prints*, and it generally takes a couple tries, although you only pay one flat fee for as many attempts as it takes. When you accept the color timing, the print they then make—with sound—is the *final answer print*. As a note, all of those trial answer prints don't belong to you; they belong to the lab that then throws them out. It doesn't really matter, either, since the trial answer prints generally don't have sound on them, although you can request it—if your optical soundtrack is complete, and you want to make sure nothing is wrong.

The Inter-Positive (IP) and Inter-Negative (IN):

Making an *inter-positive* (*IP*) is an expensive process. It costs about $1.25 a foot, and the average 35-mm feature is 10,000 feet long (equaling about

100 minutes), so that's $12,500. The IP is a positive version of your negative, but with all of the color timing built into it. From the IP you can make an *inter-negative (IN)* —also known as a *dupe negative*—that's an exact duplicate of the IP, with the color timing in them but in negative form.

Should your film receive a *theatrical release* where you need a number of film prints to show in movie theaters, then you'll probably need an IP. You can make a few prints right off your original cut negative (also called the *camera negative*), but they're over double the cost of *release prints* that are made at high-speed off the dupe negative. The common lab wisdom is you can't make more than 100 to 200 prints off of a dupe negative before it begins to scratch and break down. Well, a big movie these days will be released with 3,500 prints, and that's just in the U.S. Should you be so lucky as to have that occur, the distributor will bear the cost of all the prints (which is part of the *P&A* or *prints and ads budget*). Nevertheless, you have to have the proper elements to be able to make the prints if the need arises.

You will also need an IP if you want to make a top-quality video transfer. You can make your transfer off of the cut camera negative, but you'll have to do all of your color timing again. Since the cost of a decent video transfer is minimally $350 an hour, you really don't want to do that. You could also make your transfer off of a film print, as many people do, it just won't look all that good. A film print has much more contrast than the negative or an IP and doesn't transfer nearly as well. This is particularly important if it's going to DVD, where you can distinctly tell the difference between a negative or IP transfer and a print transfer.

Also, if you make a distribution deal, the IP will be one of your delivery elements, meaning that it's required you have one.

35-mm Blow-Ups:

I have had two *35-mm blow-ups* done from the 16-mm negatives on *Thou Shalt Not Kill . . . Except* and *Running Time*. On *Thou Shalt Not Kill . . . Except*, I had the cut 16-mm camera negative *blown-up*, or enlarged, to a 35-mm IP from which I then made 35-mm dupe negatives and as many prints as I wanted. This was a $40,000 process, and the same thing was done on *Evil Dead*. I haven't heard about this process getting any cheaper in the intervening years.

On the other hand, I had the cut 16-mm camera negative of *Running Time* blown-up directly to a 35-mm print, and that cost $5,500. But there's only the one print and, should it get chewed up during projection, that's all she wrote.

Nevertheless, I think the latter method was a better idea. It was significantly cheaper, and then I could show the film in any movie theater in the world. No, I couldn't make any more prints, but if I'd gotten a theatrical release (which I didn't), then the distributor could have borne the expense of the IP blow-up.

On a purely aesthetic level, however, the IP blow-up of *Thou Shalt Not Kill . . . Except* looks superior to the print blow-up of *Running Time*. I did shoot high-contrast film stock on *Running Time,* though. This wasn't the best stock to use for a blow-up as it severely increased the contrast, and it came out with far too much contrast for my liking.

Delivery Elements:

When and if you make sales of your film, just what are you selling people? What is it that they actually get? These items are called *delivery elements* and are an absolute requirement to complete a sale. If you don't supply these things, then you will either lose sales or have someone else (like a sales agent, should you be so lucky) create them for you, charging you three or four times what they legitimately cost. As I've mentioned, the IP is a delivery element. The other delivery elements are:

The M&E or Music & Effects Only Track:

To make sales of your film overseas, you will need an M&E track, which is a soundtrack of just your music and sound effects without any dialog. The M&E allows foreign distributors to dub your film into other languages. Without an M&E, you would also remove all other sound when you remove the dialog, leaving you with nothing. A foreign distributor will not recreate your entire soundtrack for you—instead, they just won't buy your film.

If no one is speaking, the sound from your original soundtrack can be grabbed and put right over to the M&E track. If there are people talking right over the sound effects, then the background sounds must be recreated. If you've put in presence tracks everywhere and done all the foley, it's not a very big deal—you've already done most of the work—but an M&E must be done.

The Dialog-Continuity Script:

The *dialog-continuity script* is a transcription of every line in your film, exactly as it is spoken, with the footage count of exactly where it occurs. This is what the foreign distributors will use for both the dubbing and the subtitling.

This is not the shooting script—this must literally be what the actors are saying, including all the *ums* and *ahs* and *y'knows* and everything, with the exact footage count of where each line begins and ends. That way the person doing the subtitling in some foreign land doesn't even have to know what anyone is saying. Someone else will translate the dialog, right there on this script you're supplying, and the person plugging in the lines drops each one at the number you've given them. It actually works, too, so be very specific in your footage counts.

The Trailer:

The *trailer* or *coming attraction*, the two-minute preview, is an entire art unto itself. The producer and co-writer of *Thou Shalt Not Kill . . . Except*, Scott Spiegel, and I honestly spent more time working on the trailer for that film than we did on the film itself. It's a good trailer, too, in the let's-tell-the-entire-story mode of coming attraction.

Most trailers these days begin like this (please imagine a low, resonant male voice): "In a world . . ." that can go on to " . . . where wrong is right, and right is wrong . . ." or, "In a world where robots rule the earth . . ." or whatever.

Many trailers these days conceptually keep zooming in, with narration like this: "A town . . . a street . . . a family . . . a secret . . ." and then generally goes into a montage of fast cuts with thumping music.

The trailer for *Thou Shalt Not Kill . . . Except* goes like this: "In the beginning God created light, then God created man, and he gave him ten commandments, amongst them, thou shalt not kill. But evil forces arose, ignoring God's commandments, and wreaked havoc on the world. There are times when the laws of God and man must be put aside. *Thou Shalt Not Kill . . . Except.*" Followed by a montage of horribly violent action.

That took forever to come up with, by the way. But we did sell every overseas territory with that film, so it was worth it—even if I personally never got any of the money.

The Press Kit:

The press kit includes: four or five black and white 8x10 stills from the film, with a description of whom or what is pictured printed on a label stuck to the bottom edge or back of each photograph; a synopsis of the story; the complete cast and crew list; biographical pieces about the director, the producer, and the film's stars; and any press clippings you can wrangle together. All of these items are put together in a folder, frequently with the film's artwork on the cover.

You'll need many more stills than the four or five in the press kit, as well as 35-mm slides that can be made off the negatives. A sales agent will probably ask for twenty still photographs and ten slides.

If you end up needing a lot of press kits—twenty-five or fifty of them, let's say—and each one contains five 8x10 stills (being sure there's one still of the director), you'll go broke making that many 8x10s by photographic enlargement. Having a 35-mm negative enlarged to 8x10 costs between ten and twenty dollars each (I just paid sixteen dollars each). If you have 8x10 *copy negatives* made, however—a negative that's the same size as the print—then they can make high-speed *contact prints* that are a dollar or two each. This little maneuver will save you hundreds of dollars. I have frequently gone to Duplicate Photo in Hollywood who are always prompt and reliable and print the 8x10 headshots for probably half the actors in Hollywood.

The One-Sheet or the Poster:

Since the advent of digital enlargement and printing, having the film's poster (or *one-sheet*) made doesn't have to be a very big ordeal anymore. This used to be a rather large lithography job that was quite expensive. Now, any decent sized printing facility can enlarge your image up to poster-size. You do want to work with a sharply focused photograph, or you can create artwork for your poster as many movies do. This is about a $500-$750 expense, excluding the artwork.

Copyrighting the Film:

It's very important to copyright your film as soon as it's been transferred to videotape, but *before* it's been shown at any film festivals, or has been four-walled (more on that later), or had any paid screenings (free screenings don't count). The copyright office considers any paid screening of your film as "publication" and, once a film has been "published," it then must be copyrighted in its original form—either a 35- or 16-mm film print that you will never get back. Well, a single 35-mm film print costs about $4,000, and a 16-mm print costs about $1,500. If you copyright the film before publication, however, you can send in a VHS videotape or a DVD, which is about ten to twenty dollars.

You also must put a copyright notice, with the copyright symbol ©, on your end credits, and it generally states, "All Rights Reserved," too. Until recently, if you didn't put a copyright notice on your film—and you showed it to a paying audience—your film was now automatically in the public domain, and you had lost all rights to the copyright. That loophole has been closed, but basically, if you don't state your copyright, then it's not copyrighted. The two most famous examples of films with no copyright notices on them are *It's a Wonderful Life* and *Night of the Living Dead*, and that's why you see ninety-nine cent versions of them in all the bargain bins. If a film is in the public domain, anyone can duplicate it and sell it.

On your copyright notice, you generally use Roman numerals for the date, although you don't have to. The reason for this is if you copyright your film when it's completed, as I did in 1985 with *Thou Shalt Not Kill . . . Except*, and it takes a few years to sell the movie, the film's age is a lot less apparent as most people can't decipher Roman numerals easily.

Once again, copyright forms can be gotten at www.loc.gov/copyright.

Title Clearance and Error and Omissions Policies:

Should you be so lucky as to get a theatrical release, someone will un-doubtedly demand that you get a title clearance and an errors and omis-sions insurance policy, called an E&O policy. A title clearance is the process of getting a legal firm, most often Brylawski and Cleary in Washington, DC, to search the records and give you a legal statement of what uses have been made of that title over the years. Ostensibly, this needs to be known to make sure you don't infringe on anyone's copyright, even though you can't copyright a title. You can get a registered trademark for a title—like *Star Wars* or *Star Trek*, so you can sell a line of toys or other ancillary prod-ucts under the name—but you can't get a copyright. The title search tells you everything they can find about the title. For instance, the original title of *Thou Shalt Not Kill . . . Except* was *Bloodbath.* The title search revealed that a recent Charles Bronson film, *10 to Midnight,* had begun its life entitled *Bloodbath,* and the script was copyrighted under that title despite the eventual change. Therefore, Brylawski and Cleary would not give the title *Bloodbath* a thumbs up, and we had to change it.

To get an E&O policy, which costs multiple thousands of dollars, an insurance company (found in the handy LA 411 Book or on LA411.com) makes sure all of the liabilities issues concerning your film are confronted and dealt with. This includes the title clearance, clearances for the songs, the actor's contracts, the location releases, and anything else that could cause a lawsuit for the distributor.

The only one of my films ever to have an E&O policy was *Lunatics,* which sold to Sony, and the E&O was in the contract as a delivery element. *Running Time,* on the other hand, has been in video/DVD release in the U.S. and Canada for over five years and never had a title clearance, an E&O policy, or an IP.

When I decide on a title for a script I always run my own little title search by looking it up in "Leonard Maltin's Movie & Video Guide" to see if anyone has used it. Oddly, I think, titles are reused much more frequently these days, so maybe title clearance isn't as important as it once was. The title for Sam Raimi's film *The Quick and the Dead,* which came out in 1995, had been used for a 1987 TNT cable movie of Louis L'Amour's novel starring Sam Elliot, and that's what L'Amour's book was titled (copyrighted in 1973). The title *Bad Boys* was used in 1983 for a Sean Penn film, then again in 1995 for a Martin Lawrence, Will Smith film. The original title for *Running Time* was *Blood Money,* which had been used in 1933 and again in 1988. There was also a Roger Corman film called *Blood Money* shooting in L.A. at the same time I was, so there's a 1997 version, too.

Film Markets and Sales Agents:

There are three big film markets every year where most of the movies made in the world are sold: the American Film Market (AFM) in Los Angeles, Cannes (which is also a festival) in France, and MIFED (an Italian acronym) in Milan, Italy. There are others, too, like NAPTE and MIPCOM. They're all kind of creepy and, if it were possible, I wouldn't mind never going back to another one. I've been to AFM many times, and I've been to MIFED once. I've never been to Cannes, although I've had films shown there (at the market, not the festival).

Three kinds of people have rooms or booths at these markets: distributors, production companies, and sales agencies. There aren't any individual, unaffiliated filmmakers. To go to these markets you either have to be a distributor, work for a production company, have a film produced by that production company, or have your film represented by a sales agency. All of these various distributors, production companies, and sales agencies are listed in the big fat *Variety* or *Hollywood Reporter* issues put out specifically for each film market every year.

So, how do you get a sales agent? You call them up and send them your movie. If they like it, they'll represent it. How do you know if you can trust them? Beats me. I got ripped off blind on *Thou Shalt Not Kill . . . Except* by a sales agent and never got any money out of them. I made my last two deals myself directly with a video distribution company, and that was fine, but it had nothing to do with film markets. (The video distributor, Anchor Bay Entertainment, contacted me due to my *Evil Dead* affiliations.)

The deal for *Lunatics*—the only one of my films I don't own—was made by a sales agent (whom I had nothing to do with) at Cannes. The deal was with Columbia Tri-Star who bought all the rights to the film in perpetuity, which still seems like a crazy deal to me. I've made standard seven-year deals with my other films. The only thing that's saved my ass at all in the world of distribution and, admittedly, I've never performed very well in this realm, is having the rights to my films revert back to me after seven years so I could make a new deal.

Ultimately, though, you've got to trust somebody, or your film will never see the light of a projector bulb. I was so gun-shy after my first encounter with a crooked sales agent/distributor that I did a very poor job getting my films distributed for the next ten years without a sales agent. Finally, a couple of years ago I signed back up with another sales agent. They have made sales of my films and even got *Running Time* onto Independent Film Channel; but just like my first sales agent, they have not returned one cent to me so far, nor do I expect that they ever will. Here's their scam: They tell you they need to spend about $30,000 up front on promotional materials—a trailer (unless you already have one they like), a poster, fliers, press kits, etc.—and then they subsequently never break even. This sales agent had some assistant spend about an hour or two on PhotoShop making a flier for the film, where they took Bruce's head from one photo and pasted it on his body from another one. It didn't look that great, yet the charge was $6,000.

Distributors:

People are always making film distributors out to be the bad guys, and no doubt some of them are, too. I've had most of my trouble with the sales agent, though, and not the distributors. At least, not the video distributors. In the weird case of *Thou Shalt Not Kill . . . Except*, the sales agent was also the theatrical distributor. This gave them twice the chance to rip me off—of which they availed themselves. They're the only theatrical distributor I've ever dealt with. Along the way I sued this sales agent/theatrical distributor and won, but never got any money. Legal costs for this lawsuit finally added up to nearly $50,000, spread out over several years. So, I personally have found suing the distributor to be a bad idea.

But the video distributors I've dealt with have all paid exactly how much they said they would pay and promptly, too. Maybe this is because video distributors are usually not dealing with vast sums of money. I'm sure this isn't everyone's experience, but it is mine.

On a small, independent, low-budget feature, I'd say it's nearly impossible to get more than a $50,000 to a $100,000 *advance*—the amount you get up front—from a video distributor for the U.S./Canada videotape and DVD rights. You are still included in what are called *overages*: Should your film make enough money to pay back the advance, plus all of the distributor's packaging, advertising, delivery, and overhead costs, you then get a percentage and more money. But even if you never do go into overages, which is likely, you at least got the advance. Sadly, advances these days are very difficult to get, but a deal without an advance is generally a bad deal. The chances of seeing any money afterward are very slim. That's why percentage points without an advance are called *monkey points*. As the late Irvin Shapiro used to say (the original sales agent on *Evil Dead* and *Thou Shalt Not Kill . . . Except*), "Get your money in advance and be sorry later," meaning you'll never be sorry later if you get your money in advance.

And remember, if you make a standard seven-year deal, then in seven years you can make a new deal. Ultimately, seven years isn't very long.

There are also overseas sales and domestic TV sales, too. To make any of these sales, you will undoubtedly need a sales agent's assistance. I don't know much about domestic TV sales, but a sales agent has the ability to rip you off blind on overseas sales. Since they contractually have the right to charge you for every single expense they accrue going to film markets, flying first-class, staying at fancy hotels, eating expensive meals, etc., I found it was impossible to ever get ahead with these people. On *Thou Shalt Not Kill*

... *Except*, we sold every territory in the world, yet all the statements I ever received always came to zero. The same thing is true with this new sales agent, but I don't know what else to do. There's no way you can personally set up all these overseas deals and service them because you don't have the operation or the know-how. At least I don't anyway. But I've avoided the use of a sales agent for setting up the domestic video/DVD deals ever since I got ripped-off on *Thou Shalt Not Kill . . . Except*, and I have subsequently received all the money I was supposed to get.

People find this very difficult to believe when I tell them, but as far as I know it's true: Film distribution companies will not watch your movie if you just send it to them—even the folks in their acquisitions department. This may seem like the height of absurdity, and perhaps it is, but I do understand where the distributors are coming from. Enough films come in through known sales agents or someone else they recognize—most of which are horrible and rejected—that they don't need to look at films coming from strangers. The same goes for scripts, by the way. If you send an unsolicited script to a production company (which is called *over-the-transom*), they're just going to throw it out unread. That's exactly what distributors do with unsolicited films—unwatched.

Four-Walling:

Four-walling is the term for renting a movie theater and showing your film yourself. Once you've rented the theater, any ticket sales you make are yours. I've now done this twice, with *Lunatics* and with *Running Time*, both times in LA. Although both times this scheme ended up costing me a lot of money, it's one of the only ways to get your film reviewed by real film critics. If your film is not actually playing in a theater so other people can see it, the critics won't review it. Sending a videotape to a film reviewer means nothing—they only review films showing in a theater.

My luck hasn't been all that terrific regarding the four-walling of my films. I opened *Lunatics* in LA the same day as *The Lunatic*, a Jamaican film. The theater where my film was showing put a sign in the ticket window stating, "This is not a Jamaican film," which I considered using as the film's slogan. With *Running Time*, I happened to open the same day as *Titanic*. Not only did my film do no business, but Woody Allen's newest film at the time—*Deconstructing Harry,* showing in the same theater across the hall from my film—also tanked. Meanwhile, one block away there was a line for *Titanic* stretching for as far as the eye could see and around the block. I considered wandering along the long line of people wearing a sandwich board that said, "If you can't get into *Titanic*, there's more movie entertainment to be found one block away," but I chickened out.

The Only Thing Positive Is the Negative:

An old expression in the world of film distribution is, "The only thing positive about the film business is the negative." What that means is whoever owns the film's negative will probably end up making the most money on the film over time. I have managed to retain ownership of three of my four films, and this allows me to keep making deals with them. None of them have been big deals yet, but it keeps adding up over the long run. (As Rocky says about his lost locker, "I must've had about twenty dollars stolen out of that locker over six years. It doesn't sound like much, but it adds up.")

Film Festivals:

The very biggest film festivals—Sundance, Telluride, and Toronto, as well as Berlin and Venice in Europe—are now like little film markets because distributors attend them. I'm sure there are probably a few distributors at the New York Film Festival, and maybe Chicago, too, but that's about it. Every other film festival in the world has no market value—you will not get a distribution deal by showing your film there. What you will get, though, is seeing your film in front of a paying audience.

For the most part, I've found you don't even get treated very well at most festivals. Film festivals are not about the filmmakers being stars—they're about the festival promoters getting to act like stars. And even if they should pay for my plane fare to get there, it always ends up costing me money to attend any festival. Nevertheless, I probably never would have had a reason to go to Helsinki, Finland or São Paulo, Brazil otherwise.

Summation:

So, with all of this information, and about $75,000 in cash and credit (half the budget), you could potentially put a really good movie in the can. Or even a classic. Or possibly a stinker. And if you've gone to the difficulty and expense of actually shooting the film, you'd be nuts not figure out how to finish it, because that can be done in bits and pieces over the course of time when you have the money. Then you'll have a feature film that has the potential to be as respected, disrespected, revered, or ignored as any other feature film out there.

Many of the finest films ever made were extremely low-budget, such as: *The Bicycle Thief, Detour, Gun Crazy, Raw Deal, Los Olvidados, Killer's Kiss, The 400 Blows, Shadows, Carnival of Souls, The Little Shop of Horrors, Faces, Night of the Living Dead, The Texas Chainsaw Massacre, Pink Flamingoes, Evil Dead, Stranger Than Paradise, Henry: Portrait of a Serial Killer, The Brothers McMullen, Slacker, Pi*, and many, many others. If you have ability as a storyteller and a cinematic vision, it will show through no matter how low your budget.

On a certain level I wrote this book out of pure selfishness. I want to see more good movies, and that means *you* have to make them for me. So go make them and don't make just any films, make classics. It's more than possible—it's necessary.

Now go do it.

Glossary

1st Assistant Director (1st AD) – The person who physically runs the set, makes sure the schedule is being adhered to, and often does the breakdown and makes the schedule.

2nd Assistant Director (2nd AD) – The person who fills out all of the paperwork with the actors, assists with extras and crowd scenes, and does whatever the 1st AD requests.

2nd Unit – A smaller crew that shoots all of the shots that the main unit hasn't got time to get.

Apple Box – A wooden box used to stand on, or lift the height of something. They also come in: *Half Apples*, which are half the height; and *Pancakes*, which are a quarter of the height.

Armorer – The person who is in charge of, and handles, the weapons, fake or real. This is a state licensed position, if you want to rent working movie weapons, that is.

Art Director – The second-in-command in the Art Department, unless there is no Production Designer, in which case the Art Director is in charge.

Assistant Cameraperson (AC) – The 1st AC frequently operates the camera; the 2nd AC manipulates the focus and exposure; the 3rd AC, also known as the *Clapper/Loader*, loads the camera's magazines, fills out the camera reports, and often operates the slate or clapboard.

Backlight or **Kicker** – Illuminates the subject from behind, giving them a glowing edge that separates them from the background and adds dimension.

Ballast – The power box on an HMI light.

Best Boy – There are often two Best Boys, the second-in-command to the Gaffer, and the second-in-command to the Key Grip.

Blather – Dialog to just have people talking for the sake of talking without any points to make.

Boom – 1. the long stick the microphone is connected to. 2. alternate name for a camera crane. 3. to move the camera up or down without tilting. 3. an onomatopoeia for an explosion.

Boom Operator – The person who holds the boom microphone. Also known as the *Boom Man* (if indeed it is a man).

Breakdown – The vital analytical stage between the script and the budget, which describes all of the needed elements for each scene.

Budget – The detailed cost breakdown.

C-Stand – A metal stand and arm for gripping and holding lighting equipment, like flags. C is short for Century, the company that first started making them.

Camera Head – The attachment to the bottom of the camera, which allows panning and tilting, that attaches to the top of the tripod or to the hydraulic head on the dolly.

Camera Report – A multi-duplicate form, generally supplied by the lab, that accompanies the cans of exposed film stock to the lab.

Characterization – That which identifies and differentiates your characters, that which makes them specific and unique.

Click-track – Like a metronome, the way the composer sets the rhythm of the scene.

Close-up – A human face fills the frame, from chin to forehead (and is sometimes referred to as a *choker*).

Composer – The person who writes, and occasionally also performs, the music score for the film.

Composition – The distance from, and the arrangement of, the elements in the shot.

Copyright – The legal registration of a script, film, book, etc. with the Library of Congress.

Core – The plastic wheel that goes at the center of a roll of film.

Cover sets – Interior sets or locations intentionally left for last on the schedule, just in case it rains and you can't shoot planned exteriors.

Coverage – The number of camera setups in a scene.

Cut – When film jumps directly from one scene to the next.

Cutaway – 1. a shot in a scene that doesn't include the actors who are featured or speaking. 2. a tuxedo jacket.

Dailies or **Rushes** – The footage shot the previous day, which can be viewed on either video, DVD, the internet, or workprint.

Day for Night – To shoot a scene in the daytime so that it passes as nighttime.

Depth-of-Field – The distance at which you are in focus.

Dialog-Continuity Script – An precise transcription of every line in your film exactly as it's spoken, with the footage count of specifically where it occurs. This is what the foreign distributors will use for both the dubbing and the subtitling.

Director – The person who decides how the script will be transformed to film, then executes it.

Director of Photography (DP) or **Cinematographer** – The person who is the head of the camera and lighting departments, and is in charge of designing the lighting. Known in England as the *Lighting Cameraman*.

Director's Guild of America (DGA) – The trade union to which professional directors belong.

Dissolve – When one scene starts to go away and the next scene comes in over the top of it. Also known as a *lap dissolve*.

Dolly – The wheeled cart for moving the camera. Real movie dollies have hydraulic heads that go up and down.

Double – An actor or stunt person who looks like and is dressed exactly the same as another actor, usually a lead, to perform stunts, fights or to appear in long shots with the 2nd unit.

Doubler – A piece of glass the doubles the focal length of the lens, so a 300mm lenses would become a 600mm with a doubler.

Dramatic Conflict – Minimally two people confronting each other, generally over a difference in beliefs.

Dutch Angle – The picture is titled to the right or the left.

Duvatine – Long rolls of black velvet used for backgrounds, as well as blocking out light from windows.

Editor – The person who is in charge of putting the movie together after it's been shot.

Exposure – How much light is illuminating the scene by coming in through the end of the lens and exposing the film.

Extra – A non-speaking actor used in the background of movies. Also known as *Background Players* and *Atmosphere*.

Extreme Close-up – Just a person's mouth and eyes, or just their eyes or just their mouth.

Extreme Long Shot or **Wide Shot** – The whole person a figure within the frame against the background. Sometimes called a *Geography Shot*.

Eye-Line – How near or far the actor is looking toward the lens.

Fade In – When the screen goes from black into the picture.

Fade Out – When the screen goes to black.

Fast-Motion – When the action is faster than normal, achieved by running the film slower. Formerly called *Under-cranking*.

Feature Film – 70 minutes or longer, although the Academy of Motion Pictures Arts and Sciences says 60 minutes or longer.

Fill Light – A soft, general, overall illumination that decreases contrast.

Film Gate – The area in the camera behind the lens, where the film is clawed down into position.

Film speed – Rated in *ASA* numbers, such as: 25, 40, 64, 100, 120, 200, 250, 500, and 1000. The slower the film stock the lower the number, meaning the thicker the chemicals, known as *emulsion,* are spread on the film, and the more light you need to penetrate it. The faster the speed, the higher the number, and the thinner the chemicals, so less light is needed to expose it.

Flag – Black cloth on a metal frame used for blocking out light.

Flashback – A memory.

Foley – The sound of footsteps and incidental noises put back into a movie after it's shot.

Forced Call – SAG has a rule that if break an actor's turnaround, meaning you don't give them the full twelve hours off for every twelve hours on, this is a Forced Call and you will be penalized.

Four-walling – To rent a movie theater and show your film yourself.

Gaffer – The head electrician, who carries out the orders of the DP, ties into electrical supplies, makes sure all of the lights go where the should and work, and also makes sure that the generators are set up and used properly.

Gaffer's Tape – Duct tape.

Glass Painting – A special effect where a sheet of glass is put in front of the lens, then parts of the background—villages, cities, mountains, etc.—are painted on the glass.

Grip – Generally the big guys who carry around the heavy objects, like lights, platforms and dollies.

General Partners – The partners who have put the deal together and will co-own it for their effort and expertise.

Genre – A French word that means kind, type, or sort, which is exactly what it means in English, too. The genre of a film is it's type, like a western, or a teen comedy, or a crime thriller, or science fiction, or a family drama.

Hanging Miniature – A special effect where a miniature part of the background is hung in front of the lens in the foreground.

High Angle – When the camera is high and looking down.

High-Hat – A short camera stand mounted on a wooden board, which allows the camera to be five or six inches off the ground.

HMI Light – A type of lighting unit that emits daylight, which is much bluer, and is rated at 5400 degrees Kelvin.

"In the can" – Means the film is entirely shot, but hasn't gone through post-production yet.

Incandescent or **Tungsten Light** – A type of light bulb, like a standard home light bulb, which emits a warmer, more orange light, that is rated at 3200 degrees Kelvin.

Insert – A close-up of anything that's not an actor's face speaking.

Inter-cut – To cut back and forth between shots or scenes.

Iris or **Aperture** – The circular hole which allows light in through the lens to the film, which can be expanded or contracted. It is calibrated in *f-stops* or *t-stops,* which are, for all practical purposes, the same thing (one is a mechanical calibration, the other a mathematical calculation).

Iris – 1. A circular wipe. 2. the aperture of a lens.

Irony – A combination of circumstances or a result that is opposite of what might be expected or considered appropriate.

Jump Cut – A jarring cut, once considered a mistake, now seen in everything. Often employed to indicate the elapse of time.

Key Grip – The head of the grips, who often pushes the camera dolly, and is also known as the *Dolly Grip.*

Key Light – The main source of illumination.

Letterbox – A video image with black bands at the top and bottom of the frame allowing for the film's original widescreen format.

Limited Partners – The investors.

Limited Partnership (LP) or a **Limited Liability Corporation (LLC)** – A legal entity, registered with the state, that clearly outlines the deal for the production of your proposed movie, the percentages of ownership, and an assurance of limited liability for the investors (an LLC is for a corporation; an LP is for a non-corporation). That means that no investor is liable for any more money than s/he has already invested. There are two kinds of partners in this type of deal: the investors (**Limited Partners**) and the partners who have put the deal together and will co-own it for their effort and expertise (**General Partners**).

Long Lenses – All of the prime lenses from 50mm up. Also known as *Telephoto Lenses.*

Long Shot – From the feet up.

Looping – Post-production dialog replacement. Also known as ADR, for Automated Dialog Replacement. Commonly referred to as *dubbing.*

Low Angle – When the camera is low looking up.

Main Unit – The film crew that shoots with the speaking actors.

Master Shot – When the shot covers the entire scene, and usually everyone in it. A master shot is a whole scene.

Matte Shot – Where part of the shot is being replaced with either film footage, a photograph, or a painting.

Meal Penalty – SAG has a rule that says all actors must be allowed to eat every five hours, and if you don't let them, you get penalized.

Medium Close-up – From the mid-chest to the top of the head.

Medium Shot – From the waist up (and sometimes referred to as a *cowboy*—that way you could see the six-guns on his belt).

Mise-En-Scene – The French term for composition, and also the French term for a director.

Montage – 1. the French word for editing. 2. a sequence that shows the passage of time.

MOS – Without sound.

Motivation – The character's reasons for doing what they do.

Pan – To swivel the camera horizontally.

Partnership Agreement – The contract between you and your investors.

Pitch – To tell your story out loud to someone.

Plot – The story in its most basic form; something causes something else.

Point – As in, "The point of the story is . . ." is generally the conclusion of the theme or subject (*Will Success Spoil Rock Hunter?* No, it won't).

Point-of-View (POV) – When the camera shows what someone is seeing.

Possessory Credit – Generally the director's credit before the title, like A Josh Becker Film, or Un Film du Josh Becker; although it can also be the Producer, like David O. Selznick Presents; or it can even be the writer, as in Neil Simon's *The Odd Couple*.

Practical or Physical Effects – Special effects done live during filming, like bullet hits (squibs).

Presence or **Background Sounds (BGs)** – Sounds like: wind, city noise, crickets, chirping birds, howling dogs in the distance, etc., which are put in during post-production.

Prime Lenses – All the fixed focal length lenses that are not zooms.

Principal Photography – The main bulk of the shooting with all of the speaking actors.

Process Shot – A shot where the action is performed in front of either a blue, green or gray screen, so another background can be inserted during post-production; or a shot performed in front of a rear-screen projection, where the filmed background is put in during shooting.

Producer – Frequently the person in charge of the entire production, although it has become a somewhat amorphous designation. There can also be: Executive Producer, Associate Producer, Co-Producer, Assistant Producer, Producer's Assistant, etc.

Production Assistant (PA) – The lowest position on a film crew; the one who runs and gets things, or helps out with anything that needs to be done. Also known as a *Gopher* or a *Runner*.

Production Designer – The person is the head of the Art Department, who designs the sets, and decides how both sets and locations will be dressed.

Production Manager or Unit Production Manager (UPM) – The person who physically arranges everything for the purposes of shooting that needs to be there. This person is generally in the office all day and not on the set. Also known as a *Line Producer*.

Push-in or **Track-in** – A slow dolly forward, frequently ending in a close-up.

Pyrotechnician – The person who sets off explosions and affixes the squibs on the actors, and wherever else they're needed. This is a state licensed position.

Rack Focus – To shift the plane of focus.

Reaction Shot – Shots of actors or extras showing an emotion.

Reflectors – Shiny, reflective boards on stands. Also known as *Flecky Boards*.

Residuals – The payments that union actors, directors and writers receive, through their unions, for television screenings and video/DVD sales of their shows and films. Music Composer receives the same sort of payments, but they're called *Royalties*.

Reverse – When the camera moves 180-degrees to the opposite angle.

Riser – Metal attachments for the camera head to raise up the height of the camera beyond where the hydraulic camera head will go.

Room Tone – The sound of your set or location without anyone speaking.

Rubbery – Dialog that's not quite in synch.

Safety Shot – An extra take in case there's a technical issue with the earlier take.

Scene – 1. A division of a play, or an act of a play, now commonly representing what passes between certain of the actors in one place. 2. a unit of dramatic action within a play, in which a single point or effect is made.

Schedule – The order in which you'll shoot the scenes.

Screen Actor's Guild (SAG) – The trade union to which professional actors belong.

Screenwriter – The person who writes the screenplay.

Script Supervisor or **Continuity** – The person who keeps the *Script Notes*, which are a detailed running description of each shot as it's accomplished: which lens was used, what was the camera's position, what directions are actors entering and exiting, which hands are they using for their actions, etc. Formerly known as the *Script Girl*.

Selects – Which takes are printed or transferred to video.

Shooting Ratio – The difference between how much film is exposed to how much film is actually used, expressed as: 3 to 1, or 10 to 1.

Shot – From when the camera goes on to when the camera goes off—from action to cut, which is also known as a setup.

Silk – A large piece of silk, frequently a parachute, used to diffuse light, or to cover the camera and the actors when it's raining.

Slate – The clapboard, used to identify the shot, and to keep the picture and sound in synch.

Slow-Motion – When the action is slower than normal, achieved by running the film faster. Formerly called *Over-cranking*.

Slug-line – The (capitalized) physical description of the scene, including the time of day.

Source Music – Music emanating from within the scene, usually from a radio or a PA system.

Special effect (FX) – An element of a movie that is created separately from the live-action shooting, frequently during post-production, to show something that couldn't be done in actuality.

Squib – A fake bullet hit, made from a small explosive underneath a condom filled with fake blood, set off by an electrical charge.

Stand-in – Generally an extra whose job is to stand in the position of one of the speaking actors so that the lighting can be set while the actor is in makeup and wardrobe.

Standard Coverage – A wide shot and two close-ups, or a wide shot and two over-the-shoulder shots.

Sting – 1. A short, dramatic music cue. 2. former lead singer for The Police. 3. winner of the 1973 Oscar for Best Picture.

Stop-Motion – To shoot one frame at a time to create the sense of movement, as in cell or clay animation.

Story – Something causes something else to happen.

Storyboards – Drawings of the proposed shots.

Theme – The subject or topic of the story, often boiled down to one word (In *Will Success Spoil Rock Hunter?* the theme is "success").

Tilt – To swivel the camera vertically.

Toe-Bag – Small, colored sandbags to indicate actor's marks.

Trailer – A coming attraction for a film.

Transitional Scene – A short scene between two other scenes.

Tripod – A three-legged stand for the camera. Also known as *Legs*. They come in two sizes: *Baby Legs* and *Standard Legs*.

Turnaround – 1. A film crew generally gets twelve hours off after working for twelve hours (your standard shooting day). 2. When a film studio or a production company decides to sell a script that they haven't produced.

Two-Shot – A shot of two people.

Tying-in – Taking electricity from a location (as opposed to using a generator).

Ubangi – Attachment to the camera head on the dolly that allows the camera to stick out away from the head, to go over things or through windows.

Walla – The background din and chatter of crowds that is put into movies after they're shot.

Whip Pan – When the camera pans so fast it blurs. Also known as a *Whiz Pan*.

Wide Angle Lenses – All of the prime lenses from the lowest numbers, up to 40mm.

Widescreen – Any screen height to width ratio greater than 1.66:1. The two main film widescreen formats are: 1.85:1 and 2.35:1; and the video High Definition widescreen format is 1.77:1 or 16x9.

Wild Sound – Sound recorded on the set or location, either before after the shooting, that's not in synch.

Wipes – A transition where one scene takes over from the next scene, usually done with a sharp or fuzzy line moving vertically across the screen, although they can go up or down, too.

Workprint – A positive print of the film, without sound.

Writer's Guild of America (WGA) – The trade union to which professional writers belong.

Zolly – So far the only term for the push-in/zoom back (or zoom-in/pull-back) camera move first devised by Alfred Hitchcock for *Vertigo*, which causes the background to either move in or away.

Zoom – A type of lens with movable glass elements inside to increase or decrease focal length. It is also the name for the use of the lens, as in "Zoom into a close-up." You can either Zoom in or Zoom back, which is sometimes humorously called a *Mooz*.

Printed in the United States
51697LVS00006B

9 780809 556458